MW01699235

ATICAL

DACH TO
TION
TINY
IFE

158.1
CAW
2015

Cawood, David (Ph.D.)
The secret sabbatical: the revolutionary approach to recover your imagination and discover your destiny for the rest

SEP 11 2016

604-926-1621
North Shore Unitarian Church
370 MATHERS AVENUE
WEST VANCOUVER, B.C. V7S 1H3

THE SECRET SABBATICAL

THE REVOLUTIONARY APPROACH TO RECOVER YOUR IMAGINATION AND DISCOVER YOUR DESTINY FOR THE REST OF YOUR LIFE

DAVID CAWOOD, PH.D.

Bookstand Publishing

www.bookstandpublishing.com
www.TheSecretSabbatical.com

Published by
Bookstand Publishing
Morgan Hill, CA 95037
4234_8

Copyright © 2015 by David Cawood, Ph.D.
All rights reserved. No part of this publication may be reproduced or transmitted in any form or by any means, electronic or mechanical, including photocopy, recording, or any information storage and retrieval system, without permission in writing from the copyright owner.

ISBN 978-1-63498-051-7

Printed in the United States of America

Preface

The central story in this book reached out and grabbed me years ago. Although the storyteller lived in the thirteenth-century, the fate of his tale's main character stunned me. The similarity to my own life, and to life in modern times was too obvious to ignore. I realized that commitment and ambition had led many of us to a certain kind of worldly success but, what I hadn't grasped, was how all this could lead to a crisis. The alarming truth was that our means of shaping the future—our imagination—was being rapidly and systematically eroded. Worse yet, this apparent imaginative decline was, it seemed to me, spreading throughout society, in organizations of all kinds—business, universities, the professions and not-for-profits. It was everywhere.

Another important influence in my life at the time—a poet and community leader who also lived 700 years ago—wrote about this same sense of urgency. He saw the emerging issue with striking clarity. But, what was more important, he knew a way out of the crunch. He spoke of renewing commitments based on the rediscovery of one's freedom, and it was as though he spoke directly to me.

An awareness of an imaginative decline and the resulting problems came together in my own midlife search and led to the evolving *The Secret Sabbatical Course* on which this book is based. Over the decade it's been offered, I've found there's a **required level of depth** for meaningful change to happen. On the Course, participants attend either tightly organized sessions on a monthly one-on-one basis or in small groups over several months. Most are fully employed. In between sessions they read short novels and watch selected videos, including movies. Attendees come from diverse backgrounds in management, the professions, and the sciences.

There have been many changes and improvements to the material—some suggested by the participants—and this book is based on the current version.

The Course presents a reintegration of three aspects of modern life that should never have been separated. These include the vast and often repetitive field of material on **managing organizations**, vital but neglected insights from the **humanities**, and the intermediate realm of **applied science,** which is growing in importance in the modern world. I reached out to the powerful potential of interdisciplinary fields such as behavioral economics, decision theory and brain science. Because Course participants are from such varying backgrounds, the dialog is frequently intense and almost always productive. The point is, **to stir the imagination, and the heart, in order to see better and ultimately do better.**

I've included an equally diverse set of **guides** and **examples** of role models from novels, movies, practical philosophy, science, TV shows and poetry. I could see the material helping midlife participants plot the next stages of their lives and careers, or influencing the "giving back" plans of some boomers. But more than this, that it could help anyone interested in changing their lives.

My practice involves a continuing interest across distinct but related fields, while recognizing their complexity. After completing a bachelor's degree in the Humanities I worked as a manager, then head office executive, before completing an MBA and Ph.D. and serving on the faculty of a business school. I arrived in Canada as a founding member of the first North American Strategic Consulting Group with what is now Deloitte. After a few years, I built an international consulting company. This involved several decades of work with very large firms such as HP, De Beers and Deloitte. Since then, my client base has also included a wide range of organizations from engineering, health care, infrastructure, education and research. In addition to the main consulting work, I designed and then handed over Executive Development workshops for universities and in-house colleges in several countries.

The humanities have historically been directly concerned with the development of the human imagination, offering examples of successful paths to needed change. Over the years I've offered ongoing humanities-based workshops with Continuing Studies adult audiences, Jung Societies and other forums.

I’ve also taken a keen interest in that key intersecting realm of applied science in my service as an Adjunct Professor of Strategy and Leadership in Applied Science at the University of British Columbia. My university and in-house college work offer only a few ideas from this book, as this material is for readers willing to go on a far-ranging interdisciplinary journey—beyond any single faculty. I do see however that business, engineering and other professional schools show a growing interest in aspects of leadership—like the potential of the imagination.

I feel tremendous hope at this stage. There is growing evidence of the need for multidisciplinary approaches and solutions and increasing excitement in managers and professionals as they explore the potential in fields outside their own. But each of us needs a framework to assemble, and then apply, this material to enrich our own imaginations. This book offers some thoughts and guidance on that exact topic, which I call “expanding the canvas of our imagination.”

More background detail is at:
www.TheSecretSabbatical.com
and:
www.CawoodConsulting.com

Acknowledgements

The team

My wife Alexis has been a part of the thinking behind this book from day one. With her Humanities and dance background she has a rich and active relationship with literature and art. The Romantic poets have been her special love and the poetic references in this book in particular owe much to her. The final conceptual and then detailed editing of this kind of book can be challenging and, drawing on her background in graduate English studies, she dedicated herself to the task at all levels. Her artwork is also featured, with the portrayal of the garden on the cover and her fractal collage in Chapter 12. Some of her paintings are at: www AlexisCawoodArtist.com

Ian Radziejewski was one of the early graduates of *The Secret Sabbatical Course* and was helpful with this project. He has a master's degree in engineering, specializing in electronics and communications and a broad background in technology companies, with roles encompassing product development, project management, and marketing. Ian has held various leadership positions, including President and CEO of a remarkably successful organization that he co-founded. The Canadian-based company has remained the world's largest supplier of mobile video security systems for six straight years.

Janice Grout was exposed to this material through a happy coincidence of events and has explored many of these ideas for a number of years in her work in education. She kindly agreed to help edit what turned out to be initial drafts that were often workshop-based. Her ideas were invaluable.

And then there are the real authors—the participants in the Course that led to this book. Not only have they provided information and examples, but they've helped shape and structure ("in-form") the book. This material will continue to develop with both the societal challenges that arise and with the needs of the people who deal with them. And this change will hopefully happen in several ways. I'm sure we'll uncover fresh ways of presenting the ideas and discover many more rich ideas to explore. In addition, the material in this book will certainly change if you read it, and perhaps reread it, with a willingness to remain open. The Greek who said we don't step into the same stream twice meant that **both** the stream and oneself continue to change.

Other acknowledgments

Coleman Barks is often referred to as the greatest translator of the works of the thirteenth-century poet, Rumi—one of the most popular poets in the world today. If you can find a way of hearing Barks read the poetry, you will be astonished at how he recreates the living Rumi. Coleman's writings on the Sufi poet are also fascinating, as he has studied and lived the material for decades. On hearing of our project he graciously agreed to allow us to use his translations in this book, and they appear throughout. Rumi is a central and enduring guide in this project and in the lives of the millions who've encountered his incredibly wise ways.

Others who have been generous and encouraging include James Hollis—a Jungian scholar, writer, teacher and therapist. George Vaillant, in the famed Grant Study, led the longest-term and most thorough study of the life adaptations that have been shown to be effective throughout entire lifetimes. He has also kindly granted his permission to discuss his findings.

Graphic artist Russell Moore, based in Texas, was able to take my rougher PowerPoints and hand sketches and render them in greater clarity with added dimensions, which is one of our themes. He has also been a pleasure to work with and practises the flexibility and responsiveness that are the basis of any effective collaboration. Here is a link to his online portfolio:
http://issuu.com/rustlemore/docs/russell_j._moore

Wesleyan University Press has kindly granted permission to quote one of the central poems of this book by Machado. Antonio Machado, “The Wind One Brilliant Day” from *Times Alone: Selected Poems of Antonio Machado*, translated by Robert Bly © 1983. Reprinted by permission of Wesleyan University Press.

Cover painting: detail from “Reaching for the Radiance” by Alexis Cawood. © 2012

Introduction

> The imagination is not a faculty for the creation of illusion, it is the faculty by which alone [we] apprehend reality.
>
> *Harold Goddard*[1]

The idea of this book began with a startling observation. I realized a growing number of people seemed less able and less willing to craft creative strategies for personal, organizational and societal change. I asked myself: what if there is an emerging **crisis in our ability to imagine?**

In my consulting work I'd noticed that the time horizon people were prepared to reach for in our strategic planning projects was narrowing from ten years, to five, then three, and finally down to one year! This reflects the increasing tempo of modern organizational life, of course. But there's a much deeper issue.

To address this alarming decline in vision, I initiated a series of one-on-one meetings and extensive workshops with CEOs, architects, heads of school, scientists, chief engineers, surgeons, board members and others. From the hundreds of executives I work with every year, a modern modestly sized "round table" evolved.

We discussed the problems, and then a potential starting place pointing towards resolution. These questions emerged:

- Can we reclaim and nurture our imaginative powers?
- How can we be truly creative leaders in our lives, and in the groups and organizations we serve?
- How can we help with sustainable solutions—are there core values and behaviors that will help?
- Where do we begin, and how do we choose a manageable scale?

* We concluded that we could begin restoring our ability to envision by grasping what we **need** to do, what we **can** do, and **how** and **where** to begin. The discussions evolved into a Course, which is the basis of this book.

We realized that a loss of vision could result in an attraction to the quick fixes of the day. And that it may engender a sinking feeling of helplessness in the face of seemingly overwhelming odds detailed in every newscast. Some try to deny this. They then lack the energy to take on what needs changing, personally, and in organizations of all kinds.

The Secret Sabbatical Course

From these discussions I refined the Course, while allowing for individual tailoring. It's not about simply setting better goals. Sitting down to list goals over various time frames is the heart of most goal setting, time management and life planning processes. TV hosts, and even the highly regarded Steven Covey, advise us to sit right down, focus for a few seconds, and write out our life goals. One of the better Time Management gurus, Alan Lakein,[2] divides his goal setting into three categories—for which you get four minutes each! These are: lifetime, three-year and "What would you do if you were to be struck by lightning in six months?" While these can be interesting, without the needed introspection you're only likely to get more of the same.

An industry dedicated to confirming that life challenges can be rapidly resolved supports a surface level of goal setting. Magazines continually recycle tips to help us achieve wealth, health, fame, sexual triumphs and amazing abs. It's mostly snake oil. "Step right on up, folks!" Keep coming back for more workshops, more solace, more magazines.

But by merely scratching the surface we end up reinforcing the very issues we're trying to transcend. A restatement of personal challenges is likely to give us more of the same things that got us stuck in those earlier ego-enhancing life tasks. So we risk planning on more recognition from others or developing a superior personal "brand." We may just create more justification for doing what we want to do anyway.

More meaningful levels are called for.

At the heart of the matter is a buried secret. A seriously neglected key to this secret is the restoration of a particular emotional domain. Decades of work in brain science shows we can't make **any** decision without a functioning emotional life. This includes even basic judgment calls such as what to wear or where to eat. We need to rediscover the generative emotions at the source of our imaginative lives. These connect to changes in how we project power, which trigger other essential shifts that I'll outline.

With the help of a relatively new branch of mathematics, we'll learn that a belief in working on a sufficiently large scale is not an issue. Not initially anyway. The counterintuitive truth is instead to start small, to begin locally, ultra-locally—with oneself.

In the pages ahead, I'll suggest we look more closely at an older model that has Eastern origins. It describes how to redirect our personal energies through a central fulcrum of transformation. This is at the core of lasting change, as it turns out. I believe the degrees of depth I propose with this model are essential for restoring the imagination.

Other steps involve recognizing and nurturing specific sensibilities and values, including the fundamental role of qualities that have been classically associated with the feminine. As our imagination is restored, we can then reapply our power in ways that are transformative.

The journey we'll take is to rediscover and then reintegrate the garden-like, organic core of our imaginations. It's organic in the sense that it's continually refreshed and nourished through the disappearing silent springs we'll help to replenish.

Why a *Secret* Sabbatical?

Initially, the Course evolved in the context of midlife decisions. The idea of taking time to examine one's life caught on with clients, although they didn't necessarily want their involvement known. They wanted to discreetly explore the questions and options offered through the Course without making declarations or announcements. First, they wanted to know how they felt about emerging alternatives. They also hoped to avoid raising expectations or sending messages that they were ready to move on, or were dissatisfied at work, or whatever else might be assumed as a result of their interest in the material. The Course was to be a "thought experiment," which I believed would help in their search. The idea of these kinds of imagined experiences being tied to possibilities of self-discovery, and further discovery in the wider world, is a central theme in my work.

Enlightened companies were happy to support the Course for executives, realizing that it was better to have committed people on board. Because they supported my idea that secrecy was central to the whole idea of *The Secret Sabbatical Course,* it was agreed I would not report back on any of the discussions between their employees and myself. People often reaffirmed their choices. They decided to stay where they were currently employed, but with renewed vigor.

In time, the Course began to include people contemplating retirement but the secret aspect still seemed appropriate. They used the opportunity to imagine future possibilities that require the freedom I've mentioned. Like those at midlife, lots of these folks weren't sure how they'd feel once free to examine unimagined alternatives. Some didn't want to announce their interest or the fact that they were searching for a new direction. It truly takes courage to strike out and begin to develop new strengths and talents when we've reached a stage in our lives where much of what we do seems second nature.

The decathletes I discuss later in the book are a clear example. While these athletes compete publicly in 10 different events, none has completely mastered all these challenges. So there are times when each of them feels less than competent, perhaps even incompetent. Most choose to prepare in private for events where they have less mastery. Similarly, many people appreciate the confidential aspect of the Course as they practice new ways of framing their future while responding to daily life.

These times of reflection and of practicing new skills, of new ways of viewing oneself and the world are best attempted in privacy, with the suggested degree of secrecy. This is the opposite of building a brand from your existing perspective for the sake of a Facebook or LinkedIn profile. It's about becoming more grounded and effective, not just about appearances.

There's another play on the word *secret.* Throughout the book, you'll find references to ideas and tactics that have been disappearing. We're no longer aware of them. They've become secrets in need of rediscovery. And so, the book is also about *"Secrets (of the) Sabbatical."*

Disappearing springs

I realized that some sources I consulted for the revival of the imagination were in danger. Many had disappeared or are disappearing in the surge of increasingly non-curated media that flood across our desks, into our pockets and now onto some nightstands. These sources are the basis of the Course and now this book. Hopefully, some will be revived as once this material is lost it will be hard to recover. It's been said that if you want to control minds, you don't need to burn the books, only ensure that they're not read. I've listed some of the works in the blog attached to this book. *www.TheSecretSabbatical.com*

The resources are frequently outside the normal range of educational material that organizations and many university courses access. In my experience, they come primarily, but not exclusively, from the humanities. Modern science is also adding dramatically to what was once the sole province of the humanities.

Integrating the intersecting streams

Besides working in organizations, I've maintained a lifelong interest in designing Continuing Studies and other Adult Education programs showing the relevance of the humanities to modern life. I've also taken a real interest in that intersecting realm of applied science through my service as an Adjunct Professor of Strategy and Leadership in Applied Science at the University of British Columbia. Even the most technological places, such as leading university engineering departments, now offer increasing exposure to group decision making and other topics aimed at the human side of enterprise.

What's called the humanities has always been for me a great way of addressing the emotional side of life. But in a non-invasive way—it's more effective and usually a lot more fun than non-fiction. That's one of the reasons I feel it's so important. One is free to imagine oneself on stage, screen, or on the page, and can then either resolve to change or not. It's a private decision and not mediated by any therapist's urgings. The Greek dramatists were fully aware of this power and honored it under the name of catharsis.

The material I'll broadly refer to as belonging to the humanities is today often seen as restrictive—even nonessential. This is incredibly serious, as here we're talking about a branch of our culture that is about the essence of being human. C.S. Lewis, the late British author and critic, commented that in reading great literature, "I transcend myself; and am never more myself than when I do."[3] So it's not only a branch of the culture, as I've implied, but more like the taproot.

But organizational life, the humanities, and applied science are notoriously difficult to blend as the walls between these silos can be intimidating. Years ago, when I mentioned that an integration seemed important, a decision-making guru said, "Good luck!" implying it was an impractical or even unattainable mission. This book is my response, as I believe bridges between them are possible. In fact, each can benefit from new perspectives.

The material I've developed originates not only in traditional humanities sources, but from movies, a popular TV show and brain science.

The guides

I discovered four interdisciplinary guides from these resources. A guide in this sense is someone who has lived the changes we discuss in the book and returned with vital experiences to share. They are far beyond pundits. Each believed that passing on their findings was vital—and so do I.

Our main guide, Rumi, sets the tone for each chapter, stressing sustainable core values and perspectives. Three others help us along the way. The first of these teaches us how to begin "clearing the decks" for our journey. To the initial surprise of some, this is TV personality Cesar Millan, from the show *The Dog Whisperer*. He spent years mastering the state of mind required by dog owners in their interactions with their canine friends. Millan takes pains to point out that he is mainly training humans as the qualities he advocates are those vital for initiating any personal change. Another guide gives us three basic questions to bear in mind. He's Marcus Aurelius, the outstanding Roman leader who fine-tuned his practice while serving for years with his troops on the front lines of the barbarian conflicts. Influenced by one of the great philosophers, Marcus recorded his application of seminal ideas in a journal that happily survived. Our final guide is a brain scientist who offers her remarkable second-by-second wisdom to maintain perspective and handle the countless and growing distractions targeting us. Jill Bolte Taylor survived a catastrophic stroke and rebuilt her consciousness to return to us with her hard-won wisdom and her compassionate approach.

Other guides are scattered throughout these pages, in characters played by Jack Nicholson, Helen Hunt and Anthony Hopkins.

All of these teachers facilitate that original but possibly forgotten contact we once enjoyed with the deep center of our own creative energy. Vision begins to return, but not only on one dimension. To express this in engineering terms for a moment—the key is an increase in the number and depth of channels! **But the attitude in which the channels are to be accessed** is central and is beyond many current technical or even management programs.

I draw examples of others who have faced similar journeys from whatever I found that provided inspiration and help. Many of the modern sources are engaging echoes of sometimes ancient and enduring themes.

Core questions about launching

For some people, embarking on the Course turned out to be a major quest in their life. In the early stages of their journeys, they asked the following kinds of questions about implementing the outlined changes.

Is it do-able?

Can we have an impact in the world? This inquiry led to lively discussions about whether or not we are mere pawns in the hands of our appetites, our genes or even our internal ecology, which includes bacteria and viruses—our microbiomes!

We were now into classic debates on free will. Sam Harris has recently explored this, suggesting that free will is less accessible than we'd like to think. In his blog he concedes "this shouldn't depress us, or tempt us to go off our diets. Diligence and wisdom still yield better results than sloth and stupidity."[4]

When the great fiction writer Isaac Bashevis Singer was asked whether he believed in free will, he answered "I have no choice!" To me this is a humorous way of saying that I must presume there is **some** scope as a human to act on my own volition—the alternative is not to be contemplated. It then makes sense to find a niche where I believe I can contribute.

This book highlights instances of people who've made specific changes and influenced their future, in self-determined ways.

Do I have the ability?

Many executives and professionals are reticent about tackling material from the humanities, and I can sure see why. The content may have been boring or made precious through poor teaching, and some humanities' scholars have distorted or pre-empted texts in response to political or academic fads. I have attended more than my share of deconstructionist, jargon-filled analyses of what were once considered great novels.

An initial hesitation concerning one's ability is captured in the opening chapters of the classic but eternally modern novel *The American.*[5] Here author Henry James introduces us to a quintessentially American character. Christopher Newman is a self-made businessman who has dedicated the post-Civil War years entirely and successfully to amassing a personal fortune. We're told he had huge confidence and competence in business, that he "…often sat up all night over a bristling bundle of accounts, and heard the cock crow without a yawn." As he approaches middle age, he undergoes a shocking experience on Wall Street. Realizing he's earned what should be enough money, he has the sudden insight that life has many other things to offer.

An early collaborator on this Project, Ian Radziejewski, has experienced a career with a similar trajectory. In retrospect, what started out for him as a five to 10-year financially-driven career plan turned into over 20 years of steadily being pulled away from formerly important ideals. He also had the privilege of being successful in his business, allowing him time for reflection relatively early in life.

James's character, Christopher Newman walks away from one last deal in response to his renewed perspective on life. His pursuit of acquisitions and possessions is done. With time and resources suddenly at hand, he asks himself: **what should I do with the rest of my life?** He sets off to Europe on his quest.

The opening chapter of the novel outlines a disturbing lack of confidence that remains so modern. Newman's assurance in the world of commerce fails him in the unfamiliar realms of art. When contemplating the great artists in the Louvre for the first time, he is confronted with a "…new kind of arithmetic, and they inspired our friend, for the first time in his life, with a vague self-mistrust."

This kind of vague self-mistrust is unnerving for Newman and the rest of us. After all, most of us don't feel comfortable relinquishing old ways. We may easily feel the downsides of such a shift without being able to imagine any positives, particularly in the early stages of change. It's hard to give up what's provided us with our sense of power and competence—another reason the imagination is so seminal.

That same self-doubt turned out to be a concise way of framing issues facing some Course participants. Like them, many of us know there are unimagined worlds, or adventures and experiences we've never dreamed of and, understandably, we feel hesitant about approaching them. Watching the pundits on TV, with their coached sound bites and appropriate expressions, the intimidation factor can easily rise because these experts seem so self-assured.[6] As it happens, we should be wary of media-appointed gurus, as assurance and competence can be negatively correlated.

Those participants with doubts about the accessibility of the Course material found that they were often encouraged by a combination of the film plus a written version of a book or play. Working this way they not only had the tools to follow, but to thoroughly enjoy themselves as well. A number of us discovered there is hope if we're wise enough to know what we don't know, which is, according to Socrates, the foundation of wisdom.

Do I have the energy and time for this?

Rumi, in a poem that has been titled “You Are The Only Student You Have” tells us

> You don’t have to fear
> That you’ll be drained.[7]

Like Rumi, I believe the energy is latently there, and that with a certain approach you won’t be fatigued. Once involved with material of this nature it becomes increasingly apparent that a concentrated source of energy actually inhabits those characters and stories we’ll share. Imagination is enlivened and you’ll feel a renewed interest in your own life and the adventures of others.

Conquering one’s doubts requires a leap of faith and the resolve to give something a try. If time is an issue, you’ll probably find you can reclaim at least some of it by changing old habits and identifying distractions.

Please give me the benefit of the doubt and plunge into *The Secret Sabbatical*, and give yourself the privilege of taking at least 20 minutes of uninterrupted time to focus. For that matter, as an experiment, try “The 20 Minute Rule”[8] whenever you’re doing something that calls for close attention. If you don’t allow the distractions that often loom when faced with a challenging task, I think you’ll be surprised to find the material is lively and interesting. Many report they have more energy when their imaginations and decision-making skills are challenged.

How much impact can I have?

The science of fractals helps us with this question of impact. It shows how and why small initial ripples of change can grow into unpredictable and powerful waves of influence. This relatively new branch of mathematics offers potent metaphors and genuine hope for the great replication challenges that all change programs need to master. Begin at home, start small, and then see how a shift in point of view can affect patterns around you. Concern with adequate scale is not crucial at the outset, but as Course participants discovered, one’s orientation—who you serve, and how you serve—will prove critical.

Questions of impact led to the perennial issue of leadership. Over time, I found the Course had added meaningful background on two crucial features of leadership found in the best-selling book *Good to Great*.[9] The author Jim Collins reported that the few long-serving "great" leaders he identified in his studies shared two specific attributes—personal **humility** and professional **will**. He stressed that his study was not concerned with how these key characteristics could be developed. He confessed that the topic was a "black box" to him. I think I can help, as you'll find references in the pages ahead to how these qualities can be developed, nurtured and then refined. Seemingly contradictory, humility and will help us focus our energies for more effective impact. We need the humility to realize the limits and natural boundaries of living within complex sets of influences and constraints, and the will to give needed change and growth our best shot.

The book includes practical examples of people who have changed their perspectives and had a lasting impact on various scales of influence, ranging from affecting one person to an entire country. Some of the most intriguing guides may be from the past but will, hopefully, step into our present and our presence. The Postscript details further specific examples and suggestions backed by some independent work on the world's largest lifelong study of what has worked in people's lives.

Of those Course participants still in the workforce, one professional decided to sell his firm and refocus his energies from management to a more direct involvement with projects and clients. He founded a much smaller boutique firm and developed a 10-year succession plan, which gave him the freedom to spend more time on personal and creative interests. Another directed his pursuits from a practice in medicine to a broader research-based approach founded on a new set of contacts and commitments. Several recommitted to their professions and organizations with a new focus, and reported healthier home lives and wider community involvement.

A CEO of a high-tech firm found he was able to communicate on a new level with his daughter as they both pondered Shakespeare's *King Lear*. Realizing for the first time that he could easily read the play, he was cheered that his teenaged daughter found his comments helpful, and insightful. Her head of school ran into our executive at a gathering and was impressed with his interest and involvement. He's now on the board of the school and loving it. Periodic Course reunions lead to a wider sharing of how participants are navigating change.

To some extent participants in the Course became co-designers over the years and influenced the Course and my book in different ways. I'm truly grateful for their suggested improvements. Meanwhile, carefully chosen segments of the material have been introduced in certain major consulting and teaching ventures. That integration can be complex, requiring subtlety and patience because timing and the level of intervention are important for acceptance. In consulting, for example, a frequently overlooked principle is, not to intervene at a level of depth greater than that which is required for the needed change. And, of course, some organizations will not deal with this material in any form, having a specific aversion to anything but the next quarterly profit.

O.K. Let's get going!

The epigraph at the opening of this Introduction makes the claim that our imagination is not the way we create illusion, but that it's central to our view of reality. Hopefully, the book will prove helpful in showing just how profound that statement is.

We'll learn how to begin a virtuous circle where imagination uncovers our blind spots and then reveals creative new pathways. We'll begin a new adventure. We'll find guidance, and escape from the shallow and ultra-short time frames frequently inflicted on us.

Everyone's path has distinctive elements, side trips and breakthroughs. Consider this a buffet that you're being invited to sample. If something appeals, then you'll be back for more. But you may want to "stay in line" as there's a progression that makes a sequential approach worthwhile.

Our quest for the regeneration of imagination is vital for living and leading our lives. This journey may be your personal key to the changes that have proved elusive so far. Restoring a profound but neglected aspect of oneself emerges as one of the most crucial tasks **imaginable**.

I've found any imaginative renaissance first takes us to a lost garden and then brings us back into the real world. Because countless stories tell this tale, we launch our own journey using an all but forgotten classic path-finding adventure. In Chapter 1, we step back into the world of chivalry and set off to find our way.

Contents

Preface v

Acknowledgements ix

The team ix
Other acknowledgments x

Introduction xiii

The Secret Sabbatical Course xiv

Why a *Secret* Sabbatical? xv
Disappearing springs xvii
Integrating the intersecting streams xvii
The guides xviii

Core questions about launching xix

Is it do-able? xix
Do I have the ability? xx
Do I have the energy and time for this? xxii
How much impact can I have? xxii

O.K. Let's get going! xxiv

1 The Pattern of a Quest 1

Owain's quest 1

The party is on, till the past intrudes 2
Owain's first adventure 3
Back to the "real" world 4
The crunch 5
That old-time lonely feeling 5

The swamp and ashes 6

Owain's journey 11

2 Imagining Imagination 13

What *is* the imagination anyway? 15
Imagination and values are deeply connected 17
We're creating and projecting our world 19
An active middle-ground function 21
Myths—stories beneath the imagination 23

3 The Failure of the Imagination: Some Symptoms and Causes 27

Symptoms 27

Corporations squander the loyalty bonus 27
Narrowing of goals to self-limiting assumptions—single vision measures. 28
Single minded heroes as role models 31
Simply follow your passion 32
False prophets and the myth of the supercycle 35
We sacrificed elegance on the altar of efficiency 37

Causes 38

Rationality alone will not become more effective at solving human problems 38
Exponential growth is unimaginable—literally! 40
Distracted from distraction by distraction... 43
Be afraid—be very afraid 44

Where are we then? 45

4 Three Layers and the Shadow 47

Can we grow into great ideas? 47

The middle layer of awareness—the castle 50

The ambiguity of boxes 51
Dogma and addiction 53
Control vs. facilitation 54

The top layer of awareness—the garden 56

The pursuit of perfection 57
The ecological mind 58

The lower layer of awareness—the swamp 59

Projection—a key idea for grasping how we shape and distort reality 63

Denial and the vital value of our mistakes 67

Let the journey begin! 68

5 A Change of Heart 69

An observation on models 69
The classic model I've used 69
Human energy centers 71
How does the 4th center transform energy? 71

The lowest three energy centers: 1, 2 and 3 73

Center 1: Survival 73
Center 2: Sexuality and desire 73
Center 3: Power over others 74

How to find and cultivate the garden: centers 5, 6 and 7 74

Center 5: Power for others 75
Center 6: Liberated vision 75
Center 7: A sense of deep connection 75
Seven energy centers lead to the regained imagination 76

The Power Shift: from "power-over" to "power-for" 76

Howards End—the movie and book 78

Henry Wilcox's trajectory—potential and actual 81
Shakespeare power shifts and forgiveness 82
The Power Shift 85

6 From Reproduction to Elegance 89

Elegant solutions 91
Literature and beauty 93
American Beauty—the movie 94
As Good As It Gets—the movie 96
"All over a dog!" 96
"Is this as good as it gets?" 98

7 From Survival to a Sense of Connection 101

The Fisher King—the movie 102

8 The Guides Begin: The Surprising Cesar 107

Navigation guide: Cesar Millan 108

Cesar's example 110
Present-centered calm assertiveness: the flow 113
Feedback on the flow 114

9 The Main Guide 117

Marcus Aurelius 117

The first discipline: The discipline of desire 121

A.1. The cosmos as context 122
A.2. Desire within your own sphere of influence 123
A.3. Love your fate, now 124

The second discipline: The discipline of judgment 126

The third discipline: Who do I serve? (based on the discipline of action) 129

10 A Modern Real-time Guide 133

Reconnecting—how do I serve? 133

Third navigational guide: Jill Bolte Taylor 133

Left brain as potential tyrant 136
Discipline is needed 137
Ninety seconds will do it—do I need to run these chemicals longer? 137
A. "Step to the right!" 138
B. Base on the right—riding the "right" wave continuously 138

The 7 key guidance questions in sequence 140

The Guides in Summary 141

11 The Blind Navigator 143

New dimensions for a renaissance 143

Way-finding 143

Exploring multiple dimensions 147

The Vertical Dimension 152
Dimensions and emotions 153
Multiple dimensions of achievement 155

What is a renaissance? 156

Building on the foundations of tradition 156

12 Fate, Fractals and the Feminine 159

Fate, destiny and will 160

A crucial intersection 163

Fractals 164

The feminine 166

13 See Better to Do Better! 171

Flying freer 171

Coming home in a different space 175

The future of these ideas 177

Now what? 178

The summing up 179

POSTSCRIPT Studies and Service 181

The proof is in the studies 181

- Huxley 181
- The Grant Study 183
- We do all have crunches! 183
- The key findings 183
- Immature responses 185
- Neurotic responses 185
- Mature responses 185
- Marriage and AA! 186

Examples of Service 187

- Compassion with accountability 188

The narrative continues 191

About the Author 193

Notes 195

Table of Figures

Figure 1- Owain's Journey 9

Figure 2 - Imagining Imagination 21

Figure 3 - Projections 66

Figure 4 - Beyond and Before Maslow: A Model of Transformation 71

Figure 5 - Potential for Energy Changes 72

Figure 6 - From Power "Over" to Power "For" 77

Figure 7 - From Reproduction to Elegance 89

Figure 8 - From Survival to Connectedness 101

Figure 9 - Marcus's Spheres of Desire 122

Figure 10 - Summary of Guides 141

Figure 11 - Dimensions as Thought Boundaries 149

Figure 12 - Levels of Influence 161

Figure 13 - A Crucial Intersection 164

Figure 14 - The Annunciation 165

Figure 15 - Adaptations to Life 184

1
The Pattern of a Quest

So come with me into the lion's
Thicket, and be not afraid.
Where we're going, no more
Wounding, just mercy unfolding.

Rumi. Circa 1300.

Owain's quest

Around the year 1200 in Europe, near the time of Rumi, traveling troubadours performed stories for people who were largely illiterate. To hold their audiences, and to keep themselves entertained, these masters of ceremonies sought out themes that cut to the heart of the human condition and appealed on multiple levels. They told or sang and energetically mimed their episodic tales intentionally leaving their followers to mull over the adventures until they returned. Not unlike those of us trying to anticipate the next season of TV dramas like *Mad Men* or *Homeland* their devotees anxiously awaited the next action-packed installment. These storytellers were real entertainers.

A quest is the oldest form of storytelling. Owain's quest is a lesser-known story from its era, yet this timeless tale perfectly describes, in allegorical terms, the way many of us feel today as we battle for meaning and power in our modern day "castles." With heightened pressures of work, often tedious commutes and road warrior expectations there seems no end to the daily rounds. As people courageously struggle to keep their jobs, bring up their families and meet never-ending monthly payments, it isn't much of a stretch to think of them as the modern knights of our time. Just as the knights of old faced continuous pressures to perform or to be literally unseated, so it is in today's workplace. In modern organizations people are often only as good as their last presentation.

For many, the vision they held in their twenties led to great success. But later in life a disturbing event or events suggests that something is no longer working. We ask ourselves, what's happened to that wave of engagement and connection we once rode with such energy? Why are we suddenly faced with an impending sense of loss? The story of Owain deals with this question and helps us recover ourselves through the telling of his adventures. We re-identify crucial imaginative sources so the vision we're capable of cultivating is expanded. For some, it may turn out to be expansive enough to contribute to the very survival and evolution of humanity itself.

The party is on, till the past intrudes

It is a lush mid-summer's night, and King Arthur is holding court to honor one of his finest knights, Lord Owain. For the celebration there is much revelry and feasting—brimming flagons of mead, ambrosia overflowing golden goblets, the rich smell of roasted joints of meat simmering on the fire.

But for Owain, there remains a nagging feeling that all is not well in spite of his triumphs. Only last evening he returned with the king and his knights from a tournament where he vanquished every opponent. Indeed, ever since Owain rejoined Arthur's court it's as though he has never left. Certainly his sudden disappearance and strange absence three years earlier has faded from the minds of the others in the banquet hall. Instead everyone, including the illustrious king, is at pains to honor Owain's prowess, especially because he has just triumphed in the lists.

Then a shocking event unfolds. Suddenly, as though from another realm, a woman on horseback brazenly enters the King's banquet hall. A hush falls over the room, intensifying the sharp sound of hooves echoing off stone walls as she rides the length of the chamber towards Owain. Filled with an overwhelming sense of foreboding, he watches the amazing spectacle. Quickly he realizes he knows this mysterious horsewoman. How could he not? It's the intrepid Luned. At once his mind flashes back.

Owain's first adventure

Owain's quest had begun many years earlier when he witnessed the return of an eager and impetuous young knight who had left the court in search of the ultimate challenge. He had returned devastated by the awesome power of the Black Knight, defender of an extraordinary garden realm ruled by a beautiful countess. That young knight had not been able to approach the garden, let alone the legendary woman who lived at its heart.

The next day Owain donned his armor, mounted his charger and left Arthur's court. Determined to retrace the younger man's footsteps and challenge the great Black Knight, he hoped to succeed where others had failed. He would enter the powerfully defended magic garden realm and meet that extraordinary woman. He endured many battles and adventures along the way, but finally Owain found himself at the fountain the eager young knight had described as the entrance to the garden.

After wetting a slab with water at the fountain as the young man had directed, and weathering the vicious storm he had foretold, the huge Black Knight appeared. The fight was long and brutal but Owain, finally striking a lucky blow, forced the wounded warrior to flee into the forest. Galloping through the trees Owain pursued his struggling opponent, but before he could reach him, his adversary came to a great pair of gates. The heavy bars of iron swung open admitting the dark figure into the realm he was to defend. Owain rushed on, forcing his way through, but the gates suddenly swept closed behind him, trapping him.

Owain would have been put to death if Luned had not appeared to guide him. She protected him as she rendered him magically invisible and showed him great kindness when she ushered him to a room where she fed and comforted him. Luned confirmed that the kingdom belonged to her mistress, the countess, whose realm and honor the Black Knight was sworn to defend.

As the story goes, that night the Black Knight, whom Owain had mortally wounded, died, leaving the countess and her people without a powerful defender. Owain, victorious, realized his destiny and with Luned's help persuaded the countess to take him as her new husband, and her people to accept him as their protector.

So it was that Owain became the new Knight of the Fountain. His role would be to defend the countess in her garden of peace and harmony. He would be the chosen one. Her knight in shining armor would forever protect this sacred realm from invaders; defend it against those who would always be from the world of castles, where the game is to expand territory and power.

Back to the "real" world

Meanwhile back at the king's court, King Arthur and the boys were restless without a war to occupy them. Besides, they missed their former favorite champion. Three years had passed since Owain's vanishing act, and the king could wait no longer. As there were no battles for his restless men to fight, he formed a party of three hundred men-at-arms and set out in search of his missing knight.

Like Owain, they too arrived in due course at the barren old tree and its fountain. The past repeats itself and after some ceremony a heavily armored and helmeted Black Knight appeared. He challenged Arthur's best men to single combat. Owain was unrecognizable under his visor and cloak of black armor as were his old friends in their battle regalia, and so the fighting ensued. One by one they fell under the Black Knight's sword until it was the turn of Arthur's second most valiant knight, Sir Gawain. The two men clashed furiously until a chance strike knocked Gawain's helmet from his head. At that, Owain raised his visor, the two men recognized each other and ceased combat.

Removing his armor, Owain made his king welcome and invited his escort back to the countess's castle where it is said they feasted for a full three months.[10] When at last Arthur could put off his kingly duties no longer, he invited Owain to return with him to the court. Owain, seriously tempted, asked his countess to release him from his sacred guard duty for a time. Reluctantly, she gave him permission to return to Arthur's court—for as much as a year, but not a minute longer.

Owain returned to the diverting life of the castle where the busy round of tournaments and banquets soon drove his promise from his mind. Life was good amongst his comrades, and the accolades were welcome. Without much thought, he caroused and jousted away the next three years.

The crunch

Memories of his commitment to the realm of the fountain return to Owain as Luned, robed in yellow satin and mounted on a bay horse, rides into Arthur's great hall. As she dismounts and abruptly steps up to him she removes the ring the countess had bestowed on him.

"Thus," her clear voice proclaims to the assembled nobles, the king, and to those who had dallied far too long at the party, "shall be treated the deceiver, the traitor, the faithless and the disgraced. Shame to thee!" She then tells him that even if he should attempt a return to the garden, he will not find his way. It's over. Without another word Luned remounts, turns her horse and rides into the night. Silence falls on the room until hushed voices slowly begin to fill the hall as everyone wonders aloud at this strange event.

Confused and shattered, our great champion is not only denounced in front of his king and comrades but is suddenly bitterly aware of the shallowness of the court. Struck by feelings of love for the countess and her garden realm and now conscious of how carelessly he has lost both, Owain rushes from the great hall into the night. But Luned has vanished.

That old-time lonely feeling

This is where I normally pause in the story, and spend some time on what Owain is feeling. At last, our hero is conscious of the great gift he received but now has lost. Owain, this once perfect knight, had been initiated into the garden. But now having broken his word, and severed his participation in that realm, he feels unbearable sorrow. There's no going back to the court, which now seems worthless anyway. Nor can he return to the garden. Stranded, Owain is headed for despair.

We can predict a painful ordeal lies ahead when old roads narrow into blind alleys, when the crises in personal and professional life begin to race out of control. If these life crunches coincide with a global economic restructuring and a crisis of sustainability, then things can get really tough. Old ways are not working. Even worse, the old goals don't seem worth pursuing.

This point in Owain's story corresponds to where we begin our own. Our real quest starts here, where we find ourselves seriously out of whack with the world and our role in it. It's what I refer to as "the crunch"—the moment when familiar solutions no longer work, and we need to set a new course. Somehow, like Owain, we too have become distracted in the castles of competition and materialism. We've lost touch with the world of growth and fertility.

Much has been written about diagnosing the problems that we share with Owain, and I'll say more as I link them to today's challenges. But this book is about more than diagnosis—I'm interested in finding ways to navigate the rest of our lives.

One issue is that this journey will need more focus and commitment than many people may realize. Happily there are trustworthy guides and great examples from esteemed sources of wisdom in the past and present. I'll draw on the humanities to provide both inspiration and cautionary tales. But the sources are also drawn from modern heroes whose lives clearly illustrate a path of courage and imaginative expansion. And, for men, we'll find that the presence of a guide like Luned can help us achieve the change of heart that life demands at this stage. This inner change is connected to a revived imagination and to profound changes in life goals. **This is for nothing less than the restoration of our own garden of inspiration, vision and reconnection.**

As it turns out, we've not reached the end of Owain's story, and it need not be the end of our own. Now we need to know how our hero tried to recover himself and his place in the countess's garden. What further challenges did he meet? Who helped him? Did he make it? And what's most important to us here: can the patterns of Owain's adventure help illuminate our path today?

As we'll discover the answer to the last question is, yes. But first, let's see what happened to Owain.

The swamp and ashes

The troubadours tell how our knight wandered alone into the woods, scavenging for food until his health failed and, almost dead, he collapsed near a swamp. They knew their audiences would understand this to mean he gave way to a state of despair and that each step taken by our hero necessarily held the threat of being dragged deeper into dark murky waters. Terms like the swamp and ashes were understood to describe psychological conditions of loss and despair—dead embers on a cold hearth.

Owain's last failing steps brought him to the estate of a wealthy widow, where one of the servants spotted the dying man. The widow instructed that he be given a healing balm and after three months our struggling knight regained his strength. To repay her kindness he confronted a larcenous neighbor. After that, she begged him to stay, but now nothing could keep Owain from his quest to regain the love of his countess. Distraction could no longer keep him from his goal.

His quest had changed from that of a brash young knight eager for adventure and fame. Motivated by a new perspective, Owain now sought a different outcome. His was a search for reconnection; a pursuit of consciousness.

One day, while wandering on his lonely way, he heard a thundering roar through the trees, then a second and a third. Following the noise he found himself on a cliff in the center of the forest. In it was a cleft where a huge serpent held a white lion; whenever the trapped beast tried to escape, the serpent struck, and the lion let out a roar of anger and frustration. Owain unsheathed his sword and slashed at the serpent until it lay dead on the ground. The job done, he resumed his journey but soon noticed the lion was following him. Sporting about like a greyhound he had reared himself, this magnificent beast seemed determined to remain by his side. They traveled together until evening when the lion briefly disappeared, before returning with food to share.

Reading the allegory, we see that Owain built a relationship with powerful natural—instinctual—forces. These were at his service, but not fully under his control. They never are. Getting back in touch with unexplained mysteries is not for control freaks.

That night as he was preparing the food Owain heard a loud moan, then a second and a third. Following the sounds, he called out to ask whether it was an earthly creature that made such a mournful noise.

"Indeed it is." came the answer.

"Who are you?" asked Owain.

"God knows I am Luned, handmaiden to the Countess of the Fountain. And I am imprisoned for the sake of a young man who stayed a short time with my lady before returning to court and never returned. Two of her chamberlains reviled this man and called him false. And when I attempted to protect his name they imprisoned me in this stone, and said I should not remain alive unless he came to defend me by a certain day—no later than tomorrow. His name is Owain."

Needing time and a plan to free his imprisoned friend, Owain and his lion set out to find some answers. On their way they found themselves approaching a fortress that appeared prosperous, although all inside were glum. Inquiring why, the knight learned that a giant had abducted the owner's two sons, and would return the next day to demand his only daughter—or he would kill the boys.

If it's not one thing, it's another; and so the following day Owain—by now calling himself "The Knight of the Lion"—not only had to rescue Luned but confront a giant as well. As the story goes, the giant objected, complaining it was not honorable to have a lion assist one in combat. Owain conceded this was not the way of chivalry, and ordered the lion to be locked in the fortress. The battle raged for hours and was not going well for Owain and so, sensing his master's danger, the great beast clawed his way out of the cell. Fearlessly he leaped over the fortress walls to Owain's aid—arriving just in time to kill the giant.

After that, Owain moved straight on to the task of freeing the bound Luned. Once again, the chamberlains asked him to restrain the lion. They argued, "Chieftain, we agreed to fight with you alone, and that animal is a fiercer opponent than you are." Again Owain agreed, but then found himself in trouble. Without being summoned the lion burst from its restraints to save him. Here we see that the power behind life, those forces of nature on which our lives depend, are often beyond our control. Towards the end of this story, Owain and the lion release Luned.

After still further adventures that, unlike the troubadours, I won't go into, Owain, his now wounded lion and Luned finally find their way back to the garden. In the French version of the story, Owain is disguised and Luned contrives to get the countess to swear that she will do everything in her power to help reconcile the knight with his lady. Only after the countess agrees to help, is Owain's identity revealed and she is at long last persuaded to forgive him for having not returned as promised.

When Owain again leaves the realm of the fountain to return to Arthur's court, we are told, "He took the countess with him and she was his only wife as long as she lived."[11]

The symbolism in the allegory of Owain is straightforward. Shown below in figure 1 is a diagrammatic view of the story with only key points outlined.

On the left are three levels to be expanded in Chapter 4.

- ✶ The top level is the garden, teeming with life. Here, water is abundant, glistening in fountains and fresh rivers. It's a place of connection, beauty and stewardship where the waters of life flow from the gifts of nature, including the endless free energy of the sun.

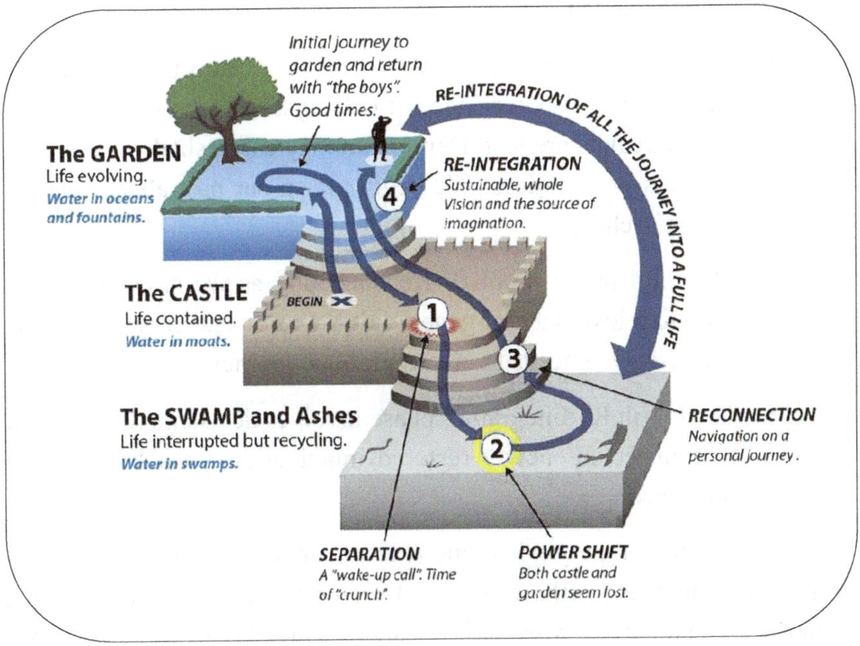

Figure 1- Owain's Journey

- ✶ The middle level is the castle. It's concerned with the basics, including power and basic survival, protection and containment. Water is restricted in moats to ward off intruders and can easily become stagnant. It needs periodic refreshing.
- ✶ The lowest level is the swamp, a place of decay. Stories often connect this region to the idea of "ashes" referring to remnants of what was once alive. Critically though, it's also a link in the recycling of earth and water needed to sustain life. It's a place of despair but also possible renewal.

In the diagram, our hero undergoes the four transformations I've identified, which are shared in other sagas.

- ✶ The first is Separation where we're pulled or even torn away from our lives through crisis. It involves a "wake-up call," accompanied by the realization of what we've done or failed to do with the original garden.
- ✶ The second is the Power Shift where we learn through adversity that our use of power needs to change. Here both the castle and garden realms are lost. Depression may cast a shadow on a review of one's past choices. We begin to see our past abuses of power and seek change.
- ✶ The third phase involves Reconnection as we navigate our way back to a lost place of generativity. There is no easy path mapped out here. One needs to create a unique journey of recovery.
- ✶ The fourth Re-Integration phase involves decisions regarding how to connect our newly restored imaginations to a life of greater substance.

Once back in the garden, one is to integrate the entire journey into a life that encompasses all three levels. It seems we are to return to the real world to serve and apply what we've learned. Part of that role, for example, is to integrate the stewardship of the natural world into everyday life.

Owain's journey

The journey to the garden is always difficult. There are hurdles and guardians. Some of these are of our own making, based on fears that we'll risk the safer world of economic and social success we've at last begun to master. But once we've arrived it's hard to stay in the garden, especially if we've been competent in the castle. It seems the world wants to reclaim you. The "boys" arrive to see how you're doing, and pretty soon they've created a job for you back in the castle. You feel you're better prepared now, you know the games, and can always easily slip back to the garden.

Compared to the challenges for access to the garden it's easy to go back to the level of the castle. It's what you're good at, after all. And it has a gravitational pull powered by great celebrations, the rewards of ambition, tests of strength and ego, fame, and possibly more parties. By contrast, the echoes of the garden quickly fade. It can't compete with experiences of combat, victory and celebration. The garden lacks the adrenaline kick we've become addicted to.

It's only when you notice the loss that you're staggered by its implications. You've had no idea what it means to be banished forever from the garden—none of us has— and the experience takes the wind out of your sails. You may feel a deep sense of having suffered the biggest loss of your life. You are adrift, without a compass—an exile from both worlds. The pain can be so great that if there's any chance at all to return to the garden you'll do everything in your power to get back. It may seem impossible (and it may not happen) but the only way to make it back is not to lose heart. And, as it turns out, to experience a change of heart.

In contemplating your return, the realization dawns that you can't just follow the same old maps. Those charts—your former intellectual "takes" on the world—don't apply anymore. You need to change how you think, feel and apply your will to discover the kind of new responses linked to a fresh imagination. Guidance is necessary too, for changing how you've used your personal energy for most of your life. And it's more than just knowledge that will change. You'll need to experience a radical shift in your moment-to-moment orientation to situations. You'll come to understand with

Aldous Huxley that "**Knowledge is a function of being.**"[12] [Emphasis added.]

You probably won't make it by letting yourself become a victim, a mommy's boy or daddy's girl, or by taking refuge in the ivory tower of pure intellect. Academics have security issues too—just think of the term "Alma Mater!"

This trip takes guts.

In our story, both Luned and the countess play roles as old as storytelling itself. These female figures have been studied, painted and featured in countless images throughout the ages. We meet them in dramas and movies. For now, I'll refer to them as guides but will get into more detail about these key figures of the imagination in the next chapters. For a man, as an example, this guiding image has been called "the anima." Women have a corresponding set of guides in this way of thinking.[13] Some other guides, like the lion, come from a more primitive animal kingdom, whose denizens are less dominated by intellect.

This ending of the Owain story is not about isolation, nor is it a happy ever after retirement in a luxury resort. It's tempting to imagine ourselves sitting beneath a tree, basking in sunshine and gentle breezes. A permanent vacation may be the travel industry's idea of bliss, but it's a state with neither tension nor its flip side—potential. No, the ending is not about hiding in the garden. It deals with integrating vital garden qualities into the world. It's about re-entering the "real world," and now being better equipped to deal with it, thanks to revealed and reaffirmed gifts. Those gifts are the payoff for the challenging work we'll undertake to renew the power of the imagination. No doubt there is a need for another renaissance. I believe these transformational periods can be nurtured and even planned. They can form patterns for the quest of our lives.

The reward is worth the trials and effort. Those who do make the journey are in the company of lions. They will acquire the intellectual and emotional heft—the true humility and personal will—to free their imaginations and fire it up in others. They will make a huge difference.

They are the catalysts of the next renaissance.

2
Imagining Imagination

Things are reversed from what they should be in this place
you live now.
One who should be hung on the scaffold is made emperor.
People stand and clap.
Tombs with ornamental plaster, self-conceit everywhere.
Palm trees made of wax, wax leaves and fruit, wax dirt.

Rumi

Centuries ago, Rumi grasped the essence of how many of us have come to feel about our culture today, even anticipating Hollywood sets and a Disneyland-view of nature.

If we're lucky, this sense of alienation helps precipitate a crisis, which can initiate change. The historian Arnold Toynbee said all civilizations face threats and challenges—it's the quality of response that makes all the difference.[14] Our globalized civilization faces a number of unprecedented threats. The effectiveness of our response depends on a fundamental human quality—the **imagination**.

The subject of the imagination—like the faculty itself—is potentially unbounded. In the next pages, I'll explore what has proved helpful in nurturing the imaginative life.

We begin from a difficult place. In today's world, every day can feel like the morning after the storm—or the calm just before one. We live, it seems, perpetually at the center of a buffeting cyclone of data and demands: overflowing e-mail in-boxes, 24 hour news cycles, always-open markets, instant messaging, live Tweeting, and a quarter-billion Internet sites (and counting). Just staying current is a full-time job. Then there's the unstable economy, fickle consumers, ruthless workplace expectations, shrinking accountability horizons, epidemic partisanship, and looming environmental calamities. Wherever you look, certainty and predictability are fading memories.

Over the years, I have written or read hundreds of book-length reports on the various problems faced by CEOs and dysfunctional executive teams. I've witnessed a few compelling visions dumbed down to bullet points and then undermined by the 24/7 encroachments on thinking time. And the idea of pursuing a lifelong career in any one company is seen as naive.

Everywhere, we see people thinking in ever-shorter frames that barely allow them to skim the surface of a problem or project. At conferences designed to address complex, pressing challenges, attention spans and allotted times for speakers have steadily declined. People clicking through texts and emails consume networking breaks. *The Wall Street Journal* reported that even when alone in their office cubicles, workers are now interrupted, or interrupt themselves, every 180 seconds on average. It then takes them 23 minutes to get back to their original task.[15] The very basis of individual and organizational vision has been undermined as surely as the beaches off New Orleans and New Jersey. A toxic change in the climate of consciousness erodes our imaginations. We used to pay attention to periods of speculation, reflections and dreams in some cases.

When we narrow the lens to examine a single organization, we often see only disconnected silos. The promises made to customers by sales staff pursuing personal bonuses deny the technical realities being wrestled with by engineering—a dysfunction that has bred years of scathing *Dilbert* cartoons. When cuts are called for, each executive is eager to respond "as long as it's not in **my** department."

The troubles we face are sometimes described as **wicked**—they are complicated, with many interrelated dynamics and feedback loops. Efforts to resolve one aspect frequently only make them more intractable in another.

No wonder we feel things becoming more expedient, and ultimately coarser. That's a predictable outcome of the loss of a compelling unifying vision.

This situation has been forming for hundreds of years with the rise in technology and secular values. The English poet and artist William Blake was a passionate critic of this kind of thinking and what it had spawned in nineteenth-century England, epitomized by grim textile mills and a relentlessly expanding empire. He called it "single vision."

The danger is that a narrow focus flies in the face of truly global interconnectedness. The deep exploitation of resources is accommodated by limited views of interdependence, despite unmistakable evidence to the contrary. Pollution in China and nuclear meltdowns in Japan are attaining global reach, even being measured in North America.

There's a phenomenon called "motion induced blindness" that demonstrates what happens to our ability to see very basic patterns when we focus narrowly on a central point in a changing landscape. The effect is shown in a beautifully set-up simple web animation with three fixed dots on a rotating background. These periodically disappear for viewers as they fixate their gaze on the center point. I urge you to check out the website shown in the endnotes to experience it yourself.[16] You'll discover just how profoundly our best "laser vision" impairs what we see, even when it's right in front of us. Today, all around us, we see the danger and self-limitation of navigating with such a single point of focus.

I won't dwell in depressing detail on issues that are becoming only too familiar. But here is a one-paragraph synopsis. The 1987 film *Wall Street* captured a decade of blow-out-the-doors excess in the pitch-perfect phrase "greed is good." In its sequel more than a decade later, Michael Douglas, reprising his role as financier Gordon Gekko, addresses a university audience. Again, he captures the spirit of the age in a phrase even more pungent. Gekko tells his eager twenty-something listeners, in a milder paraphrase here, that they are all screwed.

But it's not our inescapable destiny to succumb to narrowing, coarsening perspectives limited by a declining imagination. So how can we grasp this fluid, dynamic topic without capturing and paralyzing it in our analytical webs?

What *is* the imagination anyway?

Throughout time, great thinkers have recognized that the imagination is central to human consciousness. The Old Testament says, "Where there is no vision, the people perish."[17]

The early Greek philosopher Heraclitus viewed the imagination as a way of seeing into the flux of existence. His famous river quote, that we don't step into the same river twice, is revealing.[18] Often missed in this idea is that when you step into the stream, **both** you and the river are changing. You're not the same, and the river is not the same.

The English poets Coleridge, Wordsworth, and Blake saw the imagination as the defining characteristic of man—it's what can make us great. Through vision, Wordsworth experienced "A presence that...rolls through all things."[19] Is this the presence, often called "the way," that has inspired Eastern consciousness? These writers and their earlier antecedents influenced further generations of thinkers. In the twentieth-century, the Swiss psychologist Carl Jung described images from myth and deep ancestral roots as the very essence of our psychic life.

Happily, the dark ages of behaviorism in 1950s psychology and a desperate, doomed attempt to turn psychology into a branch of physics seem over. Today's behavioral economists and cognitive psychologists are again acknowledging the power of unconscious drives. But the imagination seems to be a topic beyond most modern research. This is hardly surprising as it's proven elusive and can't be directly probed through analysis. But that doesn't mean it's inaccessible.

And that's a good thing. The world increasingly—and urgently—needs imaginative solutions.

How is imagination defined? New references to this quality frequently appear, but differ widely or are unclear.

The Oxford English Dictionary states:

> —The faculty or action of forming new ideas, or images or concepts of external objects not present to the senses:
> —the ability of the mind to be creative or resourceful;
> —the part of the mind that imagines things.

I'm going to expand on ideas for imagining imagination. Or perhaps it's better said, for the **process** of imagining. Specifically, let's consider not what the imagination **is,** but what imagination **does,** and how it's connected to our values.

Imagination and values are deeply connected

"Values" include what we care about, and how we act.[20] As soon as we enter the realm of care we're into the emotional aspects of life. And, as it turns out, these influences—our emotions—underlie all our decisions.

Imagination has been said to be at the top of all our values.[21] Jacob Hirsh of the University of Toronto expressed this view in a program on Canadian radio and in conversation. He sees imagination at the pinnacle of our values because it allows us to envision any number of worlds.

I would argue that the relationship between imagination and values is rather one of mutual influence. For example, which world we select from our images—building a utopia or a punishment center for infidels—is a choice made on the basis of our values. These values act as organizing principles for our imaginative life and stem from more than the realm of thinking. Vision is deeply invested with emotion.[22] Take empathy, as an example, when our imaginative ability to share and understand the feelings of another may lead to change, and possibly a desire to help. So if we want someone to imagine a better future for themselves, and for the rest of us, we need them to see better and feel better. A **change of heart** is needed, and values acted upon, if they are true values.

To illustrate the relationship between imagination and values let's look briefly at Shakespeare's *King Lear.* At the beginning of the play, Lear wishes to resign his position as king and divide the kingdom. You could say he no longer wants the job. Instead, Lear's goal is to enjoy a king's life free of regal duties. "Born a king, always a king" is not quite his motto. He envisions a world where he can hunt and carouse and spend whatever time he wishes with each of his daughters, but if the kingdom goes to rack and ruin, don't look to him.

Unhappily, Lear, while attempting to hand over his power and land to his daughters, chooses to test each of them to see if their love meets his standard, proving their loyalty and worthiness as inheritors of his kingdom. These are values Lear holds so strongly that he insists on hearing them expressed. The youngest daughter Cordelia refuses to make false statements concerning her love for him. She refuses to buy her allotment of the kingdom in this way. He reacts angrily and banishes her. The other two daughters, who want his assets, but not his company, betray Lear with false declarations of love and Lear buys in. He turns the kingdom over. With the older two at the helm, he soon finds himself a castaway. Thrown out of what was once his own empire, Lear is left to his fate. An old man discarded on the road to nowhere, a king in crisis.

In this moment of truth, Shakespeare asks his audience to imagine Lear at the point of no return, hopelessly lost in a storm, or as it turns out, lost in two storms. We're not only to envision a storm raging on the landscape of the story, but also that torrent raging in the heart and soul of a man and a king who was once the most powerful in the land. Lost in our imagining of this old king, completely aware of the thoughtless deeds he has committed, Shakespeare then has us imagine an amazing circumstance that neither Lear nor his audience could have predicted.

To this point in the play we have only known a man totally ill-equipped to be king. Selfish and immature, it's as though he deserves the tragedy he has bestowed upon himself and the kingdom. But this sense of things changes. In the midst of this tumult, there's a transformation. All of us feel it; the audience and this impotent old king. In his darkest moment, Shakespeare presents a Lear who, for the first time since we've met him, begins to see. In his bitter exile, he notices and is able to identify with other creatures that, like himself, are suffering. The ex-king of all the land sees the plight of possibly the lowliest of all creatures, rats drowning in the deluge of the storm, and he sympathizes with them. He imagines their suffering, and this creates cataclysmic change. The blind king can see! The storm has opened the floodgates and the seeing king will know redemption.

Much of this play is about blindness and vision, how Lear comes to see and finally finds his way. Gloucester, another character, in a moment of personal vision tells us, "I stumbled when I saw."[23] Unlike Lear, who has lost his heart, leaving his vision impaired, Gloucester has in fact lost his eyes; he is literally blinded. But, like Lear, his imagination had failed him when he too misread falsehood for loyalty. He tells us, "I see it feelingly"[24] after this painful insight. Those four words capture a central theme of this book. For both men, we see how seeing better leads to the path of redemption.

Let's look at another example of this relationship between values and imagination. Say for argument's sake that I claim fairness as a value. I'd argue this assertion has to have arisen from some experience or set of influences that I have in mind which validate this value. When you think more about this, it gets interesting.

Here's my experience. On the playground one day, an older bully got under my skin and humiliated me in front of people I wanted to like and respect me. In this instance, I felt powerless to change my circumstances. But years later, while teaching, I saw a student about to be harassed in a similar way and so I stepped in and warned off the bully. I identified with the new victim through memory and imagination and this time I could change the outcome. The imagination is involved when values such as fairness are called on.

In a well-functioning society and a solid organization, I will be backed up. In a dictatorship, my imagination is constrained to suggest actions of a different kind—with different values in play. I may well have to abandon fairness and justice in an instance where the bully is backed up by the State or others. I can then decide whether I will keep quiet, emigrate, adopt tougher values of dominance, or risk my safety. These are the problems facing thousands of people in ongoing uprisings and situations of social unrest. I chose to imagine a different context and to emigrate from apartheid-ruled South Africa.

We're creating and projecting our world

Some cognitive psychologists stress we can only hold about five items in consciousness at any one time and that about 50 percent of our brain is devoted to the visual cortex. We process massive amounts of data to create our mental construct of reality. Each of us applies different unconscious filters to pre-screen the input that creates what we finally see as an issue. To the dismay of some clients and graduate students, it seems each one of us sees an improvised world out there—depending to a large extent on our needs, fears, and interests of the moment. This realization goes back over two hundred years to the revolutionary statement of the philosopher Immanuel Kant, who sparked a "Copernican revolution-in-reverse." He believed that objects "out there" are in fact framed by our own innate cognitive processes.[25] Thousands of years earlier, the Hindus imagined living in a world of Maya, which is a generated and self-projected set of illusions—based on our fears and desires. At 10:00 a.m. that green Starbucks logo may stand out as a beckoning, consciousness-boosting beacon!

Evidence of an improvised world also pours in from the smallest aspects of the universe. One undisputed outcome of the strange world of quantum mechanics is the startling revelation that we create a changed outcome by the simple act of observation. At this level, there is no detached observer—only one who has no choice but to be a player. Neil Turok's 2012 Massey Lecture series titled *The Universe Within* revealed fascinating views of how we co-create reality at the deepest levels.[26]

Blake and Jung amongst others, saw the imagination as a crucial aspect of consciousness precisely because it is so active in creating our realities. Blake based his mythology on the Bible and built beyond that framework in a profoundly spiritual way. The creation story accords imagination the highest place in his worlds—as the seat of the divine.

The self-creation, or at least the co-creation, of reality by our imaginations is more accepted nowadays, but the ways in which the imagination weaves this world are far from clear.

The French philosopher Gaston Bachelard points out that we often equate imagination with the formation of images when, in fact, it's about the **deformation** of images—otherwise it is just perception. What we see then triggers an abundance—an explosion—of images.[27] Imagination is essentially open and elusive and can be massively generative.

The improvisations that are at the heart of great classical music, jazz and blues are about working around a given theme to enhance the mood or momentum of the moment. Often these can't be repeated; explaining the "classic" concerts where a specific set of moments creates a unique alchemy between performers and audience. Have a look at the opening of the *Sacred Fire* concert by Santana, or listen to Glenn Gould's studio recordings of *The Goldberg Variations*. Or try listening to three different performances of "Teach Me Tonight" by Oscar Peterson, Errol Garner and Oliver Jones.

Bachelard also points out that imagination launches us on a journey. Through a gentle push, it puts us off balance and launches us into the unknown where we need an evolving set of skills to guide our lives. So as not to rush back into the familiar arms of safety, we need to learn greater confidence in wider measures. How, for example, might a new opportunity open up unpredictable connections, undeveloped skills, new relationships?

An active middle-ground function

I believe the imagination occupies a **vitally active middle ground** between two levels of consciousness. I've introduced this idea of levels in the Owain story discussed in Chapter 1.

In the next diagram, the upper level deals with connectedness and related concepts. In keeping with a long tradition of imagery and metaphor, I'll repeatedly return to the classic depiction of this higher level as a "garden."

The lower level is divided into two realms. The "real" world—the hard world of daily physical reality, of data and the body, striving and

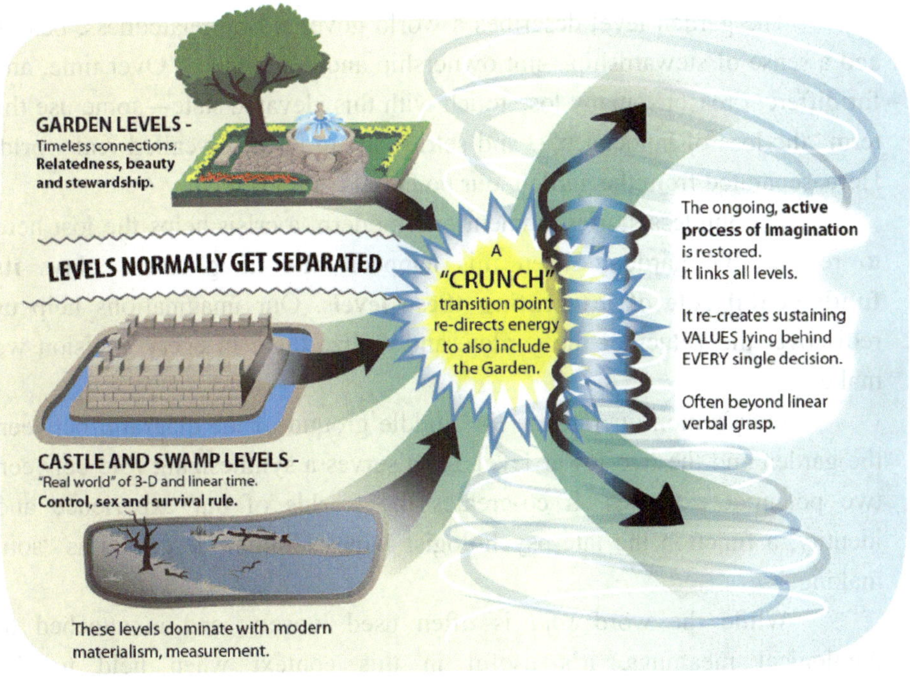

Figure 2 - Imagining Imagination

power—is imagined in the structure of the "castle." The second aspect of this lower level, characterized by images of crisis and corruption, is referred to as the "swamp."

In this symbolic topography, imagination mediates between these major levels of human concern. Without this **key intermediating function**, we risk being carried aloft on flights of inflation or unfounded theory, untethered from the practical experience of life. Alternatively we may descend into the barren, unsatisfying world of barter and materialism.

The diagram captures in visual terms how we see the imagination working in our lives, depicting the vital role it plays, and why it's critical to relearn how to engage actively, and exercise this faculty.

A key aspect of this visualization is the idea that the lower levels of the swamp and castle dominate our modern world (as shown on the left of the diagram). We see in the classic story of Owain how easily these lower levels take over our affairs. Unaware, we're ruled by our basic drives: survival, sexual dominance and other forms of control over others.

The garden level describes a world governed by relatedness, beauty and a sense of stewardship—not ownership and exploitation. Over time, and for different reasons, many lose touch with this elevated state—some use the term "the loss of innocence"—and settle for life in the so-called real world. Here, separated from the garden, our potential is diminished.

In countless stories, ancient and modern, a crisis helps the lost hero to recover the garden. When this happens, **the imagination plays its fundamental role of integrating these levels**. Our imaginations help us rediscover the values of the garden, and realize them in every decision we make.

Imagination operates in the middle ground of the diagram, between the garden and the two lower levels, and serves a synthesizing role between two potential extremes. It co-creates the worlds of our experience and identity, a function the late psychologist James Hillman described as "soul making."

While the word *soul* is often used loosely, and is attached to theological meanings, it's useful in this context when held to the psychological function of actively synthesizing our world through the imagination. Carl Jung, in fact, titled one of his most influential books *Modern Man in Search of a Soul*.[28]

We can't easily do a dictionary pin-down here, because we're describing a process, a kind of kinetic mental energy that is one of the core manifestations of consciousness. It's the way we create our world, which makes it difficult for any of us to stand outside that process and see it in action. Hillman, however, used process terms very effectively. In his description, the soul is "the imaginative possibility in our natures."[29]

Myths—stories beneath the imagination

Imagination may be elusive, but it can be accessed. The time-tested gateways include indirect means, such as myths, which are nothing less than the stories of the soul.

Anyone who claims to be free of the influence of myth is probably unaware of the narratives that drive them. Think of the unquestioning acceptance today of endless economic growth, of jobs, the market, and progress. These, collectively, are a myth that in the not-so-distant future may collapse into its own contradictions.

Think of others, the Facebook and Twitter fiends who race to catch the latest deals and news. They are driven by the myth of connectedness that the Greeks identified with the god Hermes. The Romans adapted this to their god Mercury. The addiction to checking online devices (now up to 80 minutes a day on average) and the mercurial volatility it engenders, recreates this myth in twenty-first century terms.

The Left promotes its myth. In its most reductionist form, all people are essentially equal. This idea creaks along in Western democracies (but is under siege). It is much less central in the Chinese meritocracy. This equality myth overturns the Greek ideal that our leaders need to be people of special virtue, modeling generativity, empathy, and excellence.

The point is that **myths live through us**. We're their heroes and their villains. That person standing on Main Street is Ulysses. **He is on the quest of his life.**

However, the Greeks, Romans and many other cultures, were conscious of the roles of their Gods and honored them in festivals and ceremonies. But over time things have unraveled, and as far as I can tell, the best approach to this decline is through the lens of the late mythologist Joseph Campbell.

Even without the privilege of attending Campbell's lectures, I found his writing and videos to be in a different league. A preeminent scholar of western psychology and Eastern and Western mythologies, he hosted an extraordinarily popular New York radio program for the general listener on myths that we all live by in the everyday world. One of his books in particular, *The Hero With a Thousand Faces,* found favor with the public and academics. What I appreciated was his efforts to reach out to non-exclusive audiences. He made a huge contribution.

It was Campbell who argued that we're in a time where the key integrating functions of myth have collapsed. Mythologies in older cultures used to fulfill several functions. They helped reconcile people in their relationships, their role in society, their link to their environment, and to see their connection to the cosmos. Great traditions, priesthoods, and organizations arose to help them. The myths of the day supported science and psychology, as they were then constituted.

But from around 1200, there was a breakdown in the sustaining power of myths. Dogma was questioned, and the march of science showed time and again that the old stories were not literal truths. Copernicus hurled our planet into space; Hubble lost us in a hundred billion galaxies, and now quantum mechanics questions space, time, and even causality.

The breakdown in the power of the old myths led the troubadours to tell a new sort of story. The need for each of us to follow our unique path in search of the lost grail characterized their tales. Set in this era, Owain's story marks the beginning of a new consciousness. This narrative helps us map a creative path as individuals and teaches that we need a quest to deal with the collapse of our foundations.

The Secret Sabbatical will help us on our journey. It will **reconnect** us and then help us create a **new integration** of age-old human concerns in the light of the massive and accelerating revelations of science.

In terms of reconnection it will recover our links to timeless myths that remain central to the human condition, and with how we handle questions of inevitable life changes of love, loss and legacy. If we can become more aware of which myths we are living or are living through us, we can perhaps access their power and shed their constraints. Owain is a version of the timeless myth of the adventurer in search of his soul. That is the reconnection part.

The second aspect of the journey is the creation of a new integration of classic human concerns that is not alien to science and its extraordinary findings. The scope ranges from the expanding nano-world to the churning gasses of the distant stars that harbor the same building blocks of life we've been privileged to assemble and enjoy. Joseph Campbell glimpsed a part of the new synthesis. He was still alive to appreciate, and focus us on, the mythical power of the image of the earth rising from the vantage point of lunar orbit. Talk about a new perspective! He saw NASA's "Earthrise"[30] as a defining image of the new global imagination and he's given us a wonderful impetus. This image changed the consciousness of some.

But the majority of us struggle with the great disconnect between a mythology now largely lost and the overwhelming sense of being alienated in a world of incomprehensible science. Instead of gods like Ulysses on a great journey, we have celebrities like Kim Kardashian, who is famous for being famous.

Before we take up the challenge of our own journey, in the next chapter we'll examine symptoms and causes of the decline of the imagination.

3
The Failure of the Imagination: Some Symptoms and Causes

There are those that say, "Nothing lasts."
They're wrong. Every moment they say,
"If there were some other reality,
I would have seen it. I would know about it."

Rumi

If the imagination plays a central role in how we perceive reality, some say in creating it, then it follows we should be concerned about its decline. I'll begin this chapter by naming a few symptoms and probable causes as necessary background.

Problems arise from factors such as a self-serving focus on "single vision" goals, the shallow application of psychological principles, and blind spots in our perceptual toolkits. Below I list six symptoms and four causes.

Symptoms

Corporations squander the loyalty bonus

A benefit of my consulting work is that I've had access to many companies' internal books. While the scope of each organization differs widely, the figures consistently demonstrate that customer loyalty is a striking advantage for any enterprise. The result is much, much higher bottom-line profits. How does 40 percent more profit from a five percent increase in loyalty sound? Developing an ongoing relationship, and achieving the benefits of referrals and repeat business, requires an active and flexible imagination. One has to be in a dynamic relationship with changing client demands while one's capabilities require development and renewal.

Yet in industry after industry, we see it becoming the norm for organizations to set themselves up **against** their customers. The marketers employ every advantage of scale and marketing sleight of hand to dupe customers and clients out of the largest possible slice of paycheck. The current grail is to switch to ongoing monthly payments, called an annuity model.

The most egregious example of self-defeating conflict is the music industry. As recently as 1990, this was an immensely wealthy business that paid its artists royalties amounting, on average, to a puny seven percent of the income their creative work generated. For this and other reasons, the industry was loathed. In the subsequent decade, its giants introduced the digital compact disk, forcing many of us to buy all of our music again. But in going for greed, they also unwittingly committed a grave strategic error, releasing into the world what were effectively master copies of their musical libraries in digital form. In the words of strategic planning: "they gave away the vault." These flawless copies could easily be ripped and distributed endlessly over the emerging Internet. When music downloading became widespread, rather than adopt a new business model, the industry responded by suing its customers. Now it was loathed **and** feared. Good work, guys!

Only one company addressed so-called music piracy creatively: Apple, whose iTunes became perhaps its biggest strategic coup of all. Now that model is under dramatic change as the plummeting cost of online storage has led all the giants (Apple, Amazon and Google) to rush into online streaming services hosted on their massive data centers scattered across the world. One dominant player will probably emerge and it may or may not be Apple.

Let the good times, and annuities, roll!

Narrowing of goals to self-limiting assumptions—single vision measures.

The idea of pursuing a limited number of goals arose from the Industrial Revolution, where tight and specific measures were needed to plot progress on the production lines. The metrics were founded on a number of underlying assumptions about the organization and what motivated people. Fatally, the assumptions became so deeply rooted in the culture of the companies that the required changes simply could not be approved for those who needed to implement them. Countless human and organizational casualties continue to follow this predictable barrier to innovation.

Conventional wisdom says choosing our targets and going for them is the way to get things done. It's how we measure success and cut the winners from the losers. It's also completely oblivious to any dimension other than its singular goal. Were it displayed in an individual, this censoring of the full spectrum of possibilities would suggest denial verging on clinical insanity. In a century increasingly defined by network effects, it's crazy to think the goal is all there is to pursue in either one's personal life or the corporate jungle.

As someone raised in the business environment of a great industrial and mining corporation, it was a life-changing moment to read one day that General Motors was acting on a series of unstated but implicit assumptions. Any experienced outsider could clearly recognize them.[31] They were unbelievably unimaginative and included shallow stereotypes. An example was the belief that "Cars are primarily status symbols. Styling is therefore more important than quality to buyers who are, after all, going to trade up every other year." Other assumptions were that gas would always be cheap, the environmental movement was a fad, and that strict, centralized financial controls were the secret to good administration. These beliefs proved to be fatally flawed—some literally. Yet even decades later, while GM's European, Japanese and Korean competitors boasted novel technology and styling advances, this kind of thinking still seemed evident. And when were these misguided ideas first pointed out? In 1983!

A full generation later, in the spring of 2014, GM began recalling 1.6 million vehicles for quality issues with a potentially lethal ignition switch fault they'd known about for over a decade. Problems persisted and by July 2014, GM had recalled more vehicles than they'd built in total in 2013. Recalls had risen above 29 million faulty vehicles, some now found to be burdened by other issues as well. The company admitted to 13 deaths as a result of the ignition fault. The "cost overrides quality" consciousness that had inserted itself in the DNA of GM meant in effect that the cost of the replacement switch seemed to override safety issues. The current cost of the switch for a small car is 57 cents.

This is the logical extension of a process that GM and others began in the 1960s, called "value engineering." I've seen this concept first hand in several organizations and it has a justification up to a point long passed by many companies. The goal here is to strip down the cost of every component to the lowest possible level without affecting performance. Well, at least not so much that it's noticeable.

Was it only coincidence that the 80's also saw GM's hometown rival Chrysler go through the first of an ongoing series of "workouts" fueled by addiction to the classic short-term expedient of price discounting? There is no difference at all to the cycle of addiction of price discounting to any other addictive loop. All rely on short-term patches and ignore longer-term root causes. Chrysler's white knight then was the vastly egotistical Lee Iacocca, who dismissed Chrysler's persistent quality problems with the airy confession that "Sure, we shipped some crap!" In 2010, 2011, and 2012, Chrysler again performed poorly in auto reliability rankings in *Consumer Reports*.

Then there was the powerful "strategic vision" of a former CEO of the Coca-Cola Company. Reflecting a narrowing of the imagination down to a shockingly tight focus, this fellow's epiphany occurred on a trip away from corporate HQ. Several times during the 100 mile limo ride, he noticed he was unable to lay his hands immediately on a Coke. His insight? Coca-Cola's mission henceforth was to ensure that no one on the planet was at any time to be more than ten minutes away from the opportunity to buy one of its products.

This mandate captures the essence of much of our economy. Provide a product (in this case, with no food value but plenty of habit-forming caffeine, endorphin-triggering sugar, and fizzy carbonation) and then steadily eliminate barriers to its consumption. It's called instant gratification. The distinction between this and peddling drugs is hard to distinguish on the facts. Coca-Cola is now targeting the poorest African consumers who down only a meager 39 servings of Coke a year, rather than the attainable 665 annual servings per person achieved in Mexico. The difference between this approach and an imaginative engagement with new, more beneficial beverages has taken Coke decades to launch.

This contagion of symptoms is to my mind the result of an unimaginative pursuit of narrowly defined, short-term wins. These include everything from the housing meltdown, to falsified Wall Street returns, to financial houses that knowingly sold their clients murky securities selected for their probability of tanking while the vendors secretly played the other side of the bet. Rating agencies endorsed investments so risky and toxic that their creators were shorting them personally.

The individuals at the heart of the financial meltdown acknowledge no guilt. A number of them appear in the award-winning 2010 movie about the financial debacle, *Inside Job*, giving no visible sign of remorse.

Single minded heroes as role models

Sadly, there are seemingly endless shallow appraisals and easy-to-prepare recipes for finding our personal passion splashed across the magazine covers at the checkout line. Moreover, these purported quick-fixes have their equivalents in the nominally more serious business culture. None is more central to the Western idea of management or the process of corporate reappraisal than the hallowed notion of goal setting, including sales quotas, budget targets, and not to forget another two percent from supply chain costs. To some, when their broader costs are counted, these ever-tightening targets border on the insane. Crazy—but useful. I suspect this fetish for goal setting has a very definite purpose.

Imaginatively challenged organization leaders who think short-term, love to hire motivational speakers to fire up the troops. They want employees to be inspired to pitch their goals unrealistically high and then strive to reach them. And why wouldn't they? To a narrowly focused mind, short on imagination, that looks like productivity. So they hire star athletes who have done great things by setting incredibly ambitious performance targets and forcing themselves to reach them. Financial firms were particularly fond of Lance Armstrong. Big consulting firms loved Tiger Woods.

The explicit moral being promoted is that the same practices will deliver success in the business world: work harder than you can imagine, sacrifice all else to your singular performance metric, and you too can be a winner. Maybe not at the Tour de France or Masters championship, but close! The popularity of these two particular figures as corporate role models has turned out to be quite revealing. Both men are phenomenally competitive personalities. But all of us, even celebrity athletes, have more than one dimension. It's just that when one of those aspects is so bulked up and dominant, we neglect other dimensions. These negative spaces in personal development are, in a way, the shadows of our strengths. And in the cases of both Armstrong and Woods, these characteristics came to embarrassing public light. They and their sponsors have been looking to image rehabilitation if possible. After Tiger Woods had regained a respectable golf ranking, Nike splashed social media ads proclaiming "Winning takes care of everything" quoting Woods, when asked about his game.

But the darker shadow being cast here is a set of unconscious ego-identifications that these admonitions instill in employees for the organization's benefit. "Just get on with it. Do what it takes to win and your future is secure."

This can be a devastating lie.

The truth, I've found, is that some managers who invoke such ego-inflating rewards are propelling everyone below them to drive up record profits in the shortest possible reporting period to ring up their own bonuses.

Simply follow your passion

The self-help movement churns out endless and easy recipes for finding purpose and achieving success. Newsstand magazines feature easy-to-follow guides to finding your vocation. Sometimes an accompanying questionnaire, matching hundreds of others like it, promises to identify your strengths in order to leverage them in a new career. From here it seems we're only a few steps to the carnival busker's cry "Step right up, folks!" Stephen Covey's *The Seven Habits of Highly Effective People*[32] suggests we simply sit down and prepare a personal mission statement off the top of our heads. In *The Watchman's Rattle*,[33] Rebecca Costa counters the grim inventory of the world's problems with the comforting thought that evolution has never yet failed to adapt to a crisis. Neuroplasticity, the brain's ability to reconfigure itself, will save us, the author claims. However we can help the process along, by paying attention to insight, eating well, and getting lots of sleep, according to Costa!

But there is a fundamental danger to all of these prescriptions, even apart from the sticky point that evolution regularly adapts specific species right out of the game. Usually, the person answering the questionnaire, writing the life-mission statement, or listening to his or her inner voice is **the same one who is feeling adrift** and looking for direction. This person is trying to construct a new and improved future out of the same beliefs, attitudes, and habits of mind that brought him or her to their current disoriented state in the first place. In addiction treatment circles, this mistake is often explained as "My best thinking got me here."

What's worse is that, in pursuit of our individual passion we may mistake our surface appetites for a deeper calling. The effort is well-intentioned enough. It's inspired by a laudable piece of advice from Joseph Campbell, who counseled folks to, in his words, "follow your bliss." But some in Campbell's audiences were inclined to oversimplify the insight, in my view. Many failed to follow his more profound and creative wisdom, preferring instead to take up the catch phrase to justify self-interest. The bliss we are to follow, he meant, is one discovered only after completing a journey of self-discovery and honest acceptance of our rightful place in the world. These are points he stressed in that groundbreaking book *The Hero with a Thousand Faces.*[34] Another of his books reinforces our need to create our own path. Its title, *Creative Mythology,*[35] captures this imperative.

There are many framings of the existential human journey besides Campbell's, of course. In some of these models, for example, we find ourselves playing a certain combination of roles. These originate from whatever it was that helped us to feel safest and most loved in childhood. The idea in these models is to benefit from the potential in the various roles while cultivating sensitivity to being sidelined by their possible over-use in self-defeating interactions. Often feedback from others is helpful.

One of the longest surviving models, *The Enneagram,*[36] identifies roles such as the "performer," "observer," and "helper" while describing the complexities of different personality types. In the best situations, the performer can be a charismatic presenter. But a more negative aspect may involve concealing insecurities beneath an extrovert's 500-watt persona. Under pressure, this person may stretch integrity in the service of a good impression. The observers in society can be incisive and focused artists and scientists as they apply their sharp powers of detached observation. But if the style dominates he or she may live life meekly peering in through emotional keyholes. The caregiver may hold the emotional fabric of groups and families together, but may in certain circumstances slip too easily into the sometimes crippling role of an enabler, and fail to see his or her own life narrowing and falling into ruin.

We all have these shadow elements, called neuroses, as part of our personalities. At the extreme, they may fuel the self-destruction of addiction—to drugs or alcohol, but just as easily to fame, money, success, or the jolt of adrenaline that comes between laying a bet and the turn of a card. There are many ways to become who we aren't.

Many of the shallower questionnaires counsel us to do more of what we love—typically performing, observing, or caregiving, to name the few examples I've chosen. Lamentably, this frequently reinforces the same maladaptive behaviors that brought us to the questionnaire with pen in hand to begin with. When magazines advise people to follow their passions without providing sufficiently trenchant tools to handle their real issues, it's simply bolstering the self-image that readers would like to have strengthened. In reality, we may need substantial change.

Because we might only want shallow affirmations and not the penetrating self-awareness we need, it all but guarantees that most of us will not find the resolution we seek. What is more likely to happen is that these dissatisfied seekers will keep coming back for more: more advice, more shallow analysis, and ultimately, more self-help products.

All this may be good for the self-help entrepreneur. I'm sure it is. But for consumers the real effect of the uncritical injunction to follow your passion may merely be to encourage them to do something like doubling down on addictions. **The problem is reinforced in the guise of being solved.**

Others are picking up on these points. Happily, a new wave of thinkers shares my view that "follow your dreams" prescriptions are largely hollow.[37] In a magazine article that led to several subsequent media interviews, Miya Tokumitsu takes on the "Do what you love" mantra. She is highly critical, for example, of the explosion in the use of unpaid interns who labor to enter the highly desirable fields they love.

According to Tokumitsu, the injunction also brushes aside the vast majority of workers who don't have the luxury or education to be so selective about their work.

She concludes:

> In masking the very exploitative mechanisms of labor that it fuels, DWYL [Do What You Love] is, in fact, the most perfect ideological tool of capitalism. It shunts aside the labor of others and disguises our own labor to ourselves. It hides the fact that if we acknowledged all of our work as work, we could set appropriate limits for it, demanding fair compensation and humane schedules that allow for family and leisure time.[38]

Nonetheless, the very best personal-inventory questionnaires and one-on-one interviews can help us drill through habitual psychological defenses and illuminate some of our limiting character traits. My approach is based on just such a process of steady self-discovery involving navigation through distinct stages, with the help of meaningful examples and experienced guides. What's asked of us is that we steadily see and acknowledge the shadow aspects of our behavior so that we participate more consciously and effectively.

False prophets and the myth of the supercycle

A popular theory holds that the world economy is driven by grand global waves, or supercycles, of sustained overall growth, for the most part independent of human intervention. A current supercycle promises continuing economic growth over decades with only a few setbacks for a new wave of middle class consumers in the emerging economies. However the actual countries cited seem regularly to fall in and out of favor. If we believe this hypothesis, we must somehow overlook the material reality that billions of people adopting sometimes spurious lifestyle cravings will have environmental impacts the planet can't sustain.[39]

Many of the prophets of supercycle theory are functionaries of the financial industry, health care suppliers, agricultural commodity, and other megabusinesses. They're paid to be optimistic. But besides these obviously self-interested shills, why are others not telling it like it is? Surely, one can envisage broader views, unless, of course, the imagination itself has been taken hostage.

For example, our great economic challenge is not a shortage of gainful work, it's too many people—not unemployment but overpopulation! This is starkly reflected by a human biomass 100 times greater than any previous large animal on a now groaning planet.[40]

The spiking population in countries with rising life expectancies and falling mortality rates is partially a hangover of the former need for large families in the absence of institutionalized social security (things like old-age pensions and unemployment insurance). Technological advances have also driven increases in human longevity, farm production, and global mobility. This momentum has juiced up the metabolism of natural productive systems beyond their ability to self-regulate to the point that managing climate change is now a monumentally daunting prospect. We'll be looking at how this innovation has its own accelerating dynamic.

"Prediction is hard," baseball's Yogi Berra rightly observed, "especially about the future." But the oft-repeated demographic forecast that the seven billion of us alive today will rise to nine billion by midcentury confronts contradictory trends that are no less unmistakable. These include expanding deserts, disappearing farmland, increasing crop losses to weather, and the exhaustion of water supplies in regions where irrigation is essential to bringing in a harvest. In 2012, extreme summertime heat was said to have settled over 10 percent of the earth's surface—10 times what it was in the 1950s.[41] Not to mention heavy economy-wide reliance on finite supplies of oil and other fossil fuels. Newer fracking technologies are short term; a danger to water supplies, and may introduce complex geological issues.

Set the curve of human fecundity against some of those other curves, and you quickly arrive at the kind of conflict points captured in economist Herbert Stein's tart aphorism "If something cannot go on forever, it will stop." Throw in accelerating technology curves, and you get a race between humanity's greed and our technologies.

Two promising, but still unproven, bright lights here are the commitment to pioneering green technologies of China, and India's bottom-up revolution in products designed to be simple, efficient, affordable, and user serviceable. This is the kind of thinking that once made America great. In trying to think of an American example I came up with the Model T. Are things that bad?

We sacrificed elegance on the altar of efficiency

Our ability to respond to beauty lies at the root of any recovery of the imagination. It may sound dated or even naive to state this so bluntly, but if you think of it, awareness of beauty heightens our appreciation of esthetics, design and much of what the humanities tries to protect and nurture. Consider what fired the great Renaissance in the fifteenth-century. You'll find artists and writers inspired by the infinite implications of beauty.

Dante, the major Italian Florentine poet of the Middle Ages, was inspired by the beautiful Beatrice. He raised her to such a level of adoration that he experienced her in mystical terms, and invoked her as a principal guide in his masterpiece *The Divine Comedy*. Shakespeare was heartened by beautiful qualities of character, such as the temperance and wisdom found in many of his heroines.

Captivated by the esthetic perfection they saw in the structures of ancient Greece, the great cathedral builders—creating in the same era as Rumi and the Owain storytellers—designed previously unimagined places of worship.

To this day, the best mathematicians, software designers, and engineers describe their most accomplished work as elegant. Yet where is beauty in most of today's marketplace? Look at the images in just about every video game (now a bigger business by far than the movie industry). Instead of the compelling portraits of feminine and masculine beauty that drove movies for decades, you'll find some steroid-bloated grotesques with harsh, angular features, animated by programmed motives of death and revenge. Ads feature endlessly airbrushed and perfectly duplicated blonde Barbies. The fashion industry often consciously seeks out dark, gaunt looks, sulky expressions, and seedy locations to the point that some models look like victims of abuse. Animated films invoke the harsh color palette of bad acid trips.

In the pages ahead, we'll hear from an expert on the power of beauty to inspire the imagination. She laments the strange "reproach of beauty" deadening our culture. Without the sensitivity to beauty, she argues we can't navigate the crucial stages of our journey. I agree with her. Significantly, her book is out of print.

In the following, I'll identify more specifically some probable causes of the imaginative collapse. I can name no single culprit, as there are many intersecting streams of causation characterizing this potential disaster.

Causes

Rationality alone will not become more effective at solving human problems

The silicon brain behind IBM's game show star, Watson, demonstrated that computers could be very **efficient** at processing lots of information. But they are not **effective** at pulling out key insights to solve complex problems involving hidden human agendas. Applying appropriate weightings to knowledge for truly wise decisions that account for human emotions such as fears and hopes remains beyond a computer's logical grasp.

Optimists ever since the Enlightenment have expected that rationality would one day guide us to a war-free world, where resources will be fairly distributed and suffering eliminated. We're still waiting.

In fact, we'll see that brain research is showing the contrary to be true: that the more we understand about decision making, the more we reveal its emotional underpinnings. As it turns out, we can't make any decisions at all—even where to eat lunch—if a certain part of the brain dealing with emotions has been damaged. The heart has a key role in the affairs of the mind.

We're trapped in a paradox; emboldened by the brilliance of our reason, while unaware that we've obscured a more vital illumination of our imagination and feelings. Leaders and some who train them pay too much attention to their own technical and logical development and too little to enhancing their emotional skills. As a result, we're sometimes led by emotionally stunted people. Selfishness, fear, and an all-conquering desire for power rule their decisions, and we're somehow surprised that the results turn out badly.

When these disorders reach critical levels, we encounter the psychopaths: people who lack remorse or empathy and who are detached from others generally. However, from my experience during an assignment at a large California prison system, I can attest to the fact that they can have an extraordinary and compelling ability to draw us into their narrative. They are skilled at reading others' needs and can tailor their observations directly to them, with a mysterious and sometimes compelling kind of laser-like accuracy. In extreme cases, the psychopath may not care if you live or die. Psychopathy afflicts about 1 percent of the general U.S. population, which is about 3 million people in that country alone. There has been speculation about the percentage in some organizations' top slots.[42] A British writer estimates that the incidence is four times higher among CEOs.[43]

But it's not only at the extremes where our failure to acknowledge the crucial role of non-rational insight exacts a price. Technical training may only carry a modern engineer for a few years in the field before he or she encounters situations that call for wider relational skills. No less reasonable a magazine than *The Economist* bemoaned in September 2011 how narrow, technocratic language and hasty writing had replaced elegance and reflection.[44]A former minister of culture from France has described books nowadays as no more than mere marketing tools.

Long before Freud pointed it out, our emotions lurked beneath the surface of our decisions forming the basis of those choices. And now, at last, a new wave of decision-making studies reveals encouraging signs of a rediscovered respect for transcending the purely rational.[45] Remarkably, brain scientists have led this development, including the great work of Portuguese neurologist António Damásio in *The Feeling of What Happens*, which explores the biology of emotions.[46] More recently, behavioral psychologists have designed elegant experiments to expose the illusion of rationality. In his best-selling *Thinking, Fast and Slow*,[47] the leading behavioral economist Daniel Kahneman shows, for example, how our brains are hardwired with built-in biases to make terrible investment decisions. To whatever degree possible, vision must be liberated from simplistic formulae and unacknowledged preferences.

Exponential growth is unimaginable—literally!

Moore's Law is the observation that computing capacity—and by extension, technological advance in general—has been doubling roughly every two years for several decades.[48] Defying skeptics who regularly predict that the curve will break down as the number of transistors on a single chip (the metric that Moore's Law counts) nears the theoretical limits of atomic physics, the accelerating cycle has continued, using other approaches. Formerly mind-bending quantum principles are being harnessed for calculating purposes, and the architecture of chips is raised into a third dimension.

Hard to imagine? You're not alone. The fact is that the human brain doesn't naturally grasp this kind of increasing rate of growth. It sneaks up on us.

One classic example of this rate of growth is revealed in the answer to the question: "How many times would I need to fold a piece of paper to reach the moon?" Leaving aside impracticalities, we are into the realm of a thought experiment. Because the folding takes place in a constantly doubling environment (one folded piece goes to two thicknesses, which double to four and then eight etc.) we're involved in a truly exponential growth rate. Depending on paper thickness, the answer works out to only about 42 folds. This experiment tells us that we could reach the moon with a (very large) piece of paper that had been folded only 42 times.

The failure to understand the back-loaded nature of another instance of exponential growth—compound interest—has been the downfall of millions of people who find themselves drowning in debt. Similarly, compounding growth over decades has been a blessing to the very small number of young people who "get it" and enjoy early financial freedom by investing in stocks instead of Mustang convertibles. But some of those savvy youths I've met are not quite as much fun as the profligate spenders. Who knows where the best balance lies?

Moore's Law is a twentieth-century insight, but the phenomenon it describes appears to have begun millennia ago. American engineer, futurist and inventor Ray Kurzweil claims to have charted compounding technological innovation all the way back to the invention of the wheel. Some of Kurzweil's dates may be somewhat arbitrary, and he overreaches, I think, in implying that technology is advancing so fast that computers will shortly surpass and replace much of today's human judgment.[49] Good decision-making relies on much more than straightforward logic. But the broad outline of his rising curve of innovative progress throughout history is fascinating and hard to dispute.

The thing to remember about exponential growth curves, however, is that left to run long enough, they turn nearly vertical—at the mathematical extreme achieving near-instantaneous, near-infinite rates of growth. Sometimes when viewed in nature, it's in the form of an explosion—a reaction that generally leaves all of its contributing compounds unrecognizably changed.[50]

We're certainly heading there on Kurzweil's curve. We're rocketing up in the later stages of exponential growth so fast that any activity with a technological component (and that's just about every field today) faces change of unprecedented velocity, unpredictability, and complexity. And the day is coming, Kurzweil points out, when change will occur so fast that we won't be able to forecast at all. That is part of his definition of "the singularity."

"The greatest shortcoming of the human race," physicist Albert Bartlett, a professor emeritus at the University of Colorado in Denver, believes, "is our inability to understand the exponential function." Homo sapiens' mental equipment evolved to the experience of linear accumulation: one nut, two nuts, three.... Our brains are simply not wired to imagine things that double every week or month or year.

In that sense, our inability to manage today's exponential growth rates stems from a fundamental, even biological failure of the imagination in comprehending big numbers. When these are manifest in modern economic terms, we become like castaways trying desperately to frame and relate figures beyond comprehension in our daily lives.

- A billion hours ago, we were in the Stone Age.

* A billion minutes ago, the Roman Empire was at its peak and one of our Roman guides was about to be born.
* The US government has spent over a billion dollars in just the last four hours.

This processing paralysis is quite apart from other human failings, sometimes related to greed and fear, which induce us to deny the evidence. Increasingly, economists concede that none of us make our purchasing decisions, whether for $2 peanuts or a $500 million stock trade, solely by the numbers and rational self-interest.

Neuroscience, meanwhile, is tracing the roots of our decision making in every sphere of activity—from child rearing to international diplomacy—down to a netherworld of ancient brain regions we share not only with other mammals but with reptiles. Apparently, the lizards are in charge.[51] And none of us are immune to this fate unless we pay attention. The troubadours of nearly a thousand years ago, with no knowledge of evolution, recognized these impulses at work in the hearts of men and women. In their ballads, they identified them as dragons or serpents. And the dragon, as Joseph Campbell so beautifully puts it, hoards gold and women with no idea what to do with either.

Do these so-called serpents, dragons or zombies remind you of anyone you've met or seen featured on TV or the big screen lately? It's probably no coincidence that some of the most popular media feature vampires. Here are dark forces dependent on draining your lifeblood while emanating an irresistible and fatal attraction. Not a bad image for some modern marketing? A therapist I know feels this is actually the dominant image of the past century and that *Dracula*, the novel by Bram Stoker, is a prophetic masterpiece.

The fact is that we all have our inner "dumb" processes. We should be grateful for that fact because it turns out they perform duties essential to our survival. Core basic bodily functions are carried out 24/7 in the unconscious recesses of our brains. But learning to recognize our inner lizard's claw marks on our habitual thinking is essential to improving our skills at navigating in an unpredictable world.

Distracted from distraction by distraction...

By now there's been so much reported on distraction that any commentary is itself in danger of being a distraction. So I'll be brief here, although I do see the problem growing with wider access to media on the go. There are those that seem willing to sacrifice their very lives when crossing the street in favor of not missing a status update on their phone. This is while being plugged into their computer-curated choice of continuous streaming music on their headphones. Not a second is available for the imagination to function without external input. Consumption **of** media is replacing creation **on** media—as the startling substitution of laptops in favor of tablets suggests.

A generation ago, the late academic and writer Neil Postman wrote the seminal book: *Amusing Ourselves to Death.*[52] Its message has suffered a fate that its title anticipated—buried under a flood of distracting trivia. Nonetheless, Postman brilliantly contrasted Aldous Huxley's *Brave New World* and George Orwell's *1984.* While Orwell imagined oppressive state controls, Huxley was perhaps nearer the truth. He argued that we participate willingly, even happily, in our own manipulation and submission. He believed we would not become a captive culture; we would become a trivial culture. As Huxley observed, the civil libertarians and rationalists on the alert to oppose tyranny "...failed to take into account man's almost infinite appetite for distractions."

The power of commerce to distract us is increasing at an alarming rate as each new ad can now be tested on its ability to activate deep unconscious regions of our brains. We're tempted beyond our capacity even to know it. Our unconscious minds are no match for the laser-like techniques discussed in such books as *Brandwashed* by Martin Lindstrom, one of the leading practitioners in mining neuroscience for corporate clients.[53] He stresses that the budgets available from marketers for brain research are growing at a rate unmatched by any objective research. Another book, *Influence: The Psychology of Persuasion*[54] lists specific ways to undermine our resistance.

A TV commercial for a Sony portable gaming device features two strong young men riding in a cab. They are lost in the most mind-bogglingly trivial cartoon video games. Displayed over this image is the slogan "Never stop playing." What can I say?

Be afraid—be very afraid

At a time when we may need our imaginations the most, this may be the deepest and darkest reason of all for its collapse.

Fear, cynically and consciously fanned, was a core political tactic of the George W. Bush administration and many others needing to justify aggression.[55] But marketers as well as politicians seek to leverage the same serpent-level response. Make people afraid. Get their attention, continue to stoke that fire, and then offer your product, service or program as a simplistic antidote. Just check out the next news broadcast and count the fear-driven messages. Do the same for the ads and side effects of those life-changing medications. It sounds like some could well change your life, but not quite as we've been led to imagine.

This is the worst climate in which to try to foster imagination. How can anyone be expected to leap out of the box if the box itself feels like it's all that's left floating in the storm?

Fear, whether about one's basic survival, of not getting needs met or of merely losing status, goads us into using and often abusing whatever power we might have. It justifies any measure. The response to 9/11 sparked runaway paranoia and a bull market for security services. In the United States, each new tragedy like the killing of young students in Newtown, Connecticut, spurs a fresh boom in gun sales. True heroes of both these events tended to be drowned out by the merchants of fear.

The attention we pay to media contributes to this effect. A survey in *Newsweek* [56] reported the fact that an astonishingly short exposure to stressful media stimulation—as little as five hours—can produce visible physical changes in the brain. The article detailed the increases in depression and other ailments among those most exposed. There is a real cost to submitting oneself to the media circus!

Although it's intelligent to be fearful at times, when looking at a host of frightening issues many of us succumb to feelings of hopelessness or engage in denial. We need tools and the courage to face core issues. It can be helpful to remember a shared message from both East and West over the millennia: "Be not afraid!" It's central to the Hindu god Shiva raising a hand in the posture of resisting fear. Depending on translations, this phrase also occurs somewhere around 365 times in the Bible, once for every day of the year. The problem is, if either denial or fear holds us back, then the imagination's power to move between levels is blocked. We remain stuck in basic survival mode.

Where are we then?

This heading reminds me of a great cartoon showing a visitor puzzling over one of those University orientation maps in a Metaphysics Department. The arrow points to a spot asking, quite profoundly, "Are You Here?"

Perhaps we're still at the stage described from his prison cell by the leftist Italian writer Antonio Gramsci. In the early part of the last century, he argued "The crisis consists precisely in the fact that the old is dying and the new cannot be born…." He imagined we were at a place where a cycle was being interrupted, poised at an uneasy interlude known as an interregnum and that: "…in this interregnum a great variety of morbid symptoms appear."[57]

When morbidity becomes too hard to ignore, organizations may call in guys like me. We go by different names, management consultant, strategic planning consultant, and our backgrounds and abilities may differ widely. But one way or another, we're responding to calls for help in delivering an organization back from the brink. Inevitably, this requires an organizational change. After all, its best strategic thinking is what brought it to the brink. Right? And if rescue is to be achieved, sometimes the change must be extensive. It starts personally, with change leaders. First they need to step out of the cultural boxes that have enclosed so many past great organizations. It's relevant that the average lifespan of a Fortune 500 company is 30 years.[58]

However, there is heartening news. Lots of clues to a renewed imagination have endured. Happily even in our own mind-numbing and distracting time many of these can be recovered. I don't claim for a second to have invented anything new in this regard. At most, my hope is to dig up some of these past treasures, to shake the dust off old roadmaps and link up to modern findings.

Having looked at a variety of symptoms and causes I've attributed to a failing imagination, I'll focus next on expanding our model of the three layers. Then we'll move on to the sustainable building blocks of recovery, which include **service, beauty and connectedness.**

4
Three Layers and the Shadow

Can we grow into great ideas?

Tie together all human intellects.
They won't stretch to here.
...
Nothing happens until you quit contriving
with your mind. Quit your talking.
...
You can't understand this with your mind.
You must burst open!

Rumi

Having explored the question of **why** we need to change, it's now time to look at **what** needs to change. I'll begin with how that necessary revision began in my own life because I believe introspection is central. Personal change is the root driver of transformation at every level—in one's own life, in the life of any organization, and in society. Two of the last century's milestone thinkers, Jung and Mahatma Gandhi, agreed that any real evolution in the world begins with the individual. As the latter famously advised "Be the change you would see in the world."

I used to enjoy presenting weekend or evening sessions for Jung societies and other groups of adults who showed up mostly because they shared my love of the humanities. But at some point my life began to change. My time was running short, and things were getting tough. My work as a strategic management consultant and part-time University of British Columbia Executive Programs' presenter was incredibly demanding. I was working regularly on three continents, with tight deadlines and rightfully demanding clients.

Professional opportunities had multiplied into a crazy pace of travel and work. My ego loved the strokes, but my personal life was suffering. Certainly my body was beginning to object.

One night I concluded an increasingly rare Jungian session with a poem by Rainer Maria Rilke. As I interpret "Archaic Torso of Apollo"[59] we, the readers, are (through the eyes of the poet) gazing at the headless bust of Apollo when something bewildering happens. It's as though we go from the apparent blindness of the statue to some unnerving moment of revelation. While looking at the headless form, it seems the light of that sun god enters the torso radiating a dazzling light, and the transformation begins. The figure gleams and, no longer viewing this beauty with anything remotely like esthetic detachment, we are dazed as the god bursts into life.

All translations of this poem speak in some way to this unaccountable experience and so it's impossible not to think of Rilke's personal revelation, his sudden awareness of the reality of the presence of the god. It seems poet and reader watch it happen.

Faced with this unveiling moment it's equally difficult to deny the force of this extraordinary event. In this interaction, Rilke feels himself under scrutiny as he realizes there's been a turn of events. No longer is he an onlooker, but with an overwhelming intensity the polished form in front of him pins him in an otherworldly gaze so probing that he cannot evade this encounter. There is nowhere to hide. The poet is made aware of some elevated reality within himself. Rilke has been found so wanting in relation to this immense presence that it is immediately imperative that he change his life. The poet writes "...for there is no place / that does not see you. You must change your life."

The only way to appreciate Rilke's poem and have a true sense of the full force of the poet's extraordinary experience is to read "Archaic Torso of Apollo." It's not possible to capture its essence in the few lines I've written. But the question is; if we're not ready or able to recognize the possibilities of such timeless beauty, how can we ever know or believe in this kind of transformation? Perhaps this is one of the central questions of the humanities. It speaks to the role of great art.

In a world dominated by practical or technical knowledge and education this may be an unusual view of the power of the humanities. But are we able to see the possibilities of being changed by identifying with a character in a novel or play, or an experience such as Rilke's? To have one's life altered through such an encounter just might mean to be in relationship to great works of art, and an ever-enlarging sense of life itself. Rilke's insight contains huge promise for us all.

As I finished the last lines of the poem that evening it seemed that somehow the same moment of transfixed insight had happened to me. Although I had no idea what exactly had happened, I knew I had to change my life. In realizing this, the question for me was no longer—is this poem good enough for me, but am I enough? Am I up to meeting its challenge?

Let's pause to deconstruct this moment. A dead poet presents his encounter with an inanimate stone object that I can't see, and yet I feel his shock. On top of that, I feel a transfiguring jolt of my own. Rilke's poem not only presents an extraordinary experience; it evokes a similar feeling of encounter in me, his reader. I entered a place I could not have known before this moment.

One of the powers of the humanities is to act as a conduit for emotional experience. Because of those unforgettable novels and plays, poems and paintings, we're able to walk in another's shoes across time and space and extend ourselves in ways we've never imagined. As long as people are sensitive and receptive, this potential exists. But, there's a catch. For this chance at renewal you need to show up, to be present for the effect. A sign in Vegas put it this way: "You have to be present to play."

For me, the Rilke moment triggered a chain of events that included major lifestyle changes. I quit doing more of the same and took real time off. Over that period I read everything I could get my hands on, and my brain around! Milton, Blake, Kant, detective novels, books on behavioral economics, neuroscience, you name it. I read like a mad man!

I also worked on a refocused model for my business —this time to pursue real change. The consulting side moved to working with organizations genuinely seeking sustainable ways of evolving. On a more personal note, I developed *The Secret Sabbatical Course*.

So ultimately, Rilke's encounter with the stone Apollo—Greek god of prophesy, among other powers—led to the book you hold in your hand.

The middle layer of awareness —the castle

To explore the question of "What needs to change?" we return again to Owain's story where the symbolic landscape provides an ongoing framework for examining the terrain of our own lives.

As we've seen, the castle represents the everyday world of ordinary commerce. This is a world where we at least try to be polite as we deal with the complexities of our lives and jobs. At the outset of the story our hero is living in the castle as a young, ambitious knight who will do anything to secure worldly experience and enhance his reputation. Sound familiar?

The other two levels we've discussed lie above and below the castle in this model. Our hero can't escape the lingering memory of somewhere better, a place of beauty and contentment he once glimpsed, which the image of the garden suggests. Below the castle lies an abyss, the swamp.

For a moment, focus on just the castle; one of the fears it serves is that of not feeling **safe**. Perhaps this explains why it's surrounded by a moat, where the water of life has been stilled, contained and harnessed for defense.

This pretty much describes the mind of the castle builder and dweller. Certainly it dominates corporate life when executives fail to see past the analysts' consensus forecasts for the next earnings period. "Let's annex, harness and contain resources, then defend our territory from competitors and invaders." We're talking bare-knuckle survival, lizard-level thinking, and so one probably doesn't have to deal with anything other than survival. Not exactly the home of visionaries!

Any of us who have been close to the world of financial analysts have more than likely noticed the shallowness of some of their commentaries, and how easily these insiders of the realm manipulate the media. It took until 2014 for the work of a young New York-based Canadian financial analyst to be widely recognized, having exposed the fact that every stock purchase across the nation had been subject for years to being skimmed of a fraction of its value by groups of high frequency traders.[60] These parasitic geniuses, using the awesome power and speed of rapidly escalating chip speeds, skimmed hundreds of millions of dollars in tiny increments using millisecond speed advantages. In this case too, speed does kill, and it's we who are the victims.

It's worth remembering that for several centuries, castles worked. When besieging armies were equipped with nothing more than swords and arrows, castle walls and surrounding moats kept them at bay. But when armies adopted gunpowder and cannon—technologies from a new era—the castle-moat concept as a defensive structure became terrifyingly obsolete.

The ambiguity of boxes

The castle can easily be imagined as a metaphor for protection and enclosure. Boxes too, are also a containment metaphor for a wide range of conventional wisdoms including theories, dogmas and entire business models.

Some actual boxes can serve as examples of how one can become imaginatively trapped. One of the original industrial boxes—the ice-filled icebox—was replaced by the electrically powered refrigerator. Not a single icebox manufacturer made the transition. Dell Computer pioneered just-in-time desktop and laptop manufacturing, but failed to take their eyes off these waning product boxes in time to grasp the smaller tablet and smartphone revolutions. From a consumer experience point of view, their office boxes seemed to vanish into the ether in the new world of cloud computing.

German-American psychologist Kurt Lewin developed a related idea in what he called "field theory," a close relative of systems thinking. Its key notion is that every theory has a "focus of convenience," a problem or situation that it illuminates well. But that focus of illumination is limited in range, like that of a bright spotlight. Beyond its focus, the theory's descriptive and predictive powers break down, leaving us in the dark.

The same limiting pattern of thought—call it the "to a man with a hammer, every problem looks like a nail" effect—constrains our approach to more tangible problems. And the hammer we choose may betray interests quite unrelated to the problem we face.

In medicine, today's trend to progressively narrower sub-specialties of practice leaves the patient obliged to judge what is best among competing treatment models. Let's say you seek medical relief for gastric problems. A naturopath might prescribe a range of herbal remedies (that they happen to sell) while a psychologist argues the solution is ongoing counseling for stress (at $300 for a 50-minute session). A yoga guru determines that disciplined stretching will cure the problem.

A physician may simply prescribe medications that mask symptoms. It's possible he or she may also have been paid directly by a drug company to prescribe their product, or entertained at conventions in exotic locations with long breaks for golf. Another doctor might come up with a new diet and some mechanical tactics to help suppress reflux symptoms. A third, perhaps having enjoyed the perks of a different offer from marketers, could decide to test for parasites like helicobacter and prescribe powerful antibiotics. In this case, a few years later this prescribed cure will be targeted as a cause of the problem. So while some theories have useful functions and range, many are **uninterested in specifying their own limits**, or are unable to do so. It's a jungle!

And, if patients are sick their judgment may be impaired. We know, for example, that certain parasites routinely re-wire the brains of their hosts to drive them to act in ways that may be self-destructive to the host, but serve the parasites' interests—a form of connected intelligence that we're only beginning to understand. Every month there are more examples of this with parasites now being implicated in obesity, depression, and even autism.

Some observers have extended this self-serving diagnostic issue beyond any one field and suggested that many large organizations prolong the problem they were originally established to solve.

And even when our model is correct or our theory accurate, so far as it goes, there's no guarantee that we have adequate brainpower to deal with the fundamentals of an issue. Solving a shallow definition of the problem with high accuracy has seldom helped. A client's accountant once proudly predicted the exact day on which bankruptcy would strike. I can't stress enough the vital distinction between problem-solving (that computers and most MBA classes can facilitate) and problem-finding! Looking for genuine root causes remains an art.

Ian Radziejewski once worked as a project manager in a telecom firm that had been a darling of NASDAQ, but started to experience problems with customer satisfaction and stagnating growth. Instead of addressing the underlying quality and process issues, the Executive in charge (the Senior

Vice President of Sales) decided that what was really needed was another V.P. whose role was primarily to schmooze with customers and convince them everything was really OK. The resulting top-heavy reporting structure with four levels of vice-presidents did little to forestall the company's rapid decline.

Despite all this evidence that our best thinking has its limits, many brilliant minds have fallen into the trap of conceiving elegant and complex systems, "theories of everything."[61] No less a genius than W.B. Yeats, to some the greatest poet of the twentieth-century, constructed an elaborate and all-embracing model of reality based on his wife's channeled instructions. It seems to be one of the peculiar gifts, or curses, of the intuitive mind to be attracted to grand, overarching conceptual frameworks.

Dogma and addiction

Dogma is just another kind of castle-like structure enclosing an imaginary protected space. It's a box. But in this case, the illusion of protection can be perilous. Philosopher and neuroscientist Sam Harris[62] argues that the current tolerance of diverse religious views is not always a good thing. Certain religious followers would welcome a nuclear conflagration in the Middle East as an omen of the Second Coming, in which most of us will burn while they—and only those chosen few—will be saved and taken to heaven. Other people endorsed the massive killing of civilians on 9/11 as a necessary step toward the resurgence of radical Islam on the way to destroying the sinful, infidel Western World. To say that either of these views should be condoned in the name of religious tolerance is a dangerous trap. Such tolerance for intolerance continues in the ongoing turbulence in the Middle East and Africa in particular, but may be on the increase in other countries too, as stagnant developed economies see an influx of immigrants arriving from failing states.

Things get even worse when our dogmas or faulty beliefs include self-reinforcing feedback mechanisms. This was driven home at an unforgettable workshop at MIT, conducted by Dr. Peter Senge.[63] He illustrated how organizations become trapped in addictive thinking loops that are indistinguishable from those of the junkie. The cash rebates to customers so popular in the U.S. auto industry are a classic example. By boosting short-term sales, they provide a jolt of revenue just like an addict's next hit, while preventing attention being given to larger, underlying problems. In the case of the addict, these may be stress, genetic predisposition, or dysfunctional belief systems. In certain auto companies they are likely to include poor R&D, weak quality assurance, outdated design, and failure to nurture a values-oriented culture.

In both cases, dynamics are at play over two distinct time cycles. The short-term cycle provides quick pain relief, while a longer-term cycle undermines the addict or organization's overall health. As the addict's liver breaks down, or the company's value fades in the eyes of customers, the perceived discomfort (slumping market share) merely reinforces the short-term behavior.

The addict feels he has found a solution to stress, but it's killing him. In a corporation, rebates increase quarterly sales, but undermine longer-term profit, leaving the organization with ever-fewer resources to address root problems. Beginning in the 1970s, and continuing today, just such a progressive erosion of resources leaves U.S. auto companies often unable or unwilling to match the quality of their competitors.

Control vs. facilitation

One of the most powerful ideas of the modern era is that of evolution. Yet some people have not fully grasped its critical insight.

The twentieth-century saw an upsurge in people unable to imagine any force of creation other than blind random forces. And others argued that life could not have achieved forms that appear to reveal complex designs without a guiding intelligence or forethought. Is this evidence of a failed imagination; that there are only two possible explanations, a divine engineer or random chaos?

There is another force at play here however; one that is only recently coming to light in the expanding field of the dynamics of self-organization.[64] Perhaps if more people were aware of these discoveries and emerging theories, they might find it easier to see what needs to be controlled in life and at work, and what needs instead only to be facilitated. Most living organisms are constructed "from the bottom up" by simple formulae controlling incredibly fast repetitive processes. I am referring here to the science of fractals (amazingly only discovered in 1980) by the eccentric Belgian genius Benoit Mandelbrot, who was a researcher at IBM. It's worth a serious look by anyone interested in how things are grown from the bottom up.[65]

Fractals are recurring simple patterns that repeat at different scales. They exist throughout nature—trees, hurricanes, and blood vessels all carry the imprints of their creation. Using the same principles of fast replication of simple formulae in modern computing, fractals are also how your graphics programs and video games create scenery. The pieces are self-similar and simple, but they create complex patterns through repetition. It's this aspect of repetition on different scales that I've found so intriguing as it shows phenomena happening at multiple levels.

Similarly, I've found that personal behaviors, such as openness to feedback, can be modeled and repeated in groups, and that entire organizations can emulate the same patterns. This is another reason the personal qualities of a leader are so vital. A selfish, egocentric leader can hire a team that reflects his personality and before long the whole organization gets the picture. These cultures end up defined by "Look after number one!" Now we're into toxic credit default swaps. Similarly, a gifted leader, strong in humility and drive, can help build the kind of sustainable organizations found in select studies such as those identified in the book *Good to Great*.

A subtle but crucial point is that fractal patterns replicate up the scale to produce huge effects from simple components. So individuals outside the leadership circle can still influence a whole group, even an entire organization, through efforts within their sphere of influence—if they have adequate resources and support.

Fractals shed light on two very important principles concerning leading others and oneself to more productive and fulfilling ground. First, that for sustainable growth, facilitation is often more effective than control. Given the formula in the seed, and the right resources, a tree self-organizes its own construction. And second, to make a significant difference, we need to have an awareness of the underlying structure of a system and the ability to get it back on track when it's subverted.

The castle world in its negative and all too common form involves top-down **control**. In this realm of lizard thinking we've lost regulation of the addictive loops we've set loose in the economy and our planet. The world of the garden, vibrant with self-energized biological life, is all about **facilitation**. It's concerned with enhancing the optimal conditions for life to flourish sustainably—and enhancing the resources and opportunities for life. It's where we're headed next in this book.

The top layer of awareness—the garden

Often people relate to the idea of the garden when asked to remember a night when they were young and still dating. The air was electric, and they felt life was full of possibility. Yet revisiting the place where that glorious experience occurred usually disappoints. We're not the same person, and, in any case, geography alone can't change consciousness. (Although try telling that to the travel industry.)

Portrayals of the garden, of paradise, occur in myths and tales of diverse religions and cultures, from the Biblical Eden through to many imagined Utopias. Shakespeare's late play, *The Tempest*, is a meditation on the nature of the garden. In this imaginary place, set apart from the world, we learn what's meant by garden-consciousness. Here's a realm where it's possible to find love and peace and feel what it means to forgive.

The play shows too that with unchecked appetites and dark intentions we can easily build another kind of place. Whether our experience is of an enchanted isle or a dismal bog depends on our perception—an important clue to our own efforts to integrate the three levels of Owain's story and discover what our own garden looks like. With Shakespeare as our guide we learn with some precision how to move from the limitations of castle-consciousness and find our way back to the garden.

Because the garden is notoriously elusive, metaphors and images are more able to convey its qualities. I think one of the best essays on paradise is by James Hillman. He tells us "Moments come when we feel outside time, seized by a longing, moved by an image, in touch with invisible voices. We realize we do not live in one world only."[66] Hillman asserts that these invisible voices are our impetus to create some meaning in our daily round. This vision of honoring something beyond the self is probably central to all initiations, the object of every drive toward transcendence.

The pursuit of perfection

Aspirations to perfection drive all the great quests—in art, music, engineering and organizations—possibly every project that has merit. It's the sub-text to *In Search of Excellence*—the classic study that launched a new wave of management bestsellers. A glimpse of paradise is what was revealed to us as teens, when we were first swept away by the dawning of lust and love. Not long after, we were buried in the hoops and deadlines we needed to jump through, or meet, to earn a place in the busy-ness of the world.

Owain faced the same realization. How do we lose touch with a promise, perhaps only implied, made once upon a time to ourselves or someone else? And then how we slowly or suddenly begin to realize that our moment in the garden is lost—and so are we.

Beauty is neither trivial nor marginal here. It's central to the guidance we seek. Gardens are places of beauty, and beauty is one of the ways in which the imagination is enlivened. It can then play its intermediating role described in Chapter 1.

Although it's hard to find, the garden is mostly experienced away from the pressures of the workaday world. You may have accessed, or been granted access to, Eden a few times—often through what seems like, in retrospect, lucky breaks. But the goal is to become aware of the garden's enduring presence, and then to step into it as a revitalizing part of everyday life.

One way I've found to enter the garden is first to set up the right circumstances, hoping to turn the keys provided by the imagination of others. They may open gates if we're receptive and help us with what we need to know and experience. Here I include all kinds of great minds, artists and passionate thinkers from the past and an equally diverse set of people happily still with us. Each of these individuals has discovered a conduit or doorway into a timeless world of beauty and vitality that can be accessed or perhaps co-created in real time—at any time.

In more modern terms: the garden is a 24/7 defense against the constant barrage of incoming demands from others who dwell in the castle or the swamp. An imagination supplied with that measureless garden energy helps us evade assault.

The ecological mind

Those who try to describe paradise often hit a wall because, in the final analysis, it's not possible to do in ordinary language. Music, poetry, dance, these get closer.

Is this because paradise is an emotional state more than a realm or a place, a whole brain and whole body experience? According to Joseph Campbell what it's not about, is a search for meaning. Instead, Campbell claims it's a search for an **experience** that the brain interprets as meaning.

The experience of paradise may be revealed in a world of shifting impressions. The Romantic poets, Keats, Shelly, and Wordsworth in particular, demonstrated the ecological mind, an awareness of everlasting change and interdependence. As artists, they came to know feelings of metamorphosis or transformation. They enjoyed a far richer sense of cyclicality across the seasons than the modern linear Western mind, always traveling forward on its one-way street.

There may come a time when that imaginative poetic flow is no longer felt in the same way. It's to feel stuck. It seems we need to change our sense of change, and let go. Many poets including Rumi believe we need to surrender to the world of the garden. Although surrender sounds far too much like a capitulation to the average westerner, it's essential. It's a submission first to an unidentified yearning, knowing or feeling that you're being summoned, while realizing you can no longer reach the dreamed-of place. It can drive you crazy, standing on a familiar beach flooded with haunting memories of the past while at the same time dreading you may never know old times again. This is the longing one must yield to while being fully aware it can never be met, or satisfied. It's a state of being that means, ultimately; one is awake and alive. The yearning is real, and we're called on to be conscious of it while knowing it's beyond our grasp. The song and images from "Bali Hai" in the musical *South Pacific* captured this for millions.

Hillman provided his poetic version of an added dimension to the meaning of surrender. According to Hillman, "It becomes less a matter of seeking Paradise than of receiving its gifts." What he's saying I think is we need to surrender this desire to find a place or state and shift to a grateful recognition and acceptance of its gifts.

Sound a little fuzzy? Perhaps—particularly if you've been trained to see every problem as a nail. But it's all words can do, or at least the best I can do, to outline these ephemeral but vital concepts, which is why we need the extra reach of poets and other artists. I'm grateful for their help.

The lower layer of awareness —the swamp

Sorrow goes by many names. The swamp is one. Ashes, or down in the dumps would do as well but, whatever names we use, we all know these evocative terms speak to the tough stuff most of us would rather avoid.

A participant on the Course related to the following poem by Spanish writer, Antonio Machado. For him, the poem conjured up a hard place of sorrow. He was saddened, at least initially, by the realization he'd have to change; that he too must change his life.

As with most of the poems we look at in the book, I'm not able to do an adequate reading of Machado's poem in a paragraph or two. My point is more to talk about the power of art to change our lives and hope that the poems appearing in these pages spark a note of interest for you too. Maybe you'll take some time to look at them again.

The wind, one brilliant day, called
to my soul with an odor of jasmine.

"In return for the odor of my jasmine,
I'd like all the odor of your roses."

"I have no roses; I have no flowers left now
in my garden... All are dead."

"Then I'll take the waters of the fountains,
and the yellow leaves and the dried up petals."

The wind left. And I wept. And I said to my soul,
"What have you done with the garden entrusted to you?"

Antonio Machado[67]

Machado's poem opens on a bright clear note. "The wind, one brilliant day," stirs the reader into some glimmering Elysian dreamscape that seems at once familiar. The lines conjure up a paradise we feel we know and have always known—an unforgettable breezy sun-filled day, luminous and utterly uplifting. We don't hesitate as something within us thrills to the wind's call leading us confidently on our way. We're eager to respond to that fragrant wind filled with an odor of jasmine.

Before the reader has even reached the end of the second line the wind seems to have taken the form of pneuma, our soul, and touched us, quickened us as if to alter our consciousness in some inexplicable way. There's been a shift in the language in the poem—that breeze blowing across the poem's landscape initially so brilliant and clear—is now blowing into the portals of our souls. A dialog sets up between the breath of the poem and the soul of the reader and we're astonished. Our breath, or soul, is taken away, as suddenly we are in a place the poem has not prepared us for, and we're undeniably not ready.

The tone quickly darkens and the wind and day of the poem change. The poem brings to light some unrecognized interdependence that we, the reader, have failed to consider. Something has totally escaped us and for a moment there's confusion. We're confused, and then, we're not. It seems we were to tend some unacknowledged garden left entrusted to us. How could we have forgotten?

Now it begins to sound like Luned admonishing Owain. And like Owain, we're entering the swamp. Although we've not been entirely conscious of this so-called garden of roses left in our care we are definitely keenly aware of the force of our fall as we acknowledge that we have no flowers left—that "...all our flowers are dead."

This is a dreadful awakening. If only we could wake up, as though from a bad dream. But, if the poem has reached us, if it has spoken to our souls as Machado intended, then we can't walk away. It's a poem about the life of our soul and, as it turns out, it's we who have broken with ourselves. We have been the betrayer of our inner life, not the steward of that inner garden we might have imagined ourselves as being, prior to this shocking confrontation.

Hearing of our failure the wind announces it will take everything that remains in this barren landscape. We're told "The wind left" and it's as though we're all that's left in an empty place once so full of promise. The poem begins in halcyon days, as we begin in our relationship to our inner lives, and both end in melancholy and sadness. The poem reveals this wasteland we've unwittingly brought upon ourselves.

We've entered the crunch, an experience corresponding to Owain's banishment from the garden. For Owain it was accompanied by the bitter realization that the castle had lost its power, all of its appeal. But now, unlike those earlier heady days, neither world belonged to him. For the first time, he faced a life without the usual abundance of choices. He must have felt old, like a dismal failure as suddenly, armor or no armor, he was impotent. Depressed, Owain had only one way to go. It was pretty much all downhill, or so it seemed to our once grand knight. The story tells us that Owain, filled with a sinking feeling his life had changed forever, fell into the dark murky waters of the swamp where all seemed lost—and much was. This is in part a tale about the loss of innocence, the fall from Eden, which occurs in both "The Wind, One Brilliant Day" and in our knight's tale. Not only does Owain tumble from on high, but he falls from a state of blissful unconsciousness. He descends into the undeniable knowledge of loss. Moreover, this shocking revelation can never be forgotten nor fully left behind. His life has changed.

This insight might be imagined as: life without decay is not life at all. Think of decay and transformation as representing half the processes of the universe. It seems to me if the billions of microorganisms in every teaspoon of healthy soil are really building the next layer of the garden then it's possible to imagine the crunch, or the experience of the swamp, as part of the necessary journey of the human soul. It's a question of integrating what we see as darkness into our personal lives so that we are as free of denial as possible.

Our imaginations are populated with images of dark and negative characters: from blood-sucking vampires, to the currently popular zombie, to deceptively benign ordinary folk who nevertheless destroy people. Think of Ava Gardner as the innkeeper in *Night of the Iguana*, Kevin Spacey as the cynical suburbanite in *American Beauty*.

The truth is, all cultures and individuals across the world have a shadow aspect or darker side. It's that we only tend to come up against these parts of ourselves fully when we're in the swamp. Accepting that we'll never get rid of the shadow sides of our personality, nor permanently banish the swamp within ourselves, gives us a place to begin our search. With this in mind it's easy to identify with the lost hero. Like Owain, our question is: how conscious can we become of our own shadow?

It's been said, what you don't know can't hurt you. Not true. The things you don't know about yourself and the world can be incredibly dangerous. Ignoring blind spots that invite you to walk into figurative walls and over unseen cliffs can definitely lead you to perilous places.

Employees often talk about what their managers can't see about themselves. Take for instance, a manager who procrastinates continually, but insists that everyone else meets deadlines. With every perceived act of hypocrisy, the manager is less effective. There are studies to prove this. I've replicated some in client organizations to help improve managerial self-awareness.

Our shadow is the unknown, disowned, or denied part of oneself. The best description I've come across is Robert Bly's, who contends it arises from **the unlived life.** Such an amazing description, it's as though these words call up a lost and unresolved part of each of us. Everything that was disapproved of when we were children is somehow tucked into this phrase. Bly imagines all of our unfinished issues being dragged behind each of us in a bag.[68] It contains primitive drives, dreams, anger, jealousy, laziness and fantasies. This darker self also harbors things that might have been valuable but were, for various reasons, suppressed. Traits such as vulnerability in men and decisiveness in women, or.... Fill in your own blanks here. We're never free until we realize our shadows are an essential part of us. Finding a scapegoat becomes the next predictable and self-defeating step.

The shadow is of course alive and well in contemporary life. At a critical moment in the 2012 US election race, Republican Senate Candidate Todd Akin was asked about his opposition to abortion, and in particular about a woman who had been raped. His reply, "If it's legitimate rape, the female body has ways to try to shut down the whole [pregnancy] thing"[69] suggested an entire lifetime of patriarchy, expediency and ignorance. Plus, it seems Congressman Akin was getting his science from 900 years ago! As historian Jacqueline Murray observed: "... according to the 12th-century philosopher William of Conches, 'prostitutes who have sexual relations for money alone, and who take no pleasure during the sex act, do not conceive.' They would, however, get pregnant from sex with a lover."[70] Overnight the Democrats had a bump in the polls.

It's critical that we learn to see our shadow because the qualities in ourselves that hide in the shadow, mostly the characteristics we can't stand in ourselves, are usually projected onto the world.

So now ask yourself: What do I dislike in others? Chances are, when you answer this question honestly, you'll have clues to the contents of your own shadow.

The shadow contains suppressed energies. At times these may come blasting into the light of day, usually when we're most stressed. The arc of our lives, or even the trajectory of a nation, can change when we're involved in this world of inner darkness, projecting our unlived lives onto others. For the most part, the outcome is not good.

Projection—a key idea for grasping how we shape and distort reality

Much like a movie projector works in casting pictures onto a screen, our imaginations can hurl deep unconscious images onto people and situations out there. Projections can work at both positive and negative levels, depending on the observer's inner state.

I've mentioned briefly that Jung named the feminine projection of the typical male, the anima. He was deeply immersed in mythology and history and drew parallels of the concept into ancient times. A similar set of projections from women to men led to a figure he named the animus. Whenever I use these terms, they include the qualities associated with them for millennia. The best descriptions I've come across are in the illustrated examples in the great chapter on this topic by Marie-Louise von Franz in *Man and His Symbols*, a classic and readable book edited by Jung himself.[71] These will emerge in more detail as we explore their manifestations.

Certain ancient and deep-seated processes of projection reflect what are now called gender stereotypes. Jungian psychologist James Hollis points out how ubiquitous and wide-ranging these figures are. They involve millennia of associations and to dismiss them as merely cultural or gender specific is to miss their age-old power to speak to us.[72]

The focus in the Owain story and the Course has been mostly on men and so I'll concentrate mainly on their roles here. But it's worth remembering that most figures of grace and freedom from the examples I'll quote, are feminine. We'll see a little later that it's Shakespeare's view that the feminine has the power in fact to save mankind from itself.

Jung argued that negative projections were the nuclear fuel of global and regional conflicts. An example is the image persistently projected onto foreigners in times of social unrest by sociopathic leaders. Jung believed these dark projections would continue to threaten civilization until they were tackled within the individual.

Positive projections may constellate a belief that this person we've just met will embody all we could ever hope for in a partner. How many times have you seen references to people being totally infatuated with someone representing (for them) all the positive aspects possible in a relationship? It may have happened to you more than once. Feeling less than perfect, we can project ideal positives onto possible partners or lovers—hoping they can save us from our disappointments. This frequently happens at the beginning of relationships. The projections can also involve foisting our own unacknowledged weaknesses onto others and then judging them for these deficiencies.

But if a man projects positive qualities onto a woman who possesses them, she may serve as a powerful guide to the evolution of his imagination. We'll see many examples of women guides acting positively in the lives of men as we move on. Luned guides Owain and he learns what he needs to realize within himself to re-enter the garden. When he desperately needed rescuing, Owain no doubt saw Luned in lofty ways. He believed she would save him. And as the story unfolds, she does help—but he must undergo major personal change. Curses—no short cuts!

Projecting a false image of graciousness onto a tough peasant is a major theme of *Don Quixote* and its derivative musical *The Man of La Mancha*. A rough or cruel figure can propel a man to despair—one of the darkest features Glenn Close as a true femme fatale in the movie *Fatal Attraction.*

A woman may also initiate a wide range of projections onto men. These can range from the tough he-man, to the romantic poet or an inspirational leader like Gandhi.

Even though Carl Jung elaborated on this concept of projection, there are examples in ancient stories such as *The Iliad.* Think Helen of Troy! As the stories go, she not only launched a thousand ships but caused a ten-year war. The Old Testament depicts King David compelled to commit murder after a haunting vision of Bathsheba bathing. The concept is not new.

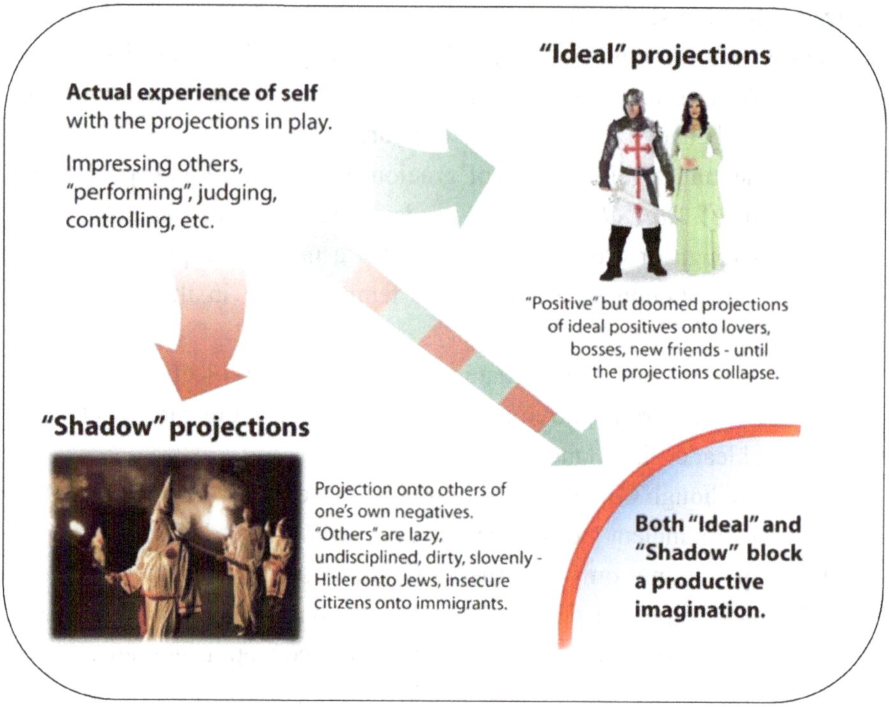

Figure 3 - Projections

The key in our close relationships is to learn what we must do to work with someone after our projections have fallen away and we encounter a normal, flawed person—much like ourselves! As we mature, we need to become aware of potential unconscious tendencies within ourselves and to free others from these ultimately unsustainable roles.

Carrying weighty projections of others can be an unbearable burden, especially if they're those of a whole culture. We witness real despair at the heart of many famous people as they begin to realize they are hopelessly bound in a vision of an entire nation that, on close examination, does not leave much room for them to be themselves. For that matter, these projections may be the result of such serious objectifications that they actively conceal any true picture of the real person. They're left to bear this hefty cross. From Evita Peron to Marilyn Monroe, the pressure can be too great.

Denial and the vital value of our mistakes

In the West most of us have been conditioned to see the dark moments in our past as shameful. Our urgency to conceal this humiliating history comes from the fear that we'll be perceived as losers—that we will end up unloved, disowned, and ultimately all alone. Our society says it's not OK to let on that you're feeling even slightly reserved about life, let alone feeling despair while questioning its fundamentals. This reflex denial is dangerous.

Periods of reflection and questioning are essential to any non-trivial change. There's no substitute for realizing that the world you have created for yourself has been composed partly out of compensation resulting from the reality that you're a really small, fragile object in the world. As well, suppressed feelings of guilt and anger can block possibilities of personal change. Also there are frameworks imposed by family or dogma that are not your own, but were designed to control you. Finally, there's the collusion in a conspiracy of silence to inhibit emotional truth, especially if you're a man. Gene Hackman brilliantly played the role of a middle-aged man suffering under the emotional climate established by his father in the classic movie *I Never Sang For My Father*. He is a heart-wrenching example of what can become of the next generation when elders fail.

Often, our mistakes serve a purpose—to someone. Maybe we've become a workaholic. That may serve a number of people, from bosses who appreciate the unpaid hours we pour into their assignments, to an alienated spouse who quietly prefers we spend even more time away from the house.

Men in particular are encouraged to become masters of denying mistakes. Sharing anything too heavy, which is negative, emotional or too personal is frowned upon in macho company. We may find ourselves living an endless loop of self-destructive behavior and being congratulated for our efforts!

I think one has to try to do the work. Here, I'm talking about the personal work involved in becoming more conscious. It's hard to face our own wrongdoings, our shortcomings, our failures, including things we've failed to do. While facing past transgressions one must also come to the realization that **it would be unthinkable to repeat them**. The English novelist and poet D.H. Lawrence knew this. In his unforgettable poem "Healing" he wrote about the importance of the "...realization of life's mistake, and the freeing oneself / From the endless repetition of the mistake."[73]

Courage is definitely one of the keys to turn the lock in the door to the rest of our lives. How we choose to confront our shadows—our fears and frustrations, our deepest disappointments—may provide the wake-up call that triggers needed change. Or, if we turn our back on them, they may condemn us to a slow decline.

Let the journey begin!

Whether we find ourselves stuck in the castle, or evicted from the garden and lost in the swamp amid the ashes of our fallen ego and stumbling shadow, the journey back to the garden is going to be a challenge. Denial is at the top of my list of things that prevent the imagination from playing its key mediating role between the levels. It's a barrier as effective as any moat to protect castle dwellers from feared relations with the rest of the world.

But the journey is less mysterious than it appears. The itineraries of successful adventurers are well documented.

5
A Change of Heart

...As when seeds break open in the ground
and act differently.
There is a hidden love-center
In human beings that you will discover and savor
And nourish yourself with. That will be your food.

Rumi

So far, we've discussed the transformative journey mainly in emotional and psychological terms. But the path that journey follows has, in fact, a basis in two physiological "maps" of biophysical energies that have a long history in the East.

An observation on models

Science and philosophy have an extensive tradition of using models to help frame more abstract concepts. From Socrates to Einstein, these simplified frameworks guided the thinking of their followers. In this book, I've attempted to use such a model, based on energy centers in the human body. If you have trouble relating to this idea, try regarding it as a less complicated framework for some fundamental ways of thinking about how we use our energy.

The classic model I've used

Thousands of years ago, Hindu and then Buddhist scholars studied the human energy centers found at the core of our biology. Because these subtle foci of energy were not easily measured, they were medically discredited in the West. But as different healing approaches, such as acupuncture, become more accepted, it's increasingly recognized that this therapy acts on bodily energy systems that correspond to dense accumulations of neurons at specific physical locations. India has long had models of these centers called "chakras" and the Chinese have complex meridians of energy, linking specific energy clusters. The models differ in the location and complexity of the pathways but both deal with the physical locations of human energy systems.

Over 50 years ago, psychologist Abraham Maslow stripped down an Indian version of these centers for Western consumption into a hierarchy of five needs. He not only left out some dimensions, but also omitted the pivotal role of one of these centers while achieving specific changes in the others. His work is largely accepted in a normally cynical West and is foundational in modern organizational studies. The acceptance of Maslow's work may have been because of his efforts to simplify things. I'll re-introduce some of the missing dimensions and dynamics below.

The model I'll use corresponds to seven centers located at specific physical locations in the body. For example, the solar plexus, which is currently in vogue with the get-fit group and referred to as one's core. The central fulcrum and major transforming center is at the level of the heart, which is no coincidence.

By now there have been many Western books and websites produced on the Indian centers, which are also featured in yoga. You'll find an amazing assortment of interpretations, including at least one set with a completely different number of centers. For our purposes, I'll base the model on the interpretation of Joseph Campbell. The key that he identified in a memorable presentation is the transformative role of the fourth medial heart center.[74] While many versions include seven centers, very few Western models show the specific reordering roles in the level of detail to follow.

All the centers represent a road map not only to human needs (à la Maslow) but also to individual emotional and moral evolution. They're a helpful model of the stepping-stones and transmutations needed to awaken the dormant imagination, amongst other changes.

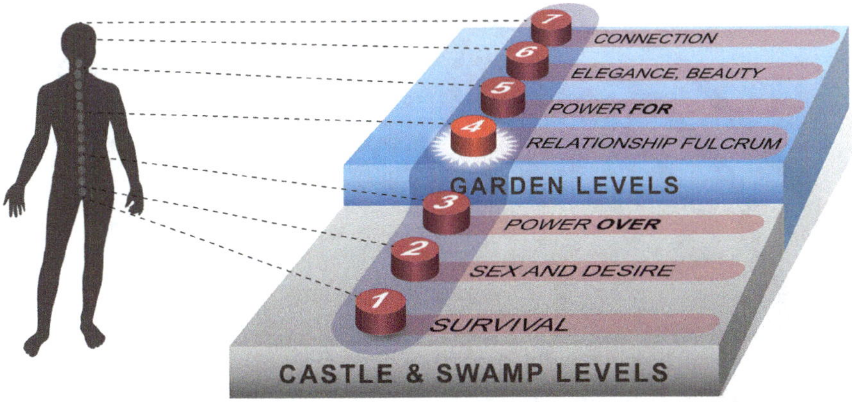

Figure 4 - Beyond and Before Maslow: A Model of Transformation

Human energy centers

The core of our model is about change and renewal through the middle center. Basic instincts (from "lower" physical levels) get renewed and reordered in more civilized ways (at "higher" levels). They don't go away. These changes free the human imagination to deal with both the pleasures and dangers of an evolving species on a vulnerable planet.

I begin with an outline of the seven centers and show that the middle one is central in its function. I'll continue in this chapter to show the transformation of the first set of centers.

How does the 4th center transform energy?

Archimedes said: "Give me a fulcrum, and I shall move the world!"—a remarkably helpful observation when trying to find a starting place for imaginative transformation. Where do we position ourselves to begin?

Because it's the foundation of personal change, I'll begin with the central energy source located in the middle of the energy centers. It can't be entirely accidental that this pivotal heart energy center corresponds to the essential organ of blood circulation, the metronome of life itself, and the

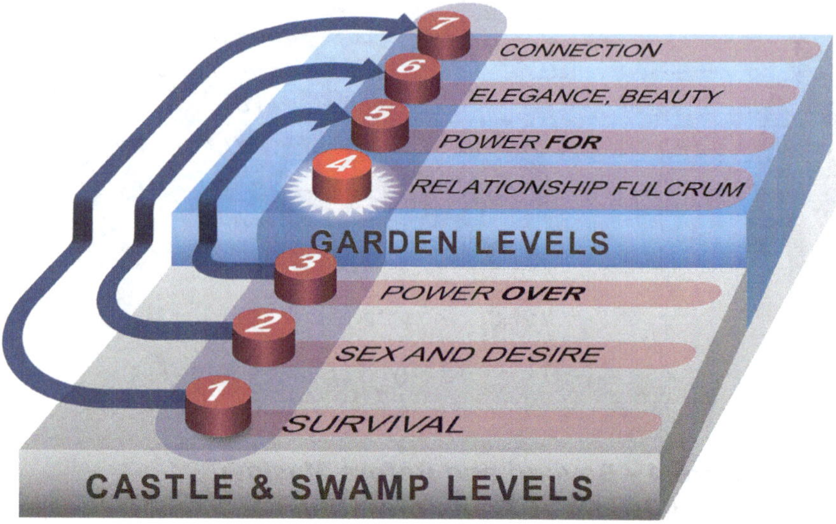

Figure 5 - Potential for Energy Changes

symbolic seat of love and courage. It's concerned with emotion and is a key player in relationships, a sense of wellbeing and longevity.[75]

Positioned between our lower and higher triads of energy foci, we share this center with other social creatures, to one degree or another. But not, I suspect, with lizards and insects. It's nothing less than the fulcrum of change, and is based on our ability to sustain relationships.

In my Course we see it in action in movies, in examples throughout literature, biographies, the daily news, and art. The energy of the fourth center—the power to reconnect with others—is essential. It's here that our personal outlook, attitude and potential may be changed from the blinkered, driven and, as we've just seen, often deluded, lower energy centers of raw survival, lust and the use of power over others.

Once we grasp how a map of the seven centers can help us navigate, I'll provide practical guides for our journey.

The lowest three energy centers: 1, 2 and 3

These play a key role in everyday life. In the East, the three lowest energy centers were traditionally described as dealing with:

Center 1: Survival

Sitting at the base of the spine, this root center drives fear and greed. Strikingly, these are two emotions now widely acknowledged as the prime movers of the stock market, and probably the whole financial system.

They are also the only motivations recognized by the simplistic psychology of Behaviorism, now happily discredited but formerly influential. A post-graduate class was once reduced to anger and some tears when I staged a debate, pretending to be Frederic (B.F.) Skinner, the father of Behaviorism, for whom stimulus and response was all. I showed how relatively easy it was to discredit more complex views of human behavior by arguing that they were the result of nothing more than conditioning. Mammals can be easily studied if deprived of food and placed in mazes. Exploring subtlety is more difficult. That problem has not gone away in our contemporary political discourse, where simplistic and self-serving catch-phrase notions like "trickle down" are hard to deal with. Jonathan Haidt's book *The Righteous Mind* makes this point, showing how readily one can drag complex political debates into simplistic categories of loyalty and betrayal.[76]

Center 2: Sexuality and desire

Located, predictably enough, in the genitals, this center has experienced its share of exploitation. Modern marketing is expert at triggering these urges into nothing more than a desire for goods or services. Think of the ubiquitous female models at trade and car shows promising an old link between a new truck or car and sexuality. The fact that women increasingly influence new car purchases still escapes some of these marketing wonders.

In traditional psychology this center preoccupied Freud, who reduced much complex adult behavior to repressed sexuality. Concerning the deep structures of everyday neuroses, Freud's thinking was brilliant but his notion of "penis envy," for instance, was based on pure speculation unsupported by any research whatsoever. I recall being told that Freud never worked with any young girls, and only met one young boy for a single hour of therapy. Meanwhile Freud's life suggests issues with his own sexuality—a classic example of projecting his own shadow onto others.

Center 3: Power over others

Seated in the solar plexus, this is the center where we gather the energy to attempt control over others, defend territory and protect possessions. Friedrich Nietzsche, who erected his philosophy on a theorized human "will to power," and his disciple Alfred Adler, father of the "inferiority complex," were both concerned with this focus of energy. Neither used this model nor showed an awareness of it in this way.

Martial artists wisely move from this physical center of the body, as do many athletes and modern dancers. Those who are in touch with this place can easily project their grounded state.

These three lower centers manifest our most basic drives—in an evolutionary as well as moral sense. They connect to parts of the brain shared not only with mammals, but with reptiles and insects, and constitute our lizard brain. Here is the home of the metaphorical dragons we met in Chapter 3 who occasionally encourage us to regress to their level in decision-making. Tyrants and dictators often exhibit the same issue but tolerate fewer restraints. Or to be more accurate, they crush constraints. In the world of ants, where the three lower chakras rule, there are many invasions and "ethnic cleansings" amongst colonies.

How to find and cultivate the garden: centers 5, 6 and 7

In mirror image of our trio of lower centers, which tend to rule us in the castle and even more forcefully in the swamp stages of our lives, the three higher chakras correspond to our capacity to dwell in and cultivate the garden.

Center 5: Power for others

Focused near the throat, the energy of this center is directed outward to other people, and to causes that extend beyond oneself. Having used our power in self-serving ways at center 3—the default setting of a lower lizard center, we move to this new focus. Having experienced the transformative potential of center 4 we find that this fifth chakra opens the possibility of joy and relationships through a rediscovered concern for others. But this emotional realm can be alarming and many men resist it out of a deep-seated fear of change. For some, there is a lingering shadow conviction that such altruism is somehow "unmanly."

Center 6: Liberated vision

The classic location of this center is near the "third eye," on the forehead. It's associated with intuitive perception, and the ability to perceive and appreciate esthetics.

Here sexuality is transmuted—not lost, but amplified, broadened and intensified. Through the shift initiated in the fourth center this impulse changes into a literally heart felt appreciation of beauty, clarity, and elegance of design. Many facets may be revealed here, including, for some, the lyricism of a sentence or resonance of a musical phrase. The very word *resonance* describes a sound (sonance) being echoed in a new way as, for example, with the lingering harmonics of a fading musical note.

Center 7: A sense of deep connection

Here is the highest chakra that Easterners are able to articulate. It includes the basic energies of sheer survival, now transformed through an emotional engagement of the pivotal center 4, into an experience of complete integration in a timeless "vertical dimension." Located in the crown of the head, its role is described as linking us to the cosmos. It's inextricably involved in garden-consciousness.

Many classic tales evoke, if imperfectly, this level of consciousness. It involves a state of universal connectedness that one of our guides was able to access and directly observe. Remarkably, this guide is a scientist who, through circumstance, found her analytic left brain shut down and no longer able to censor this center, as it normally does.

Seven energy centers lead to the regained imagination

The goal is not to extinguish the lower three energy centers—potentially creating an impotent mystic. We still need those drives of survival, sex and self-protection to function in society. But, they should no longer rule us. Instead, **all** of the centers begin to function together and in harmony—mediated by the transforming role of the heart. The key is learning to use the central pivot of the fourth center to transform—to shift—from serving only the lower centers.

At the end of the Owain story, our hero takes the countess back to the castle. Significantly, this is not about a journey up and out of the world. The aim is not to bliss out in nirvana. The whole point is to continue to strive for more inclusive levels of integration so that one's life in the real world is more productive and gratifying, and inspiring to others. It's to be truly generative.

The Power Shift: from "power-over" to "power-for"

The first major change is from power-over to power-for, from force of will to willing-ness. It's central to shifting the focus of our power from fear and desire to love and creativity. This shift will come up repeatedly as we realize that our task as individuals and leaders is to facilitate the emergence of new dimensions, not to double down on protecting those we have only apparent (and fleeting) control over. It often begins with an experience in which our compassion is aroused for some reason. It may be our child or a pet that is at risk; suddenly we find strength, which feels like it comes from outside ourselves. But power-for can encompass entire ecosystems.

This transformation is not illusory. Science has discovered that when we step outside ourselves and imagine the experience of another person, so-called mirror neurons in our brains activate just as they do in the brain of the person we're empathizing with. Correspondingly, narcissism, which is a fascination with and elevation of self, makes this effectively impossible. Here's another reason the ego-boosting strategies so popular in modern life are effectively fatal to our creativity and potential.

As the diagram below attempts to illustrate, the change we're describing—one that countless narratives have captured over the centuries and that I have witnessed in many of my Course participants, and in myself—is almost literally a change of heart.

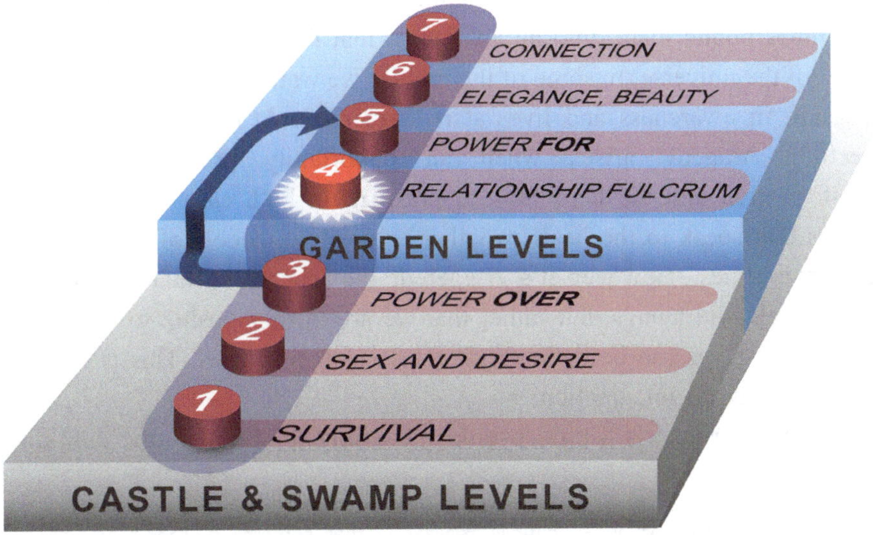

Figure 6 - From Power "Over" to Power "For"

This change is the essence of what Joseph Campbell observed in numerous sagas: the fourth chakra, or energy base, always plays a central and essential role. Typically, the heroes he studied experienced some event or events that caused this fourth center to become highly activated. When that intensity was engaged—changing from power-over to power-for—it redirected the self-serving aspects of the lower centers into transformed energies to create a more compassionate person.

Modern marketing has played ruthlessly into perpetuating the myth that we all deserve instant and endless gratification because we're special. We've earned it and we crave the prizes of success: the $75,000 auto, the second home, the safe, sanitary and legally sanctioned extracurricular adventure somewhere exotic. Clearly a recipe for human and social disaster. If you want to create a tyrant out of a pet, or child, just adopt this attitude and step back! The truth is that—in spite of the ads—it's **not** all about the individual. Life is not a right based on entitlements. It's a gift lasting for the blink of an eye in a 14 billion year ongoing process. Why not reach out?

For many protagonists in ancient and modern narratives of personal redemption and transformation, something happened to forcefully drag them, sometimes pound them, into an awareness that they were not, after all, the center of the universe. In some of the movies we watch in my Course, there's this shift in awareness and lives start to recover. At the other end of the spectrum, tragedy arises when an opportunity presents itself for transformation and the hero fails to grasp it. In both cases we're offered images that speak to the heart, whether as positive models of change or as cautionary tales. However it's triggered, the awareness that we are not solitary splendid beings, but rather that we are in relationship to something beyond ourselves can be the catalyst for a change of heart. This is the first step to freeing the imagination.

The writer Iris Murdoch links the ability to love with the unfolding of reality:

> Love is the extremely difficult realization that something other than oneself is real. Love, and so art and morals, is the discovery of reality.[77]

Howards End—the movie and book

As we saw earlier, Owain was shown a way of accessing the garden. But the lure of the Big Leagues proved too much. Winning tournaments in the castle is great sport and feeds the ego, so the drive to power and dominance had him on his way to fame and success within the establishment. Luned—an anima figure if ever there was one—carried the message of eviction from the garden. It's she who, like poet Antonio Machado, effectively asks the question: "What have you done with the garden that was entrusted to you?" And only when Owain experiences that change of heart is she at last liberated.

The Power Shift involved liberating Luned from the cave in which she (like many anima figures) has been imprisoned. Think of the role of women in many video games and movies. They've been stereotyped, objectified and imprisoned in the minds of hopelessly unimaginative game designers. The Hollywood PR machines frequently capture the young spirit of women and imprison them in confined roles, plastic surgery, and designer gowns. One has to wonder: who will rescue them? Where are their Owains?

The freeing of Owain's imagination continues. He's helped by the lion to realize his power is to be directed in the service of others. He qualifies for re-admission to the garden and to the countess's realm. It's interesting, in the end, that they both return to the world of the castle, presumably to help with its reformation. Owain directs his power beyond himself, while his change reflects the deep and enduring role of the feminine guide.

On the other hand, E. M Forster's *Howards End* is an extraordinary portrayal of Henry Wilcox, a top executive wandering deep in the swamp of the soul. His fiancée Margaret both overtly and unconsciously tries to show him ways he might become more effective by expanding his range of emotional experience. But despite her consistent efforts to enlarge the field of his imagination, he remains blind. Unlike Owain, he doesn't make his way back.

In terms of power-over, all the characters correctly see Mr. Wilcox as a dominant power player in the commerce of England. The country has become less about those with culture and more about people with economic clout. Henry knows about control and the use of power. He can comment on the real estate market and give advice on the stock market and jobs. He has business interests in Africa (exploitation of others across the globe is not a new phenomenon). On the other hand his new fiancée and her younger, less mature sister Helen, are connected to the world of the arts. Unlike Henry, they attend concerts and hold "artsy" discussion groups. Wilcox sees these activities as frills that keep women amused but which are not at all central to his understanding of the real business of life.

A recurring theme in the novel is a widely held concern about who "has the ropes" in society. In a telling portrayal of how the classes and genders see each other, Forster shows how each group (in some sense) admires and wants contact with those who have the power to make things happen in the world.

Another of the layers in the plot concerns an overall unstated theme that an era of civility and tradition is coming to an end in England (and now the world). Global business interests dominate. **Commerce triumphs over culture.** This has enormous costs, although Wilcox would not agree.

Finding himself walled behind his ego and opinions, Wilcox is incapable of extending beyond mottos and formulae. Margaret, like so many optimistic women, hopes to reach him and find a way to a true marriage of mind and soul:

> Mature as he was, she might yet be able to help him to the building of the rainbow bridge that should connect the prose in us with the passion. Without it we are meaningless fragments, half monks, half beasts, unconnected arches that have never joined into a man. With it love is born....[78]

But for Henry this revelation was not to be. We're told it was "...hard-going in the roads of Mr. Wilcox's soul." From boyhood he had neglected his interior life. He explains, "I am not a fellow who bothers about my own inside."

A lack of concern for one's inner world is a boast heard in many forms from those who see this attitude as a point of strength. Some men avoid the inside or hidden domain because they're concerned there might be nothing substantial there! Or they dread that anything unleashed might veer out of control. One client told me that he could not allow himself to cry in case the tears never stopped.

Again we think of Henry:

> Outwardly he was cheerful, reliable, and brave; but within, all had reverted to chaos, ruled, so far as it was ruled at all, by an incomplete asceticism.

We discover even more about the roots of Henry Wilcox's frozen emotionality in the following:

> Henry had adopted a half-baked belief from religious instruction that passion was not a good thing; it was to be stolen secretly.

> This robbed him of an ability to love expansively. And it was here that Margaret hoped to help him.

The extract then describes Margaret's imaginative but doomed plan for helping him change into a broader person:

> It did not seem so difficult. She need trouble him with no gift of her own. She would only point out the salvation that was latent in his own soul, and in the soul of every man. Only connect! That was the whole of her sermon. Only connect the prose and the passion, and both will be exalted, and human love will be seen at its height. Live in fragments no longer. Only connect and the beast and the monk, robbed of the isolation that is life to either, will die.
>
> But she failed. For there was one quality in Henry for which she was never prepared, however much she reminded herself of it: his obtuseness. He simply did not notice things, and there was no more to be said...he never noticed the lights and shades that exist in the greyest conversation....Once...she scolded him about it. He was puzzled, but replied with a laugh: 'My motto is Concentrate. I've no intention of frittering away my strength on that sort of thing.' 'It isn't frittering away the strength,' she protested. 'It's enlarging the space in which you may be strong.' He answered: 'You're a clever little woman, but my motto's Concentrate.' And this morning he concentrated with a vengeance.

To **"...enlarge the space in which you may be strong"** is a wonderful description of our journey as it suggests that we can learn to inhabit the upper reaches of our imaginations. We can bypass the narrow band of personal power concerns and extend into wider dimensions.

Henry Wilcox's trajectory—potential and actual

Henry begins in the castle at Stage 1 as a high-functioning power-over person who pays little attention to others. He has energy and influence. There are many CEOs at this Stage who are frequently well-rewarded for results that are bereft of any human considerations. In a short-term turnaround or a crisis they can be valuable, but they're not builders or mentors.

Margaret wants to help. Here the anima plays her role through trying to introduce changes in ways that penetrate Henry's defensiveness. She needs to be subtle to cut through that cold steel of character armor with finesse and charm. She works "by quiet indications" as she imagines building that rainbow bridge.

With due respect to Forster, it's not in fact Margaret who fails. It's Henry—and it costs him everything. Both the film and novel version of the story chillingly document the exact moment he fails.

Faced with a fulcrum decision regarding Margaret's sister he refuses a request to show compassion. There is no rainbow bridge for Henry. The wake-up call closes him down. He cannot cope and so the chain of painful events continues into further family calamity. With roots in the toughness of the business mindset that has driven the Wilcox family, our hero finds himself unequipped to handle his fate.

In the end, tragedy. Unable to realize those unconnected gateways Margaret hoped to help him build, Henry Wilcox is a broken man, someone justifiably cut off by the younger generation.

Some commentators see Wilcox softening into a more caring person at the end of the novel, but I feel this is too simplistic. I've worked with several Wilcoxes, and the conclusions of their careers are not peaceful for themselves or their families. I'd say over the decades their numbers are rising. How could they not, if the only measure of success is growing profits (sometimes technically termed EBITDA)[79] to increase the multiple[80] for a sale and get-away? "Once we have sold this sucker I can move on to the next job, or retire with my stash."[81]

Shakespeare power shifts and forgiveness

For me, *The Tempest* presents an intriguing opportunity to witness what it means to renounce power. Here we meet someone not only in the process of changing the uses of power, but giving it up.

The play concerns Prospero, a nobleman who has been betrayed by his brother and exiled to an island. Expelled from the kingdom with his only daughter Miranda, his treasured books, and a sprite named Ariel, he is a conjuror capable of manipulating reality. Ariel is a fanciful and illusory character, at once formless and formed, a kind of nymph-like energy suddenly appearing and as quickly disappearing throughout the play. Ariel might be seen as an aspect of Prospero's imaginative power.

Prospero wields this power for his own ends using the sprite as his personal servant. He manages to arrange events to have all his enemies, including his brother, shipwrecked on his island during a violent storm he calls up with Ariel's help. A key theme throughout is that this island appears mysteriously different to its various inhabitants, as I've noted. To some of the castaways the island is a garden, to others a swamp. We make the world up according to our projections.

Prospero's relationship with Ariel at the beginning of the play is undeveloped. Shakespeare invites us to see the alliance between these two characters as one based on power. Prospero is not yet able to see things in any other light except one that keeps Ariel servile. Even though the sprite is central to the nobleman's magical skills, Ariel is a servant he feels free to abuse. This enchanting being is held captive while our aristocrat uses his power.

We witness another subtle power struggle as well. Before Prospero can free himself of his views of superiority and sovereignty, he must first undergo a shift within himself. To liberate his imagination he must learn to let go of his desire for vengeance. Setting Ariel free will be his final redemption.

There is an interesting detail in *The Tempest* that I've not seen mentioned before. Besides forgiving his assembled enemies, Prospero decides not only to bury his staff of power, but to do this to a "prescribed" depth and renounce his magical arts. The burial of the staff is not a careless process for him and perhaps it's not to be for us either. It seems certain aspects of power are to be retained, while others unequivocally abandoned.

The change in Prospero happens on several fronts. He sees his beloved daughter making a fresh life for herself. She falls in love. The beauty of the young lovers moves the old man, sparks his imagination and, caught up with the next generation, Prospero begins to forget himself. Later in the play, as he prepares for his big moment of revenge, Prospero asks Ariel how his captives are faring. Ariel shocks him by describing an old mentor suffering from the imagined punishment and crucially Prospero asks Ariel for advice for the first time. He is now compassionately listening to his imagination, rather than commanding it. Ariel says that if he were human he would forgive them all. Astonished that a mere sprite could know such tenderness, Prospero relents and forgives his so-called enemies for past transgressions. This is the magical moment in the play when Ariel, like his master, is destined for freedom.

Forgiveness is not simply a naive forgetting. It's a dynamic process. After changing one's power goals, the act of forgiveness is linked to a liberated imagination.

My reading of the play expanded when I read an essay by the Vancouver theologian John Stackhouse Jr. on forgiveness.[82] He elaborated on what seemed to be two key further steps. His comments point to some things I hadn't read into Shakespeare's play. Stackhouse argues:

> If you've forgiven a painful injury, you know how much it hurts to refuse to get even, let alone seek vengeance, and instead to forgive. Forgiveness always entails suffering.

For me, this was a reminder that brought some unforgotten and unforgiven moments of the past into focus. It takes guts to give up one's right of revenge. This sense of painful injury is what keeps one smoldering, stuck in anger and resentment. Hanging onto our losses and our pride, we end up staying in the same old place thinking about what "they" did instead of letting go and moving on. We're all Prosperos, at least as he is in the earlier stages of the play.

And then Stackhouse points to a further step in the process, that forgiveness is alone not enough. "What? There's more?" I asked, feeling somewhat unsure of where this whole thing was going. But for Stackhouse the order of things has been disturbed by the very nature of such a hurtful event occurring, and so someone has to set it right. His point: having forgiven the transgression there's a further requirement of the sufferer to act in the world to undo this wrong. I'm not sure I welcomed it much—this clear call to further responsibility.

It's Prospero in *The Tempest* who grasps these levels regarding forgiveness and change, but it's taken him a lifetime. I think Shakespeare, through Prospero and Ariel and all the fun of the other amazing characters, hopes to help us move more quickly.

There is a version of *The Tempest* directed by Julie Taymor, which is perhaps the best film of the play ever. The success of Helen Mirren's creative "Prospera" brings home that these great changes in the human heart and imagination are not gender specific, although the triggers may be. It's a given that we all need to embrace these qualities as part of our developing inner life.

The Power Shift

In Henry Wilcox we see the psychic shell we must shed, while admitting a willing and potentially painful vulnerability. In Prospero we witness that transition, a true readiness to give up the old. After an empathic response to these characters, I guess what we learn is that, like them, we must let go. Metaphorically speaking, we need to get off the couch and step into the world and allow that larger community to influence us. What can we learn through an interaction or connection that may be uncomfortable? This may become more difficult as we age or gain status and progress in an organization.

Current research suggests that gaining power can indeed lead to a lessening of empathy.[83] Examples come to mind easily, from Nixon to Rupert Murdoch. But this book is based on our ability to overcome that predictable lure of power that leads to corruption.

Rollo May, the great existential psychologist, pointed to a fundamental and positive connection between empathy and power. Decades ago in his landmark book: *Love and Will*[84] May wrote:

> The interrelation of love and will inheres in the fact that both terms describe a person in the act of reaching out, moving towards the world...

May goes on to stress that in both love and will one seeks to affect others or the world, and also exposes oneself to being affected. He points to an etymological root at the heart of both these words that use the linking concept of "tend." One can tend to something one cares about (caring) and one can tend towards a course of action (deciding). The Latin root *tendere* is about reaching out, and extending.[85] It links love and will at their very roots.

The idea of leaders using their power to serve those they care about is behind the classic study *Servant Leadership*[86] by May's contemporary, Robert Greenleaf. But it's at risk of being forgotten. Even Jim Collins's best seller *Good to Great* failed to grasp the link in trying to explain how great leaders developed both professional will and—paradoxically, it seemed to him—personal humility. This freedom from pride is based on a respect for others.

What seems clear to me is that these leaders somehow achieved a Power Shift. Taking a first step out of the cage of the self, they were able to apply power for others.

I've just attempted to describe the shift in consciousness taking place between the energy centers most closely connected to power. Clients, whose professional life is often preoccupied with the exercise of power, easily relate to that experience. But we'll see shifts between the other centers. The sequence can change. What matters is that the transitions happen.

Adam Grant, in his new book *Give and Take*[87] argues that good guys may finish first, after all. Grant points out how Abraham Lincoln withdrew from an earlier Senate race to allow a colleague his chance. Having done that, Lincoln then won support for himself in the next election. And business is not all about win-lose cut-throat dynamics either. There is the legend of John Hunstman leaving $200 million on the table in a deal with someone who had lost his wife. Because this loss moved Huntsman, it seems his heart could rule his head. Grant's research adds to a growing body of support for the win-win ways of people learning how to give for the benefit of themselves and others. With powerful and brilliant people like Warren Buffet deciding to reach beyond family and give to the Bill and Melinda Gates Foundation because of their excellent managerial skills, we are into a new dimension.

These are examples of a new kind of imagining and resolving of global problems, connected to a change of heart. They involve the ability to share one's power and resources, by selectively giving away assets. The power shift connects the heart and imagination. Here is the rainbow bridge—a place where, through empathy, one transcends oneself.

We now move on to another type of shift, and explore the origins of a renewed appreciation of elegance and beauty.

6
From Reproduction to Elegance

When you feel the qualities of Gabriel in you, you fly up quickly
like a fledgling not thinking of the ground.
When you feel asinine qualities in you, no matter how you try
to do otherwise, you will head towards the stable...

Always search for your innermost nature in those you are with.

Rumi

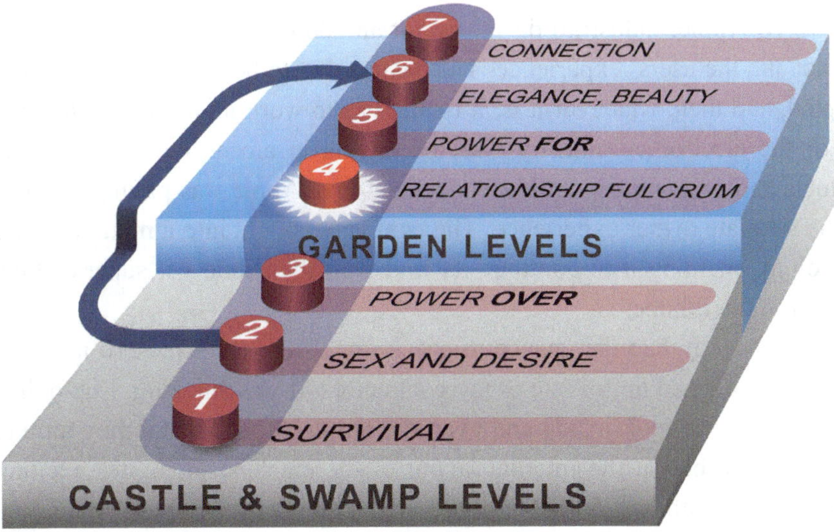

Figure 7 - From Reproduction to Elegance

In the previous chapter we discussed the transformation of power. Now we'll see how sexual energy translates at the fulcrum of the fourth energy center and is reconstituted as an appreciation of elegance and beauty.

Does this change to heart-centered energy sound completely far-fetched and unrealistic in the world we see around us? Where, after all, does beauty figure in the bottom-line metrics of interest to shareholders or market analysts? Whether you call it elegance or maybe design, it turns out beauty is important and very much alive and well in our world today. However you want to name it, this quality is incorporated explicitly in the strategy of the biggest company of the moment. For Apple, it's central to its success.

A key to the success of Apple's founder, Steve Jobs, was an ability to integrate modern technology with the best of what he'd learned from his family, the counter-culture of his youth, and a visit to India. From his stepfather, a carpenter, he learned to care about every surface, visible or not, of everything he built. This well-learned lesson translates to the clear layout even inside Apple products. From Eastern philosophy he learned the significance of beauty, and the fact that design is embodied in the thing itself. He made sure these insights guided Apple's engineers and kept them focused on whole-product excellence.

To Apple, industrial design is not an add-on. It's at the heart of the product and the users' experience. The balance has to be satisfying, the edges sculpted, and then, whatever it is, it finally has to work intuitively. While the rest of the electronics industry was foundering in arcane bells-and-whistle products and user-impenetrable technical set-ups, Apple was paving the way for the ultimate owner experience. The company bought into a metal pouring technology enabling it to continue its lead with the subtle yet superior look and feel of the iPhone.

I recently had the chance to check out a high-end Mac Pro machine when it was opened up for one of my contractors. It was amazing. I'd not had an opportunity to look inside and even the non-tech people standing around at the time gasped at the internal layout of the machine. It invites exciting modifications with easy access to hard drives and memory. Someone in the group commented that it was really just so "sexy," an example of that exciting kind of energy leading to an esthetic thrill. It seems when something is both beautiful and useful it's a pleasure to experience. This appreciation triggers awe at the elegance of the design, engineering and interface.

Industrial design is a modern version of what craftsmen have been doing throughout the ages. The continuing goal is to create objects that are not only utilitarian but which contain, in Joseph Campbell's words, a "divinely superfluous beauty." Is there possibly an echo of Rilke's beautifully carved statue in an iPhone?

Elegant solutions

I was lucky enough to be taught Statistics by a German master mathematician, Dr. Herbert Sichel. He helped me understand—through this rigorous discipline—that one needs to know the underlying assumptions behind any technique. He argued students could not apply even a correlation unless they first understood how the formula had been derived and what assumptions it rested on. His advice gives any of us dramatically more scope to apply formulae in innovative and elegant ways. We then have a feel for what it can offer and don't end up following what Sichel disdainfully called a mere recipe book.

A failure to apply this underlying principle turned out to be one of the major causes of the 2008 financial meltdown. It seems the so-called "quant jocks" in the financial engineering firms were not aware that their models relied on normal distributions, nor that these distributions no longer applied in a universe where paper securities could be created endlessly. They simply assumed that normal statistical curves would apply to infinitely expandable financial instruments—a monumentally basic flaw! As a result, the banks were unable to measure the risks contained in the financial products they were promoting.

One of these jocks, Nassim Nicholas Taleb, conceded as much in his extraordinary book *The Black Swan.*[88] Significantly, Taleb dedicates his account to Benoit Mandelbrot, the father of that new branch of mathematics called fractals, which I discussed in Chapter 4. It turns out that the financial wizards should have been using fractal math!

The book (and subsequent Oscar-winning movie) *A Beautiful Mind*[89] stresses how the real solutions in mathematics are constantly being sought in parsimony—in minimalism achieved through elegance. In architecture and furniture, the elegant solutions of mathematicians influenced the spare, uncluttered beauty of Bauhaus Group designs. They in turn inspired Steve Jobs.

A current study published in *The Frontiers of Human Neuroscience Journal*[90] explains the brains of a group of mathematicians were studied to see how the participants responded when they looked at equations they had identified as "beautiful." These particular equations lit up (in fMRI terms) the same regions of the brain known to be associated with appreciating art, including music. The principal author, Semir Zeki, points out that as "...we have evolved in this universe...the experience of beauty may be a pointer to truth about the universe."

This thought reflects something poet John Keats said nearly 200 years ago.[91] Keats was contemplating an ancient artifact, thinking of its many associations and its inherent perfection of form when he concluded: "Beauty is truth, truth beauty– that is all / Ye know on earth, and all ye need to know."

The two quotes are wonderful examples of the underlying congruence of science and poetry as these apparently disparate views approach one of nature's truths regarding truth and beauty. One difference is that the scientific paper needs to be pages long, backed by high-tech electronics, while Keats was able to compress his insight into two elegant and unforgettable lines.

The author of the research discussed above, neuroscientist Zeki, concluded "Relegating beauty to the study of art and leaving it out of science is no longer tenable." This view is central to the emerging field known as neuroesthetics, which focuses on the connections between brain science and experiences of beauty. To put it more precisely, it studies the neural bases for the contemplation and creation of art.[92] Zeki's study emanates from the Laboratory of Neurobiology and is supported by the Wellcome Trust in London, England.

Paul Dirac was a brilliant mathematician and theoretical physicist who shared the Nobel Prize when he was 31 with Erwin Schrödinger. He argued the principle of beauty that he found in relativity theory would need to take precedence over simplicity.[93]

> What makes the theory of relativity so acceptable to physicists in spite of its going against the principle of simplicity is its great mathematical beauty. This is a quality which cannot be defined, any more than beauty in art can be defined, but which people who study mathematics usually have no difficulty in appreciating. The theory of relativity introduced mathematical beauty to an unprecedented extent into the description of Nature...We now see that we have to change the principle of simplicity into a principle of mathematical beauty.

I found some promising initial work on the power of esthetics in the *Journal of Consumer Research.*[94] Two marketing professors devised an ingenious set of studies to test the impact of choosing products that have good esthetic design. They found, in controlling for other factors, such as function and brand, that it was only esthetics that positively influenced self-affirmation. It seems that choosing a well-designed product affirms a particular value—one's sense of self-worth. As values relate to the imagination, this caught my attention, and I feel the study begs further work.

Literature and beauty

A classic example in literature of the power of beauty is the role Dante assigned to Beatrice, his guide in the final stages of *The Divine Comedy.* Earlier in the poem, Dante's guide has been the ghost of the Roman intellectual Virgil. But in this final and ultimate phase through the celestial spheres of Heaven he needs an image of pure beauty. This great epic demands a symbol of transformed love—the elusive effect that later psychologists would reach for in their idea of "sublimation."

The thing to remember though, at this Stage of our quest, is that it's not just about redirecting energy, as Freud saw it. It's about transforming energy. Here, sex and desire are refigured and directed towards an appreciation, often first perceived in nature or art, of a deep and pervasive order. But the basic energies are not lost. Thankfully! What tends to happen is that once we've recognized we're part of a larger whole, our own narrower concerns begin to diminish so we're more able to appreciate that greater view and possibly contribute to it. Hopefully, our commitment to beauty will eventually grow beyond personal horizons—possibly our vision will finally reach beyond the scope of our own life span.

American Beauty—the movie

In a premonition of dark economic times, the final career blow descends on Lester, the central character played by Kevin Spacey. At the outset of this award-winning film, released in 1999, Lester appears as a small, insignificant character sitting in a low chair facing a bombastic boss who seems to tower above him. Later, no longer able to repress his widespread disgust with big business excesses, the Spacey character lashes out at the company spokesman with accusations and tales of expense account fraud and hookers. We're not surprised when he's out of a job he's come to hate. We're also not too surprised when we learn he's losing his marriage and has pretty much lost anything that remotely resembles a normal relationship with his only daughter. His wife is equally desperate.

It took me several viewings to get a take on the Annette Bening character, Caroline. She's living with a man who is disenchanted with his life. He's bitter and withdrawn. She works hard to make a go of a career in real estate. We witness agonizing scenes of her efforts at self-motivation to forestall a deep depression. We learn too that Caroline is a quintessential consumer and member of the New Age fraternity. She devours tapes that talk her "up." And then, subsequently she beats herself up for not achieving the prescribed goals. Wealth and success are the promises of these well-worn tapes. She listens frequently and so, in her mind, all she has to do is perform. Perform; and all will be hers. Easy, but it's just not happening. She must be the problem.

The promise of wealth made by this whole New Age school of marketers is I think a deep betrayal. What we are sold is that it's a means of developing higher consciousness. It's not. And Bening's character has yet to learn this truth. When a message is turned in this way, we need to be wary. Dostoevsky forcefully described this kind of misrepresentation as the very soul of evil.[95]

Caroline is easy to stereotype. It's so tempting to characterize her as simply compulsive. The way she handles herself generally, her efforts in real estate, even her relationship to the glorious roses she grows makes it difficult at times not to think of her in this light. We feel her extreme intensity as somehow off balance and, in some ways it is. But another perspective reveals her to be a caring woman. Growing her roses with such care and attention, and then arranging them on the dinner table in a moving attempt to create at least some kind of positive atmosphere, reveals this other less obvious side of her personality. This in fact is her view of American beauty and she does whatever she can to keep the spirit of beauty alive. The only ones who seem to appreciate her efforts or recognize this almost fragile or delicate sensibility are the gay couple living next door.

Her red roses in all their brilliant beauty appear throughout the film, and the contrasting sets of images are unforgettable. The earliest signifies a yearning for beauty expressed in different terms for Lester and Caroline. The color then spreads, finally seeps, into blood at the movie's end. The imagery ranges from garden to ashes.

A highlight of the film is an extended video scene of a simple plastic bag caught in a wind vortex. It was the beauty of this unscripted dance that nearly broke the heart of the young Wesley, who filmed and proceeded to play the trance-inducing fragment for Lester's teenage daughter. And it's this young neighbor who then acts as a male guide or animus figure for the daughter. It's when he comments on how unbearable the beauty of it "all" can be, that she reaches for his hand and realizes she has found a connection to beauty and love in her own life. Finding this much beauty in the present moment carries more than an echo of zen awareness.

The memorable experience in *American Beauty* of sexual desire being transformed into esthetic appreciation comes when Lester's longed-for moment with his daughter's Lolita-like school friend is about to come to fruition. At last he's arrived, or is about to! The opportunity for the dreamed-of sexual encounter presents itself. It's perfect, except it isn't. No sooner is this chance to score bestowed upon our immature hero, than it disappears. Poof, and it's gone when he wakes up to the realization that she is innocent. She is beauty, in and of itself. His moment has passed when his desire for power-over her feels not only ridiculous but no longer acceptable. His lust for a child becomes obviously inappropriate. A genuine appreciation for her vulnerability and for her blossoming womanhood transforms him. She's beyond being imagined as a kind of sexual conquest. Or he's at last beyond it. This scene suggests the anima's positive influence on a man's imagination. She then asks him: "How are you?" He replies that it's been a long time since anyone has asked him that. He means, has asked with a genuine concern for the answer, of course. We see him thinking about himself but now there's a profound change. He recalls what he's just done—or not done, and actually feels OK, possibly even quite good about himself. He's ready to grow up, to move on to the next stage of imaginative questing, just before the movie's shocking conclusion.

As Good As It Gets—the movie

This 1997 film is a romantic comedy featuring Jack Nicholson as Melvin Udall, the cynical and neurotic writer. Helen Hunt plays Carol, a single parent working as a waitress burdened with hefty medical bills for her sick young son. And Greg Kinnear plays Simon, a gay artist. The opening scenes portray Melvin as an obsessive compulsive, an entirely self-centered writer successfully churning out romantic fiction. In a loveless life he explodes with anger when interrupted while defining "love" in one of his novels. When an admirer accosts him later in the film he responds with a chilling indictment of what he thinks of his readers, and worse, of women in general. He is a nightmare of projections, unleashing lethally well-crafted, scathing comments on blacks, Jews and just about anyone else who breaks his routine and who's not from what he considers an adequate background—his own.

"All over a dog!"

Melvin's wake-up call is from the animal kingdom in the form of a small spoiled dog that's thrust upon him after he's only recently literally tried to dispose of it. Unaccountably he falls for the dog, which responds to his shameless bribery of pure bacon snacks. When Melvin recalls the dog later in the movie, he weeps and shakes his head in wonder (and some terror) at the fact that this is "All over a dog!" The moment happens against his will, which is key to many of these personal epiphanies, from Jonah's calling in the Old Testament onwards.

The dog is a perfect mirror for the tensions that exist between the two men in the movie, and "Dog Whisperer" Cesar Millan would have a great time commenting on the little fella's behavior. Simon's life is in crisis—the dog senses this and avoids him, although his preference for Melvin is at least partly explained by the bacon treats. After all, dogs are human too!

Melvin's second guide is Carol who takes him to the mat after he's uttered one of his unbelievably thoughtless comments. Initially he finds himself helping her, if only to ensure uninterrupted service in the restaurant she's working in, but then finds himself noticing some of her extraordinary qualities. His awareness of her emerges towards the end of the film in a compelling description of her specific qualities and those of many anima figures. He realizes she appeals to what he values, which as a writer is clean, straight speech. "I might be the only person on earth who appreciates you" he comments. "You always mean something about being straight and good and true. Most people don't get it. The fact that I do makes me feel good about me."[96] Carol helps him not only to see her better, but to see something more positive in himself. In this way his own potential is revealed.

This passage connects to something I've repeatedly found. Many people need to be acknowledged, to be actually comprehended, and the pace and direction of the modern world denies them this experience. For many, Facebook seems to be mainly about broadcasting an upbeat self-image. The real losers though are those not caring "to see" others. Melvin is initially a completely failed older guy, who aggressively denies any guidance or nurturing to the younger people around him. Simon's parents have cut him off, presumably because he's gay. Until a doctor is fully and well paid by Melvin, all the professionals in Carol's life have been unavailable, untrustworthy, expensive and ineffectual. The right doctor can get her son up and running in days. This may be a starkly accurate observation of the state of professionalism in the world today.

The movie sees Melvin slowly grow out of his state of gross self-absorption. But it operates on other levels too. When Simon is robbed, badly beaten and ends up with money problems, he decides to reach out and ask his alienated parents for help. Melvin and Carol accompany him on a trip to ask for the bailout cash. Melvin runs into predictable problems with Carol when they attempt to go to dinner together. He makes a characteristically inappropriate comment and she storms back to the hotel. Back at the hotel, Simon inadvertently catches a glimpse of her while she's running her bath. He's struck by her beauty and an informal modeling session ensues. Acting as Simon's muse (another term for the anima) his artistic inspiration is re-ignited. As it turns out nothing overtly sexual happens during this time away together. Instead it's inspiration that's unleashed on this trip. Here's the anima at work. In this case, Carol moves the hearts of both men, making their transformations possible.

Re-animated vision is in full force as Simon re-establishes how he is to re-ignite his imagination and return to his art. When he calls his mother he's able to understand her need to whisper to protect them both from his overbearing father. He feels her awkwardness around his call and he understands. Simon is healed in some way through his interaction with Carol and now is able to help heal the rift between himself and his mother.

Both men have been moved through the intervention of the same woman, but in different guises. The stage is set for a new level of imaginative freedom. Now Melvin can know love, as opposed to defining it for adoring readers of romantic fiction, whom he's despised. Whether either of these men can sustain a life in Stage 4 is left to our imaginations. Will either of them live happily ever after? Who knows, and anyway, what does that mean? These life changes are about learning to navigate differently while hoping to arrive at new, and up to now unimagined, destinations.

"Is this as good as it gets?"

The film's title comes from a classic scene where Melvin has visited his psychiatrist during a panic attack. On walking out through the waiting room he asks the assembled patients: "Has it occurred to you that this is as good as it gets?" There are layers of possible meaning in this great moment.

One that struck me is that being in a waiting room to see a shrink is as good as it will get if that's all you're doing—waiting! Perhaps what we learn from this movie is that we have to step out into life, or be dragged out by a dog or our love for a woman or a man, or perhaps a child. But mostly we must be willing to change, to move along in some way. In Melvin's case even this has a double meaning as he has trouble literally "stepping out." Sidewalks are one of his endless issues as his OCD neurosis prohibits him from stepping on cracks in the cement. I wondered at the time if we were to be reminded of that childhood rhyme—"If you step on a crack you'll break your mother's back!"

The other meaning is more zen-like. Life now **is** the present moment and being in a waiting room is an analogy for all of us if we line up to wait for a better future. Don't wait.

7
From Survival to a Sense of Connection

Be patient.
Respond to every call
that excites your spirit.

Ignore those that make you fearful
and sad, that degrade you
back towards disease and death.

Rumi

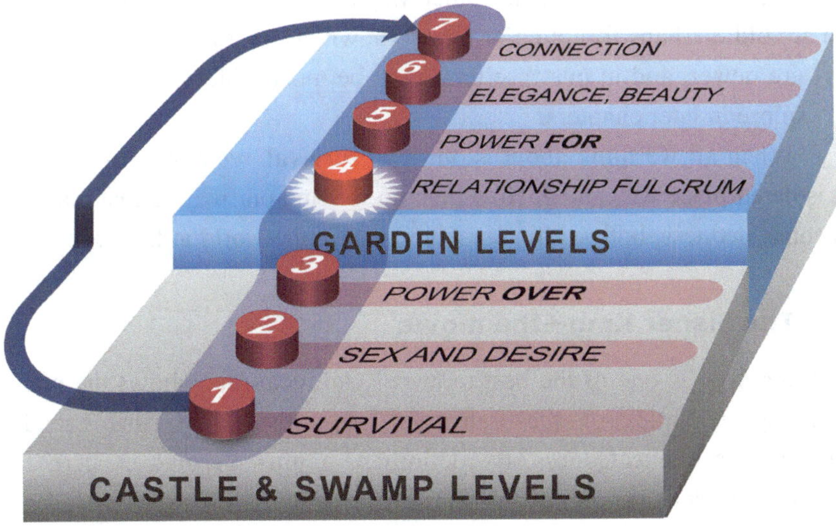

Figure 8 - From Survival to Connectedness

By this point, we've discovered it's not simply about getting what we want and then getting out. Hopefully by now it's more about making a contribution, about giving—other than just to oneself. This change involves transmuting the pure reptilian survival instincts of the lowest chakra because our drive for power has shifted. We're motivated to exercise it in another way. Physical lust and material desire have transformed as well and re-emerged as an appreciation of beauty and elegance.

Through a new sense of relationship with oneself and the world, we're definitely more likely to experience a connection to wider and deeper realities. But it's worth noting too, that as we expand our horizons it's also more likely we'll feel lost, at least initially. It makes sense, as this is a voyage we've never made, and no one can show us the exact way. We've already concluded that a narrow, one-dimensional approach to our lives or that of any organization holds little hope, so there's no holding back. Once we've left the safety of old shores other wider vistas appear. As our vision is again inspired it's possible we'll begin at last to see better because we see more.

In this section of *The Secret Sabbatical Course* we learn that although there are no charts, no exact signposts, or even old maps to help us, we can figure this out. There are other ways of imagining available to us. Some are old, perhaps forgotten or never known, at least not by many of us. Others are newer, and in our case these will be mostly ideas on time, which we'll explore in later chapters.

When all we think about is our own survival, we're probably at the most isolated place we can be. How then do we find our way to that place of calm connectedness, both within ourselves, and in the world at large?

The Fisher King—the movie

The Fisher King is one of the best movies I can recall that shows the many overlapping examples of the transition from survival to that broader encounter with connectedness. By definition, it must involve concern for others. This modern version of the tales of the Arthurian Knights includes a specific retelling of one of the great stories within the narrative of the film. Here both male characters are, in their own way, close to the edge. Each is struggling to survive but, sparked by an authentic concern for the other, they go through a transforming experience that subsequently lifts them into new levels of awareness.

The wake-up call occurs when a castle-dwelling ego-encapsulated radio talk show host (Jack Lucas, played by Jeff Bridges) advises a caller to take out his pent up frustrations on the world. Our genius "life coach" unthinkingly advises this guy to go after the establishment fat cats. The caller takes Lucas's cynical advice literally and the outcome is tragic. Jack, feeling it's his fault, is devastated and descends into a drinking-fueled depression. Beyond the reach of his partner or anybody else, he's on his way down. There's no stopping this descent, at least not at this point. Cratering into the swamp, our hero is about to end up on the street. He's a lost soul.

One of the survivors of this tragedy is Perry (the Robin Williams character) who goes into mourning over his beloved partner. She is gruesomely shot along with those other so-called fat cats. Perry is left reeling by the absolute horror of the event. Disappearing behind a curtain of blind denial, he collapses into a catatonic trance. Now seemingly schizophrenic he descends into total survival mode. His descent occurs in more than his immediate and unbearable inner life. Because his grief is so pervasive, he's driven down to what seems like the nether world of Hades. Alone, beneath the streets of New York, he lives in a sunken concrete wasteland. He too is lost.

Terry Gilliam of *Monty Python* and *Brazil* fame directed the movie. In typically stark Gilliam fashion the film unfolds with unforgettable visuals and tough emotional moments. A relentlessly pursuing fierce dark knight on a huge fire-breathing horse symbolizes Perry's unconscious terror. Consumed by the repressed memory of that horrific event, Perry cannot truly forget. With archetypal power, the memory finds a form that repeats in Perry's mind. There's no escaping the spell of this apocalyptic horseman. Raging, never giving up, this potent malevolent figure, like something out of some mad nightmare, has the power to take Perry out. Here lies annihilation and Perry should be terrified. This imagined brutal knight on his massive warhorse, deadly lance in hand, destroys everything in his path. In his current state Perry is not a worthy opponent. Unlike Owain, he cannot defeat the Black Knight. Not yet.

But, there's another unremembered side to this dark horseman, although Perry can't know it, not just yet. Gilliam however certainly does. He hasn't forgotten that the fiery furnace is also a place of transformation and change, a promise of hope and rebirth. Think about it. What else breathes searing, raging fire? The dragon. According to Carl Jung, this creature has many connotations, including being a transforming symbol with the potential to induce change.[97]

Like the Lester character in *American Beauty,* Perry regresses to an earlier state, in his case a fascination with questing stories for the Holy Grail. He's obsessed with the Grail, which incorporates the power of healing and transformation.[98] He also compulsively tracks the movements of an awkward young woman, who is well beyond his reach in his current state. He believes somehow that both—chalice and anima—may offer him redemption as he plays out this classic myth.

Perry projects the ancient Grail symbol onto a photo he's seen in some magazine of a chalice-like cup in a rich stranger's home—which looks remarkably like a castle as it happens. At some point in this story Jeff Bridges' character, Jack Lucas, is drawn, **against his will**, to helping Perry. What ails Perry is isolation and survivor's guilt. He desperately needs healing. As Jack takes on the bizarre task of getting what Perry sees as the Grail, he is moved beyond his grief and guilt. Jack is now using his physical power and ingenuity to take on a task he would never have dreamed of prior to meeting Perry. He wants to help this man. There's a dangerous burglary one night in pursuit of Perry's Holy Grail. Successfully relating to one another to complete their objective, both men are changed. The movie ends in an amazing scene of confirmation where the possibility of wholeness for Perry and Jack is a reality.

Like the old grail stories, in Gilliam's telling it turns out the actual finding of the physical object isn't what heals our seekers, but the spirit in which it's found. Or, in this case, in which it was found for Perry. That's one of the secrets of the quest. In one version the various seekers had to learn that finding the majestic cup at the end of their extended and difficult journey involved asking an empathic question. Finally they arrived at the sought after destination where they encountered their wounded king, but still the journey was not complete. It was here, at this late stage, that they could not neglect to ask the heartfelt question, "What ails thee?" In other words the kingdom in our hearts and the world out there can't be healed unless we experience a transformation **within our own hearts**.

Here is a perfect example of the **turn** created by the fourth energy center. In this case Perry's quest is inspired by more than his view of the very nearly unattainable chalice hidden deep within the castle-like walls of that stranger. It's also driven by his unaccountable empathy for Jack, the man who has caused his grief, and by his exalted vision of the young woman. So it's love, the ultimate connection to the kind of relatedness that the Grail has always stood for, which has fueled this broken man's search.

"What ails thee?" is another form of the question that the young girl asked Lester in *American Beauty*. In this context, "How are **you**?" is a truly healing question.

The characters and experiences in *The Fisher King* are grittier than those in *As Good as it Gets* and *American Beauty,* but there are parallels as each film explores the possibilities of recovery. Perry and Jack, Melvin and Simon, and Lester are all Owains in action in our modern world. All these men learn profound lessons to do with love and giving.

For each movie (and lifetime) that finds a creative ending there is another that unfolds in a grim alternative. So we need to be vigilant and ready to apply what energies we have to our issues. In a powerful play by T.S. Eliot,[99] a psychiatrist quotes the Buddha at the end of one of his therapy sessions. His concludes his sessions with "Go and seek your salvation with diligence!" Good advice for anyone, especially those of us caught in the shallows of the swamp.

In the last three chapters, I've laid out the model of change and shared some hopefully interesting examples of its dynamics. A quote from Dan Dennett, philosopher, writer and cognitive scientist, encapsulates the model, "The secret of happiness is: Find something more important than you are and dedicate your life to it."[100]

I've found having a guide or guides is essential as we move on to applying the model to our next stage. In the day-to-day navigation of our lives, it's their help we need. Let's see if we can glean some advice from people who've "been there, done that."

8
The Guides Begin: The Surprising Cesar

Don't worry about repenting.
Do the work that's given,
and learn from it.

If you become addicted to looking back,
half your life will be spent in distraction,
and the other half in regret.

You can live better than that!
Find happier friends.

Rumi

In the above classically simple, but not easy prescription, Rumi concludes by advising us to find happier friends. I took him at his word and introduced a set of guides for the Course. In the next three chapters I'll present these heroes and a heroine who will not only help us navigate through our daily lives, but stir our imaginations. They offer an invitation to somewhere new.

Below, Rumi beckons us again, but this time he points out the essence of this place or state we're looking for—the homeland of our newfound friends:

Out beyond ideas of wrongdoing and rightdoing,
there is a field. I'll meet you there.

Seneca, the great Roman philosopher, saw guides as indispensable. Even in his day, long before our modern world of relentless and never-ending distractions, he was concerned with how the majority of people were wasting their lives. Seneca felt that choosing and consulting reliable guides would secure the bedrock of a productive life and suggested the Romans should take time to attend to the guidance of philosophers.

> From them you can take whatever you wish: it will not be their fault if you do not take your fill from them. What happiness, what a fine old age awaits the man who has made himself a client of these! He will have friends whose advice he can ask on the most important or the most trivial matters, whom he can consult daily about himself, who will tell him the truth without insulting him and praise him without flattery, who will offer him a pattern on which to model himself.[101]

To stress that our navigational bearings can't come from any one field of specialization, I've selected guides for our journey who are from wildly different backgrounds, including one very practical Roman leader and philosopher. You're free to choose your guides of course, but what just might be interesting about your choices is that they may evolve over time. But for sure this book and *The Secret Sabbatical Course* are anti-dogma! The guides I suggest are not about leading the faithful. You retain your judgment and sense of responsibility all the way. In fact I hope these are qualities our guides help all of us develop.

Navigation guide: Cesar Millan

Our first major guide is Cesar Millan, the famed dog whisperer. You may have watched his TV program *The Dog Whisperer* on the National Geographic Channel. But before you become alarmed, I need to stress that while he's a gifted animal trainer, he sees his role as more than that of simply helping us better understand our pets. He has the unusual gift of perceiving the underlying psychological issues at play between the dog's all-too-human family members. By revealing the reasons for our troubled dog's behavior, Cesar guides us into the larger arena of self-knowledge. The fundamentals of his training rest on changing the dynamics of human behavior. It's the owners who need training. The rest will follow, including the dogs!

Cesar is our first teacher because he's foundational. This genial and talented TV personality helps us with his fascinating demonstrations of how humans need to act for effective relationships with their dogs. The fact that he is on the surface a dog trainer only adds to the impact. By initially convincing us we need to shape up, he so graciously teaches us how to gain self-control over the demands of our lower energy centers—those dealing with fear, desire and control. He shows that it's possible to override instinctual demands; something confirmed in recent research.

Dogs make great companions because they pick up on primal non-verbal signals. They still have those mysterious skills that cut through thousands of years of language barriers. Cesar teaches us to think of our relationships with our dogs as active, filled with imaginative possibilities. He makes us aware of their needs and how central our response is to those needs. Put simply, he shows that dogs are pack animals that need a capable leader. He asks us to imagine things from their point of view. Thinking of things this way, an imaginary conversation with one of our canine friends might begin with our being asked (by our dog!) the two following questions. First, "Can you lead?" and, if the answer is yes, then, "How can I serve you?" Of course it's not really a matter of putting words into our dogs' mouths, but instead a means of becoming aware of what's demanded of us in this relationship. As it turns out the skills we need here aren't much different from those we need in the world—a keener awareness of what's demanded from us and others, in this case a dog. A clear response from us is called for and Cesar stresses that many people are unaware of, or unwilling to consider, that first key non-verbal request—can you lead?

It's important to note that some aspects of his model of how dogs see the world are controversial. For example, Dr. Carolyn Walsh, of Memorial University of Newfoundland believes that we have misunderstood cues of dominance and submissiveness between dogs, while we have ignored other characteristics like the centrality of playfulness.[102] She and others argue that dogs are very removed from their wolf ancestors and have much more complex and idiosyncratic patterns of behavior than people like Cesar might concede. However that may be, whether or not they're strictly pack animals is not the focus of my argument concerning Cesar's key contribution. What

I'm interested in is his acute understanding of the human skills needed for leadership.

Cesar teaches the elemental leadership skills of being "calm and assertive," by stressing these are essential in our relationship with our dogs. But what he can't teach in a half an hour or so is what we are to be assertive about in our lives. That's our responsibility.

Cesar's example

One day in late 1990, a Mexican **coyote** (slang for a trafficker in illegal immigrants) escorted a small group of Mexicans across the border. Among the handful of migrants risking their lives in search of a better future was a short, stocky youth from the agricultural state of Sinaloa. Only 21, Cesar Millan Favela, barely speaking English, entered America. He knew no one. But he had a talent. Having a remarkable affinity for dogs, which he'd gained on his grandfather's farm, he had already earned himself the nickname of "Perrero," or dog boy. Two decades later "dog boy" became one of America's most successful—and certainly renowned—new citizens. His reality TV show was watched in more than 80 countries until 2012. Around the globe, millions of people are familiar with its provocative tagline: "I rehabilitate dogs. I train people."

I stumbled onto Cesar by accident one day while idly flipping channels. What caught my attention was his intuitive knowledge and outstanding skills while dealing with his guests and their dogs. Although the situations were dramatically different from any I'd known, somehow his style reminded me of great managers I'd worked with. Something about Cesar's manner is captivating: the set of his shoulders, his way of walking these dogs, how he engages the dogs' owners. I began to see more and more in Cesar's message. Eventually I came to appreciate just how well he embodies the two elusive characteristics of great managers I've already cited from Jim Collins's book *Good to Great.* Personal humility and professional will are underlying themes throughout *The Secret Sabbatical.* But Cesar starts us out with even more basic components. Perhaps he conveys the most basic of all—bodily awareness and visible clarity of purpose.

I found two episodes of the show particularly moving—and illuminating. One dealt with a Dalmatian, that dappled breed many of us know as the fire-engine dog. It had been abandoned as a pup at a Los Angeles fire station. The eager young dog quickly won the hearts of the station's fire crew, as tough a group of professionals as you'd ever wish to meet. They adopted it as a mascot and named it Wilshire, after the station's street location. But then trouble began. At first it was with food. The fire crew would return from a call-out only to discover that their pet had wolfed down the half-eaten meal they'd left behind when the alarm rang. Then it was the dog's behavior with children. Kids are encouraged to visit fire stations and sometimes the station crew visited schools, mostly with the intention of helping youngsters learn to recognize—and not fear—firefighters in their alarming firefighting gear. When their over-enthusiastic mascot began knocking children over, it sent the wrong message altogether. Unwilling to give up on their new canine teammate, but unable to accept Wilshire's undisciplined behavior, the firemen called in an alarm of their own. This time, it was Cesar Millan to the rescue.

What Cesar showed the members of the Wilshire Avenue Fire Team was that they'd encouraged and eventually unleashed their dog's troubling behavior. They were responsible for the bumptious puppy's lack of manners. In a mood to release their stress after a call-out, the last thing on their minds was showing consistent discipline with the station mascot. After a few lessons from Cesar, the firemen started to attend to Wilshire's canine needs and expectations. But more than this, they became aware of what was required of them, including the calm and assertive rule. They made sure he got enough exercise—even acquiring a treadmill for the purpose—and began leaving notes for firefighters coming on shift to ensure Wilshire received consistent treatment by everyone in the organization. The closing scenes of the episode showed Wilshire working out on his treadmill with one of the firemen, then happily joining his human colleagues in demonstrating fire drill techniques to a group of adoring children. The tangible pride in both men and dog as they worked together was incredibly moving.

In another episode, a dog was experiencing intense anxiety whenever his master dressed for work. The sight of his owner slipping into leather shoes sent the dog into a frenzy. Once again a desperate owner called in the dog whisperer—only to discover that he was the one most in need of training. Within minutes Cesar uncovered what was happening in this pet's household. His owner, anticipating another stressful day at the office, began steeling himself for work even before he'd donned his business suit. The change in this dog-owner's energy was so acute that his pet—exquisitely attuned as all dogs are to human energy—picked up on his owner's emotions and became anxious as well. That triggered a vicious cycle. Anticipating his dog's stress, the owner then became more anxious—feeding that emotion back to the now additionally stressed-out dog. Cesar's prescription included desensitizing the dog to the visual trigger of business clothing, suits, ties, etc. But the real cure lay in its owner realizing how the anticipation of work was jacking up his emotional pitch.

The message I took away from both these shows—really from all of the episodes—is the importance of calmness and assertiveness in every moment of the day. If we're unable to accomplish this, then the aim is to strive for this state while being fully aware of ourselves when we haven't managed it. In Cesar we find a kind of hands-on teacher. His lessons are not abstract, philosophical or scientific. It feels like we can learn something from the way this soft-spoken dog-handler reveals the human errors behind most "bad" canine behavior. What dogs need, Cesar constantly reminds his clients and viewers, is exercise, subtle discipline that is never harsh, and then (and only then) affection and rewards. Exercise expends an animal's excess energy and helps forge a bond with its human companion. An exercised dog is more receptive to accepting boundaries, and later, affection and play. "Problem" dogs in his model almost always turn out to be the result of humans who have a problem sticking with that regimen.

We don't need to be dog owners to learn from this. Groups can behave like pack animals too. They frequently need direction, guidance and something worthwhile to do. And just like the dogs Cesar "rehabilitates," we respect leaders who calmly make the tasks clear, whose expectations are consistent and who welcome feedback. But there are deeper layers to the lessons we can draw as leaders from Cesar's success with dogs. There are two powerful insights at work.

* the state of mind and body required from us, and

* the powerful feedback that animals provide regarding our ability to reach and maintain this state.

Let's look at each of these insights more closely.

Present-centered calm assertiveness: the flow

Cesar Milan repeatedly emphasizes the importance for dog owners of maintaining a state he describes as present-centered calm assertiveness. We'll see this message emphasized again. It's the same state that our next guides, Marcus Aurelius and Jill Bolte Taylor deem essential (while using totally different frameworks). It's necessary in any role requiring the exercise of influence.

In Cesar's terms, present-centered—being present, being in the now—means not anticipating what a dog may do next, or reacting with increased tension leading to a negative outcome. This is something you can't fake. Tension is frequently expressed in a person's stance, and further transmitted through physical contact. In the case of a dog, it easily feels the tension of the leash. Being in the present in this sense means you're not thinking about other things; you're not repressing anger, or experiencing pity or regret for any events in either the dog's or your own life. Certainly, the dog isn't. In fact, healthy and well-led dogs are beautifully centered in the now. To see how it's done, just pay attention to a dog as it pays attention to you!

Projecting calmness is about conjuring a lack of tension in the body. And it's not as hard to summon as we've been led to believe—especially when we have a moment-to-moment spiritual guide in the form of an animal. This is the lion equivalent in the Owain story!

Assertiveness is not aggression or passivity. The key is simply being clear about one's intentions. Assertiveness is the golden mean between passivity and aggression. It's to be constantly reached for—like finding one's balance, riding that wave. A non-assertive, passive person is unclear about their needs and their voice and body language usually convey this uncertainty. Their non-committal vagueness often elicits arguments in others. Passivity concedes power to others and leaves followers justifiably afraid of being exposed to exploitation. Aggressive people make judgmental statements, attribute negative intentions to others and neither listen nor compromise. They often act too forcefully and provoke counter-aggression. Aggression involves the use of power for personal gain through threat and intimidation. Assertiveness, on the other hand, involves the calm, clear way between these two dysfunctional extremes. An assertive person makes clear non-apologetic statements about expectations and feelings, criticizes in a descriptive and non-judgmental way, persists and listens to others while making needed compromises.

Assertiveness training was big in the 1980s, as men and women signed on to workshops believing they needed to practice influence, while insisting violence and aggression were unacceptable. Later the topic became simplified, seen as another fad and regrettably faded. In coaching executives I've found it's one of the least mastered skills. It's required in many "hard" fields, such as Project Management, where deviations from schedule need a focused human interaction. Through Cesar we learn how effective and elegant assertiveness can be.

Cesar has also mastered another zen idea in a practical way. It's about moving into the flow. When a dog in a group shows early signs of distraction it often only needs gentle correction, and then the whole party can be reminded to move forward. So Cesar, in his intensely practical way, stresses moving on. The movement is not onto "the great wonderful future out there." It's about being with this moment and not getting stuck or distracted.

Feedback on the flow

So we try to maintain this balance called assertiveness, and being calm is part of that. Animals can provide ongoing feedback on how we are coping, moment to moment. The dogs are a sensitive meter of our progress at achieving calmness and clarity. It's fascinating that the producers of Cesar's show sometimes feature a timeline to stress that the elapsed time from a problem dog, to a team of human and dog that "gets it," can be as little as 10 minutes.

Dogs read energy. They also process vastly more with their sense of smell than sight or sound. They do not function best with spoken commands although they can learn these. So energy and smell (particularly the hormones we secrete from our “lizard” centers when fearful, anxious or over-excited) can’t be faked. And dogs are magnificent instantaneous readers of these true indicators of our state of mind, and the state of our hearts. Millan’s genius is to liberate both species. The dog gets the leadership it needs, and we get the guidance we require to maintain the centeredness and focus of a good leader.

By teaching some fundamental skills Cesar has helped us in our revival of the imagination. These directly influence the level of stress we feel and project. They are also at the core of our readiness to be both open to the new, and at the same time, to stand firmly on our values. Once we are in this space of “collectedness” we can more easily move on to our next great master-teacher. In his time, he was the most effective leader in the world. Happily he kept a journal and in the following pages he returns with some hard learned lessons to help us continue on our way.

9
The Main Guide

...The beloved friend
is a river. ...
[It] doesn't rest. In it, if you grab a branch,
the river breaks it. Any attachment you have,
take hold strongly and let it be snapped off!

If you can't see the huge sky turnings,
Look at the broken sticks moving by,
And the foam bubbles around you.

The giddy wind, the constantly reaching up
Of the ocean, these are parts of the same motion.

Rumi

Marcus Aurelius

It's late, and a lone figure is writing in a tent by candlelight in a professionally built military encampment. Something about the way he works is unusual. He takes time to gaze into the fire as if in deep thought, and then records a few words with utmost care. This is not a military dispatch to fulfill a duty; it's a personal recording of what is of profound importance to him. He has no idea who, if anyone, will ever read it.

He's near the front lines of an ongoing fierce battle between the massive Roman Empire and yet another group of invaders constantly testing the will and competence of the Empire. The man in the tent is the most successful Emperor of all time and has spent years in the field with his troops. He's no Commander in Chief in a distant White House but is responsible for the lives of these centurions in every encounter.

He was taught by the greatest minds of his time and was gifted enough to take their advice diligently and passionately to heart. He knows that a daily period of reflection and writing based on certain profound questions is essential to maintaining balance and mission. Without this, he would be dragged into the demands of the moment and lose the perspective that it's his to provide as a true leader. What he writes in these lonely and dangerous nights will be preserved by some miracle and inspire people for millennia.

We're looking at a man who overshadows many modern heroes. He was tough, successful and fully aware of his shortcomings. He commanded the massive Roman Empire during grueling times in the second-century and was revered as a wise and caring leader. He was central to the golden age of Rome. A group of Emperors, of whom Marcus Aurelius was one, "...abandoned themselves fearlessly to their...destiny as supermen. For if ever supermen have existed, we have to look for them among [these] Emperors...."[103]

No stranger to the crunch, Marcus frequently confronted impending disaster. In his first year as Emperor of Rome there were floods and famine, earthquakes in Asia. Barbarians pressed the northern frontier, and the British legionaries rioted. Armenia was threatened, and Syria was attacked. The Goths drove other tribes across the Danube, and Marcus was to spend most of his time fighting to the north and to the east. In the last ten years of his life he was continually absent from Rome. During a particularly austere time, he contributed family possessions for military spending.

Our second guide, from the cradle of Western Civilization, is possibly one of the most competent CEOs of all time. His wisdom and leadership, based on the underlying structure provided by the teachings of Epictetus, were amongst the many traits that make him memorable.

Originally brought up in Rome as a freed slave, Epictetus was banished with all the other philosophers of his day and spent 50 years teaching from Greece. He lived around 100 years after Christ and was more influential in his day than was Plato in his. His works governed a major school of Philosophy, Stoicism. However, through the reduction of the word *Stoic* to mean someone who bears his burden grimly, Stoicism has been poorly represented in the modern world. This is not what the ancients meant. In their day, the Stoics were a force.

The Stoics were not interested in the dry pursuit of academic philosophy. They were "lovers of wisdom," which is the meaning of the word *philosophy*. They wanted their work to be a basis for specific and direct life changes. Theirs was a therapy in the wider sense, a healing of the mind, body, and soul. For them, philosophy was unquestionably to be a way of life. The decline of philosophy into an intellectual and academic enclave was the result of specific historical misfortunes, and a measure of human vanity. In fact, Marcus showed that an active and challenged leader could apply a solid structure to his life and receive enormous help from it.

Stoicism is currently undergoing a revival. For example, towards the end of 2013 a team of academics and therapists funded by the British Government launched "Live Like a Stoic Week." It's described as "...a global self-improvement experiment...that aims to spread Stoic virtue across the virtual world."[104] A pilot program based on these ideas showed a 10 percent improvement in psychological well-being. The article describing this initiative correctly links Stoic emotional attitudes with modern Cognitive Behavioral Therapy. After his return from the Vietnam War, General James Stockdale wrote relevant essays about practicing these ideas with his men while in a Vietnamese prison.[105]

In his lively novel, *A Man in Full*,[106] Tom Wolfe, who is never tedious and always entertaining, salutes Stoicism. Cleverly he introduces his themes through a prison inmate who is accidentally handed a book on the Stoics only to find he instantly resonates with Epictetus's idea that we are all self-imprisoned. The inmate proceeds to change his life and that of others.

Epictetus provided Marcus with some of the most effective questions I've seen for personal and leadership development. These questions, which I've adapted in one instance from the writings of Marcus, help build our foundation for envisioning.

Nearly a decade ago I began asking Course participants to consider keeping a daily diary, using Marcus and the following questions as a guide. Marcus did not phrase the last of these questions in this way. This is my paraphrase of his work on action, which I'll enlarge on later.

What do I desire?
What am I judging?
Who/What do I serve?

The questions are intended to be top of mind. Few Course participants have felt they could have made much progress without them and apart from attempting a daily journal practice. Emperor Marcus Aurelius served as our constant example, having done this himself every night while barricaded in those distant encampments.

Marcus had a secret weapon: not a sword or lance, not a gun, not a fleet of drones but instead, his pen. This means of contending against the enemy—both within himself and on the battlefield—was to be named the *Meditations*. Marcus's daily writings during the last years of his life are brilliantly brought to life through a set of commentaries by the late French master philosopher, Pierre Hadot.[107] Reading Hadot, Marcus declares himself a modern man on a truly noble quest.

If you were to pick up an older translation of Marcus's works, you would likely be disappointed. The language is often obscure, but worse; the three underlying structural questions that Marcus was working on are not apparent. Hadot has carefully teased out the deep structure behind Marcus's *Meditations*, based on who the mighty Roman's teachers were. After a lifetime of teaching, Hadot felt that the whole thrust of Greek and Roman thought was in danger of being lost. After all, the original idea of philosophy, as I've mentioned earlier, was to be a way of life for all thinking people. That's what the Greeks knew, what Marcus practiced, and what we can learn. Hadot's background and his highly authentic tone make the work relevant today.

Epictetus taught around the three foundational questions Hadot unearths. These are like a buried key to a lost treasure. In his *Meditations,* Marcus writes a series of answers designed to explore Epictetus's original inquiries, and in light of these, to transform his character or, as he put it, to "dye his soul."

> Such as are your habitual thoughts, such also will be the character of your mind; for the soul is dyed by the thoughts. Dye it then

> with a continuous series of such thoughts as these: for instance, that where a man can live, there he can also live well...and so to transform his behavior and his entire way of life. [108]

By reflecting upon the three core questions and writing down his thoughts, Marcus engaged in a repetitive process intentionally designed to cultivate a new way of thinking and acting in the world. He believed we are what we think and feel, what we imagine and fantasize and that, together, these processes can be said to make up our spirit or soul.

Marcus's comments on the composition of the soul bring the novelist and poet, D. H Lawrence to mind. Lawrence pointed out that what we read when we're relaxed is just as important to framing who we are as any more serious input.[109] So junk reading is not exactly all that different to junk food. It doesn't nourish one and possibly does real damage. Who knows? *People* magazine and its more extreme checkout counter cousins are perhaps not harmless fluff after all. According to Lawrence, they're not.

In his mind, Marcus was building an "Inner Citadel" of self-reliance and strength to help him cope with the turbulence of his times and ensure that he faced these as a worthy leader and mentor. It was about having the courage to learn new things and apply them, while recognizing the complexity of every circumstance.

The first discipline: The discipline of desire

The thinking here is that one is perpetually distracted by ever-changing desires. Well in advance of modern marketing, Epictetus taught there is no end to desire. Today the designers of the next iPads are carefully plotting enhancements on specific technology roadmaps that are curves of future enhancements that will never end or fulfill. There will always have to be another version in the pipeline with just enough that's new to act as the carrot for the next Black Friday. This is part of the grid into which consumers are herded. So if you know this, the question you might ask yourself, is how do I manage this constant escalation? As Epicurus knew 2,300 years ago: "Nothing is enough for the man to whom enough is too little."

Marcus's Discipline of Desire had three components.

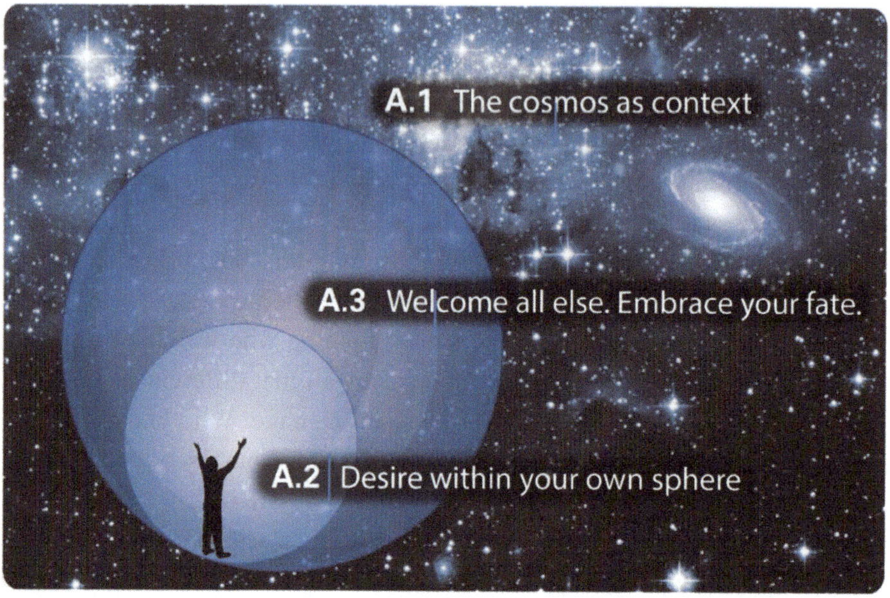

Figure 9 - Marcus's Spheres of Desire

A.1. The cosmos as context

The first deals with how we imagine ourselves in the world. A sense of proportion is always key to positioning ourselves in the big picture at the start of any journey. Here we could ask ourselves a question that goes something like the following— how big is my boat, and what is the scale of the ocean I'm attempting to sail?

Knowing the most current view of science was important to Marcus. He believed it was not only pivotal in one's effort to understand the world but, also, central in a more personal context. Joseph Campbell pointed out that all old mythologies were successful to the degree that they were able to link the individual with a view of the cosmos that made some sense. One of our problems today is that the link between what science is telling us about the universe and our day-to-day reality is tenuous. We find ourselves mid-way on a size continuum from the interstellar spaces of a possibly expanding Universe or multiverses, and the sub-microscopic worlds of mostly empty spaces between fields of energy and dark energy. We gasp, realizing how small humanity is in the grand scheme of things, but simultaneously, how precious our space bubble is in terms of what has been achieved along the road of evolution.

That said, it seems many of us simply prefer to think about buying a more fashionable pair of sneakers. Or, a newly styled car with 40 more horsepower, and acceleration and cornering abilities that are impossible to use outside a professional racetrack.[110] I confess the latter holds a lingering appeal for me!

Marcus had a sophisticated view of the cosmos and was adamant that we try to place ourselves in harmony with its massive forces. As far as he was concerned this sense of relatedness promised an experience of a real kind of joy in our amazingly complex and beautiful universe. In some fascinating sense, this is how Marcus saw himself as practicing physics. Knowledge was not something to be left to the specialists; it had important implications for the day-to-day. Attaining and holding a sense of perspective was foundational to his thinking. You may want to think of this in terms of **keeping the context constant**.

Suggested Journal question:

Where do I see myself in the big picture today?

A.2. Desire within your own sphere of influence

The idea here is to recognize our desires and aversions, and to figure out which of these are truly within our control. Marcus found his list was small if he was honest with himself. He specifically excluded fame, wealth, even health from this category. For sure we can have some impact on these, but in the final analysis, fate is fickle. It's not all a matter of choice. The road to fame is scattered with casualties. Elvis, Janice, Kurt, Michael, the list goes on.

Another way of viewing this idea is to appreciate that everything that doesn't depend on moral choice within one's sphere of influence is to be treated with indifference. Marcus did not use the word *indifferent* in the modern sense, which has connotations of coldness and is probably part of the negative image of the Stoics. What he meant was that one would see "no difference" between these things—no special appeal, no particular prejudice. In other words, we should train ourselves neither to desire nor to be averse to that which is out of our control.

What one does **within** one's control is the subject of what will follow.

Suggested Journal questions:

What do I desire that is out of my control?

What am I resisting that is out of my own sphere?

A.3. Love your fate, now

One day a wise friend and therapist, the late Ellen Tallman said to me: "If you don't say 'Yes' to it – it has got you." Borrowing directly from the Greeks, the idea Ellen was referencing comes down to us from Nietzsche.

> My formula for what is greatness in a human is *amor fati* [to love your fate]; one wants nothing other than that which is; neither forward nor backward, in all eternity. Not just to tolerate the inevitable—still less to hide it from oneself...but *love* it.[111]

It's very instructive to look at what aspects of fate we resist as this has formed the basis of an entire approach to personal change. James Hollis has a subtle and helpful chapter on the topic in his book *What Matters Most*.[112] He looks at the paradox of fighting our fate while, at the same time, loving it. Fighting fate, in Hollis's view, is the ability to continue to express ourselves no matter what the world throws at us. It's more than an acceptance of fate but, crucially, it's also a dynamic process of pressing on, of not giving up. Hollis's view is not a passive one.

For the purposes of this discussion I've found it helpful to separate fate from destiny—perhaps a potentially baffling distinction as the terms are often used interchangeably. But certainly others, besides myself, have drawn on this difference. I'll argue that fate is that which is outside of one's control. Destiny is different. In fine-tuning the contrast between the two, I found it helpful to look at the etymology of the word *destiny*. From its Anglo-French origins, it's related to the French *opportunité*, which includes connotations of timeliness or opportuneness. Given this, it's quite possible to say it takes on a meaning not implied by the word *fate*. Destiny, in this way of thinking, is what you are able to grasp at the appropriate moments, given the limitations of your genes, background, and acquired wisdom. Here lies the possible birthplace of free will.

Suggested Journal question:

Can I accept what's happening now, even though much of it is out of my control?

The Greeks mastered the idea of "the now." They believed it's all we really ever have. Centuries later the brilliant pioneering psychologist William James (brother of the novelist Henry James) turned his attention to the question: How long is it that we can feel something exists in the present?[113] Quoting several studies, he found 12 seconds to be "…the maximum filled duration of which we can be both distinctly and immediately aware." Anything outside this window was either past or future. He contended **this is all we have of now**. James, writing in the 1890's, agreed with the Greeks but he went on to quantify his observation, pointing out that we have precious little of it.

Marcus was writing about ecological connections two thousand years before the scientist Lorenz found that tiny changes in initial conditions were critical to his weather models. These spawned the concepts of the "butterfly effect," and chaos theory. Marcus said:

> Constantly regard the universe as one living being, having one substance and one soul; and observe how all things have reference to one perception, the perception of this one living

> being; ... and how all things are the cooperating causes of all things which exist; observe too the continuous spinning of the thread ... of the web.[114]

He realized that what happens to any one of us is woven into the web of fate and so it's critical to feel and respect these profound linkages. This connection of the present moment with all of time past and future is one of the great triumphs of thinking. From being a tiny trivial sliver of time that has little importance compared to our vast stores of memories and desires, the present becomes the central key to experience and change. The present moment is one of the pivotal themes in rediscovering the garden. To be a little mechanical for a moment, it's the base of the fulcrum for whatever levers we'll choose to influence things. Or to put it more organically, it's the only fruitful place to plant a seed.

But the really big idea here is that, **if we can say yes to one moment** of what's happening to us, and happening in the universe, this action is possibly our connection to the whole—to the ebb and flow of the entire cosmos.

The second discipline: The discipline of judgment

The second discipline deals with how we judge. According to Marcus we generally go too far in allowing our personal (and often short-term) concerns and wishes to influence our judgments. As Hamlet puts it:

> ... for there is nothing
> either good or bad, but thinking makes it so...[115]

We see most things through a lens of opportunity, risk, or personal gain. Within minutes of 9/11, airline and other stocks plummeted, while some others boomed. The game here is to grasp profit from crisis. "A hurricane? Good, let's load up on Home Depot stock!" Some consume news 24/7 just to capitalize on events. It doesn't take much to see where this path leads. But it's not only the distracting anxiety caused by this self-interested scanning—it's what else we're missing. We fail to see what's going on around us when everything is colored by judgments related to self-concern.

The passage below is about as solid an introduction to the so-called twentieth-century discovery of systems thinking as you'll find. This was written 2,000 years before Karl Ludwig von Bertalanffy introduced the topic with such fanfare. Marcus suggests we take great care to try to be as conscious as possible of everything, including its place in the environment.

> ...see distinctly what kind of a thing it is in its substance, in its nudity, in its complete entirety, and tell yourself its proper name, and the names of the things of which it has been compounded, and into which it will be resolved.[116]

He goes on:

> ... nothing is so productive of elevation of mind as to be able to examine methodically and truly every object which is presented to you in life, and always to look at things so as to see at the same time what kind of universe this is, and what kind of use everything performs in it, and what value everything has with reference to the whole, and what with reference to man...

This material on judging is subtle. The Stoic approach requires reflection and practice to find a balance. I try to supplement *The Secret Sabbatical* Course with other helpful examples while remaining within the tradition.

A philosophical view borrowed from the ancient Chinese Book of Changes, the *I Ching*, is helpful in practicing a non-naïve but compassionate form of Marcus's discipline of judgment.[117] In the following I'm paraphrasing, knowing it's impossible to do justice to the idea. This holy text presents a necessary process concerning the importance of seeing the different sides of human nature, while not judging. It instructs us not to discount another's darker side, their misdeeds or flaws, but in light of this knowledge, to keep in mind their full or highest potential. Simultaneously we're to ensure that we make every effort to see exactly what's going on, including another's possibly "evil" intentions, without becoming entangled in them or judging that action. Be astute, always keenly aware—don't deny and don't judge what you see. If we think about this in the language of fate and destiny, it's possible to say we are to recognize, concurrently, another's destiny in the full light of their preordained fate. I explore these themes in Chapter 12.

This discussion on the *I Ching* is a variation on Marcus's idea of what value everything has in reference to the whole. Holding potential in mind can initiate a new cycle and is the basis of many creative thinking approaches.[118]

Another approach to Marcus, one that's a bit more fun, is to have a look at one of a series of fundamental ancient teaching stories designed to bring us perspective through humor. These are attributed to Mulla Nasrudin from a manuscript dating from the seventeenth century.[119] Here's one I can recall on judgment and time frames.

> A villager had a horse that ran away. All the neighbors gathered and said "How unfortunate that you've lost your horse." The man said, "Maybe."
>
> The next day the horse returned leading seven wild horses, and the neighbors said "How fortunate you are to have eight horses." The man said, "Maybe."
>
> Then the man's son was thrown and broke his leg when trying to break one of the horses. The neighbors said "How unfortunate that your son has a broken leg." The man said, "Maybe."
>
> The next day soldiers arrived to conscript troops. They rejected his son because of his leg. The neighbors said "How fortunate that your son's leg is broken." The man said, "Maybe."

Suggested Journal questions:

What am I judging as good and bad based solely on my needs?

How did these needs arise?

The third discipline: Who do I serve? (based on the discipline of action)

"You're gonna have to serve somebody!"

Bob Dylan wrote a song about action based on discipline. He highlighted an inescapable fact, we all "Gotta Serve Somebody!" Dylan wailed: "…it may be the devil, or it may be the Lord / But you're gonna have to serve somebody."[120] This takes us all the way back to Owain. The castle and its power games were not a sustainable source or a long-term goal for our hero. King and country needed to be reimagined in light of the generative powers of the garden. The question for us is not whether or not to serve. It's a question of who and what we serve. Another way of putting this, perhaps more in the language of the day—what is our mission?

Marcus's first principle was to ensure that we know we're here to serve something beyond ourselves. He believed we had to be in sync with our wider human community and to act according to its best interests. So now we've moved from the interior world of Marcus's earlier realms of desire and judgment into the world of action.

Marcus also believed we get involved in far too many actions, and that we need to focus our energies with extreme discipline. This "funneling effect" of our Roman Emperor is a way of imagining how we might deal with the time pressures of today. According to Marcus we must limit our commitments, and to do this it makes sense to use the question of service to sort our priorities. Only then can we set adequate and appropriate goals.

Marcus taught that even if an action were to be interrupted by death it would still be complete, because what marks an action is "…the moral intention by which it is inspired, not the subject matter in which it is exercised."[121] Remember, he was no armchair philosopher. Here was a man who was on campaign for years, away from the comforts of home while facing the toughest imaginable rebels. Nothing you see in movies like *The Gladiator* comes close to what historians of the time described.

The idea of fractals is connected to Marcus's argument that we're here to accomplish something larger than that which lies within the small world of the self. Just as our planet isn't the center of our solar system, we're not a center either. We belong to something much larger and grander, but what we do in terms of scale is another matter. In this context the size of our actions is not the criterion. Whatever we do—help save a species or adopt a rescued animal—demonstrates that self-similarity of all actions when they're exercised for the good of another.

This question of service is a tough one. Shakespeare explores it in several of his works. Through a kaleidoscope of characters and situations we scrutinize this pressing issue in a cultural and family context. The concerns that come to light remain relevant today. Do you serve the voices of the established culture—the adults and traditions of the past, or the needs of the present? Harold Goddard wrote the following on this question, as framed by Shakespeare. "With rare exceptions, man has been a slave to the past, but refused to understand and love it. He ought to love and understand it but refuse to be its slave. This is irrational but it is true."[122] There needs to be a respect for culture and history, as well as the imperative to take courageous fresh stands. Honoring the past is sometimes the best route. At other times one must break free, unbind old ties. There's no formula. However, **the ability to embrace seemingly contradictory ideas is both the hallmark and enabler of an expanded imagination.**

Shakespeare's Hamlet reveals a man torn precisely between the command of a father from the past, and the imperatives of the present. In *King Lear*, Cordelia refuses to obey the command of her father, and in so doing inherits an undeserved fate. The demands of an ambitious and ruthless mother ruin Titus Andronicus. Romeo and Juliet are victims of ancient family feuds. These are all tragedies based on the central issue of whether or not to be driven by voices from the past. Again and again we see Shakespeare's characters faced with making this choice. Modern "honor killings" continue the tragic theme when enslavement to the past remains the only choice.

In Marcus, we meet a man who advocates scrupulous honesty with oneself. Through Shakespeare we meet aspects of ourselves through characters who, in their plight, are called to respond to the demands of Marcus and his inescapable question: Who do I serve?

Suggested Journal questions:

In all honesty

Who do I serve?

Who do I wish to serve?

My next chapter places us in the company of a woman who puts a modern spin on our journey, based on brain science. In light of advice from Cesar and Marcus, but from a different perspective, she'll suggest some basic ways to sustain our balance as we deal with the day-to-day pressures of serving.

10
A Modern Real-time Guide

What is a real connection between people? When the same
knowledge
Opens a door between them. When the same inner sight exists
In you as in another, you are drawn to be companions.
... ...
Always search for your innermost nature in those you are with.

Rumi

Reconnecting—how do I serve?

In this chapter, we enter a new stage—one of Reconnecting—where we'll concentrate on a modern and uniquely experienced brain scientist. She answers the question "What do I need to know, and practice, to be effective out there?"

Third navigational guide: Jill Bolte Taylor

Jill Bolte Taylor may disagree with me about herself and her work. To begin with, I'd suggest that if there's one book, and one book only, you read from my referrals, *My Stroke of Insight*[123] is the one. The book is an insider's perspective on one of the most extraordinary human adventures ever recorded. It also lists specific ideas on how to benefit from what she's learned—and what she alone could have learned.

Jill was an established brain scientist in her 30s when she was hit by a sudden, massive stroke. As a brain expert, she was uniquely qualified to follow the slow progress of the unfolding catastrophe in her left brain. (Along with Dr. Bolte Taylor, I'll use the terms "left brain" and "right brain." This is a simplified division of functions but it helps define core issues at the level we need.) She was completely conscious during the entire process. While blood leaked into her brain cells she observed and understood the escalating damage occurring in her left hemisphere. She could feel parts of her mental and physical processes shutting down. As an expert in the field she knew beyond any doubt how each minute that passed successively damaged some portion of her left hemisphere and impaired other functions in her body and mind.

Miraculously, her life was saved. But given the harm she suffered, the task she was left with was huge. Over a period of eight long years and with the help of her extraordinary mother, she slowly rebuilt her life from what amounted to an infantile dependency. Jill is someone who can talk to us about the miracle of neuroplasticity—the brain's innate ability to self-heal. Through personal experience she came to know (in her words) how things "go away" in a disaster, and how they may be healed or "come back."

In addition to all of this, her experience of trauma was one that presented more than just terrible limitations. During the hours of her stroke what she encountered was beyond any normal experience of reality. Rather than the stroke simply shutting down her entire world, a second place opened up to her, that she had no previous knowledge of, a place of extraordinary bliss. She was delivered to the garden. The garden of Owain, the biblical Garden of Eden, the Nirvana of Buddhism, the "ground of being" of others like Huxley, whatever you call it; Jill discovered a paradise. This happened intermittently, when the terror of sensing the steady and measurable collapse of her left brain was punctuated by ecstatic experiences. These episodes only occurred when the stroke suppressed the left brain's normal functions of sustaining our life narrative (through the language center) and identifying our personal boundaries.

When Jill experienced this mysterious world, she seemed to leave her body and enter the territory studied these days with modern methods by people like Newberg and D'Aquili.[124] These experiences of so-called timeless zones arise in the previously uncharted areas of the brain where highly trained meditators have only recently been shown to have some control. Using brain imaging technologies such as functional magnetic resonance imaging (fMRI) we're gaining scientific knowledge of specific and enhanced potential that is possibly within each of us. What Jill offers, is further evidence of the realities of these ambiguous and miraculous moments. It's as though she worked hard to come back from that paradise, or brink—however one chooses to think of it—to do something very important. And on top of that, she's probably the best-qualified person to do this.

Bolte Taylor says she came back (rebuilt her left brain) partly to tell us what she learned about how the brain can help or hinder our effectiveness. It turns out she has specific and practical ideas to share with us on how to lead more creative and fulfilling lives. She entered brain science to help understand a problem in her family, and she retains this sense of mission in her ongoing work.

I know of no one else with the following combination of skills and experience:

- advanced training in brain functioning
- total immersion in disaster and in "heaven"
- a slow rebuilding of key functions with a loving guide
- the willingness and ability to tell her story in a compelling way
- an ongoing mission to advance brain research.

For me, it's difficult not to see this brain scientist as a modern day prophet. In the past, prophets were said to be people who could read the future. They spoke of what was to come or, put another way, what one needed to know. Beginning with a fearless look at the problems of their day, they helped point the way by extrapolating forward. To read the future one must first see into the present, and Jill certainly had the presence to do just that. In the language of our day and age, the language of science, Jill tells us what we need to know. And, like those past diviners who had undergone rigorous personal training and extreme experiences, years of meditation, months in the desert, Jill earned her way. Her knowledge came through revelation. As a result, like those of the prophets of the past, her values were in sync with what mathematician, Charles Muses,[125] describes so well. According to Muses, once one has passed through that door of perception, the duty is to turn and help others on their way. Jill meets all these tests. She shows us our inner world and reaches to point us on our way.

Left brain as potential tyrant

These days all kinds of sources describe the left brain's functions, many are now well known in management circles. I'm not going to repeat all the facts about the degree of detail and linearity that this part of the brain encompasses. It facilitates great things, particularly when it shares its capabilities with the more fluid and creatively potent right brain. But discipline is one of its major accomplishments; which is why Marcus, with his focus on discipline, plays a role in the Course.

Our more recent problem in human evolution has been the suppression of the right brain. As the dominance of the left has been reinforced by the scientific revolution, we've increasingly lost sight of the value and power of the other hemisphere. The problems I've identified in Chapter 3 on the failure of the imagination could be placed at the door of a super-driven left brain and a low functioning right brain. We're missing the holistic view. We're missing that sense of interconnectedness. We're out of "the zone," and so life isn't much fun. That zone includes the two halves of the brain being in tune with each other— not driven by the lizard concerns.

The key to understanding the left brain is that it's the source of the creation of sequence in separating out the wealth of stimuli pouring into our brains. Someone said that time is useful because it prevents the feeling that everything happens at once!

In Jill's opinion it's "By organizing details in a linear and methodical configuration, our left brain manifests the concept of time whereby our moments are divided into the past, present and future."[126] Having created time, we then go on (in the left brain) to create the saga and narrative that's the story of our life. As though that's not enough to occupy half a brain, the left then asserts that it has total authority over the domain it has itself created. The Queen in Lewis Carroll's *Alice in Wonderland* is a similar tyrant. What she insists on goes something like: "I've created this reality, and you'd better shape up and follow suit!"

Jill partly lays out what possibly the greatest philosopher of all time, Immanuel Kant, had intuited in his monumental *Critique of Pure Reason*,[127] in 1781. He insisted that the mind does more than create time; it also creates space, causality and other categories that many still suppose are somehow "out there."

Discipline is needed

We need the left brain in order to function in the world, and Jill spent the better part of a decade regaining hers. As she felt the old issues returning during this reconstruction, she was able to map her body's responses. So she learned to be sensitive to what the build-up of tension from the left brain's concerns felt like. Moment-to-moment, as the age-old survival chemicals coursed through her body, Jill was aware of their effect. A critical finding of Jill's is that "Without structure, censorship or discipline our thoughts run rampant on automatic." Here is a key to why we need the disciplines of Cesar Millan, Marcus, and Jill. Some studies on the origins of obsession, compulsion and addiction show that once a circuit has begun firing, it can then continue in the future with less external stimulation. Sound familiar? Long before MRI imaging was available, people had intuited this. Habitual patterns that self-reinforce have been noted for millennia.

The primitive structures of the brain, which are linked to the three lower energy centers, are fascinating in one crucial way, according to Jill. **They don't mature!** Unlike the left brain (which showed amazing neuroplasticity in rebuilding core functions for Jill) these centers that generate fear, anger, desire don't necessarily change from those of a young person. The uncivilized aspects of the shadow, in my view, also never give up or mature, unless we deal with them. So a workshop instructor who yelled at a group during a session I was attending: "You are all emotional infants!" may have had a point. There are other change strategies however!

Ninety seconds will do it—do I need to run these chemicals longer?

Jill's single biggest insight for me was the 90 Second Rule. It takes about 90 seconds for a stressor to hit the "physiological/emotional" system and trigger the chemicals (including cortisol) that respond to stress in the bloodstream. They are toxic if we allow them to run continuously. So, we have a choice. We can allow the chemicals their 90 seconds of action and then recognize they have done their job of alerting us to danger, at least as perceived by a more primitive brain. We can then ask ourselves the critical question, "Do I want to run this loop again or not?" Probably not!

A. "Step to the right!"

The 90 Second Rule is applied by learning how to "Step to the Right"—meaning learning to invoke the calming and perspective-granting wisdom of the right brain. When you feel the urge to over-plan, judge, or over-react; step to the right! The left brain is still crucial for going to work, preparing a meeting and getting results on time. Few of us would dispute this. The Hippies of the 60s didn't get this vital aspect and some flamed out, or dropped out.

One of Jill's chapters is called "Owning Your Power." This ties in with the idea of mediating our use of power-over. As we've seen, dominance can transform into power-for, ensuring not only self-discipline but also the use of one's power for helping others. The 90 Second Rule helps us deal with the distraction of our negative emotions. It connects to James Hollis's relevant advice not to allow your voice of authority (meaning your own acquired wisdom) to be silenced.[128]

Stepping to the right is the primary core discipline in Bolte Taylor's second-to-second advice on finding our way; riding that wave we call our life.

As a real-time observer, she reads and gives direction to her body as she steers it away from the shoals of anger, aggression and the need for power-over. She does this through awareness and gratitude for the possession of a fully functioning body-mind system—through a sense of heartfelt thanks.

B. Base on the right—riding the "right" wave continuously

I was born in South Africa, which has five mile long ocean surf breakers and solid winds. It has become another home of surfers, windsurfers and kiteboarders. One of these legendary surfers was Shaun Tomson who wrote *Surfer's Code*.[129] One of his twelve codes is "I will take the drop with commitment" referring to the courage and precise timing needed to judge, and commit to big waves. But, the wave has to be the right one. So he's mindful every second of how to position himself at the right angle to capture the optimum energy from nature, to enjoy its thrill without the wave crushing him.

In my transitional efforts from windsurfing to kiteboarding, I was made acutely aware of how having less equipment makes for an upgraded second-to-second challenge. To stay in control, a kiteboard, having no centerboard, keel, mast or rudder, demands continuous attention. Propelled at 40 mph attached to a harness there can be no question of daydreaming. It's like the difference between flying helicopters, which are inherently unstable, and most other recreational airplanes. The riders and pilots of these particularly sensitive craft need to be in touch with the present moment as both activities are a completely hands-on experience. Whatever is going on out there in the wild blue yonder, it's not grounded in logic.

We're like kiteboarders in our own lives, I think. It's as though we also need to change our skills to stay in touch with the demands of this new craft we sail. We need to identify the right place from which to **base** and navigate our lives. Most of the time, that place needs to be the wide-ranging right brain, tuned to the other receptor areas of our brains and bodies. This is the challenge. Can we actually live more on the right side with less anxiety, and then step up and move into the world to deal with its business?

Jill covers this call to action specifically in her book. My shorthand name—perhaps a clumsy attempt to capture the essence of what she's saying—is "Base on the right." But I do want to stress that there are two phases we're working on with Jill. These include: (a) stepping back when we've "lost it," and, (b) a more fundamental positioning as we cultivate living on the right.

She in fact ends her groundbreaking book by describing our moment-to-moment task of "tending the gardens" of our minds. The idea is to nip the weedy comments of the critical mind's "peanut gallery." This brain region is after all only the size of a peanut!

Jill assigns a special time each day to listen to inner critical concerns and then disciplines herself (that "D" word again!) not to tune in to these voices at other times. Several cultures have had their version of small, sometimes petty and demanding mind-creatures that need managing. In Hawaiian mythology it's the menehunes; in Western myth the gnomes.

She also reinforces the circuits she wants. She lives mostly within those environments dealing with creativity, dance and gratitude. And, yes, when necessary she very effectively calls on those other "left brain specialists" with their ability to organize, plan and deliver compelling lectures that, amongst other things, advocates bequeathing one's brain to research. (See her presentation on the TED network for example.)[130]

With Jill Bolte Taylor, the need for life navigation gets clearer. Although there is not one simple answer, we learn from her that every moment involves sailing between the considerable domains of both brains' hemispheres. These are powered by the energies of the body, hopefully transformed through compassion, beyond the illusion of the freestanding self.

So, let's look back for a moment at the three guides we've explored. Each has suggested questions that help focus on leading a life with transformed power and purpose.

The 7 key guidance questions in sequence

Given that we're trying to sail in the present moment, how we navigate second-by-second is fundamental. We need to monitor the tides of our feelings as we ask ourselves these questions:

- Am I calm?
- Am I assertive?
- Am I judging?
- What do I desire?
- Who or what do I serve?
- Can I step to the right?
- Can I base on the right, while working on the left when necessary?

The Guides in Summary

In the following diagram I've attempted to locate the main contributions of our three guides.

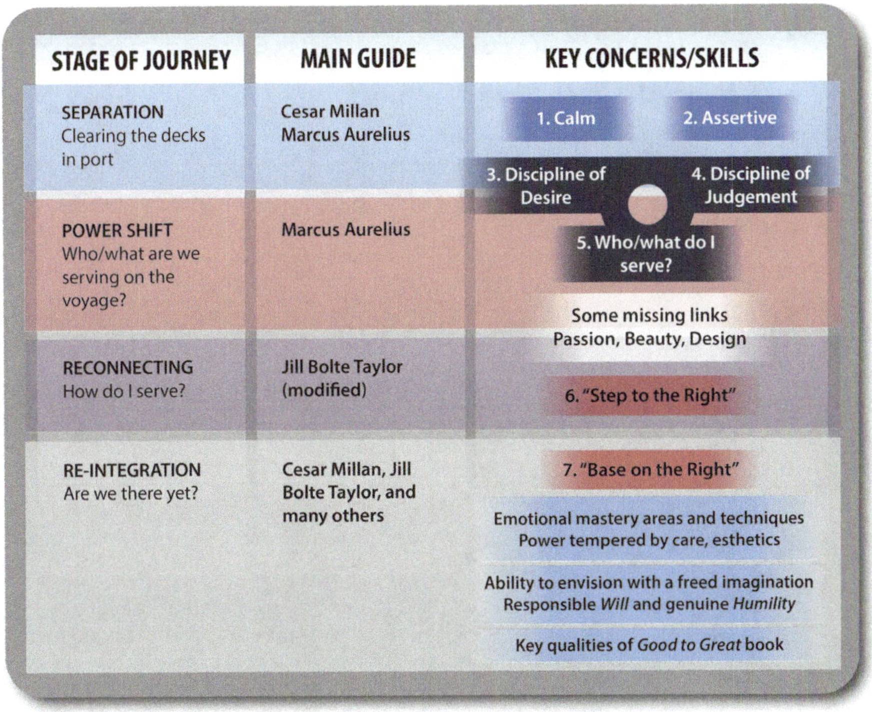

Figure 10 - Summary of Guides

Now let's become navigators and sail on!

11
The Blind Navigator

Humankind is being led along an evolving course,
through this migration of intelligences,
and though we seem to be sleeping,
there is an inner wakefulness
that directs the dream,

and that will eventually startle us back
to the truth of who we are.

Rumi

New dimensions for a renaissance

Way-finding

In the vast western ocean, a palm-fringed atoll, a third the size of New York's Central Park, was hardly more than a mote in the great circle of blue. Of even less significance were the few humans standing in a circle around a small tidal pool. Above them a mild wind ruffled the palms, bringing with it the salt mist and distant boom of waves breaking against the island's sheltering reef.

But what held the small group's attention was none of these. Instead it was a wriggling brown infant, barely a year old and plainly impatient to break free from his mother's arms. As the elders in the group made prayers of their thoughts, the young woman knelt, leaned out over the pool and offered her child to the water moving back and forth in the rough coral bowl of the bay.

There the child was left to splash and play, to bob up and down on his baby-fat legs in the supportive warmth, to loll and drift and doze, neither disturbed nor directed by grown-up intervention (if closely watched from a little distance by his mother) as the sun moved slowly across the sky. Over the months to come, he would spend many days—and nights—in the pool. As the sea became almost a second womb, the growing boy learned its infinite moods and movements: the long, slow breath of swells from the deep Pacific storms, the slap of sharper waves pushing up the atoll on the incoming tide. He felt the waning of the water's confidence as the tide followed the moon past the island and around the world. He acquired sensitivity to the hidden power and changing moods of the sea, without need for description or analysis.

Later, at around the age of eight, the boy will make his first deep-sea voyage on a fishing outrigger. As the slender craft slips past the atoll's reef into the ocean swells, nausea will overcome him. When that happens, the boy will be lifted overboard into the sea. As the boat makes its way through the water he will be towed behind, lying on his back to allow the familiar rhythms of the waves to flow over him, cradling him in the ocean's trust. Soon the nausea will pass. He will never again feel strange on the restless, surging surface that is his destiny. Indeed, land will become a foreign place for him. He will become one with the ocean he has been bred to navigate, the ocean where we were all once at home. It's the highest honor his village can convey—to become a navigator and lead the way.

Centuries later a man named Mau Piailug will be called to follow the ancient tradition and accomplish a critical task. Just as those navigators who've preceded him, he'll learn to navigate across the trackless ocean to other islands of the Pacific. For millennia his ancestors sailed in search of trade and exchange of news, ideas and marriage partners. Sometimes, even to found a new world, and now it's Mau's mission to find the way. The world has changed. The mission has changed. Born in the early twentieth-century he will, however, still be depended upon to carry this tradition forward.

And still, it's the highest honor. To be a modern navigator, Mau Piailug must have the old knowledge. He too must know the names, rising times and paths across the sky of more than 200 stars. He must let his vision fly with the sea birds and know their routes. He must distinguish between five different kinds of swells and learn to sense the ocean's deep currents.

Mau will learn to read subtle changes in sky color above remote atolls, and understand how cloud patterns change as they approach island hills. He will know how the salinity and taste of specific parts of the ocean change in subtle ways as they're affected by currents, far-off rivers and temperature gradients. Like a gifted musician, he'll train himself to detect the infinite fluctuations in the rhythm of the swells slapping endlessly against the hull to identify the distinctive patterns created from the ever-changing shapes of shorelines.

There are patterns of photoluminescence that surround certain landmasses at specific times and places to help the navigator. A particular bird seen at a certain distance out at sea is key. A white tern indicates land within 150 miles, a brown tern ventures out only 50 miles, and so on. Ancient chants tell what to look for in stages as he crosses the equator and faces a totally transformed sky—a new Universe. As the Southern Cross disappears and the nebulous Arcturus rises, like those mighty navigators before him, Mau will feel exposed and vulnerable.

Only recently have we had confirmation of another secret known to these ancients. Anyone visiting Hawaii will have noticed that the prevailing winds come from the north east—most of the islands are settled on the leeward west sides. But the Polynesian settlers came from Asia in the west. Tacking these boats into the wind is possible but difficult, and few craft could continually push against the powerful Trades. A modern Polynesian navigator confirmed that the explorers waited for the big intermittent westerlies. A very smart move. They recognized what has only recently been referred to in Earth Science as El Niño![131]

In the world of massive way-finding, Mau Piailug embodied knowledge of millennia. With it, the Polynesians sailed an area one fifth of the world, from New Zealand to Hawaii to Easter Island. Two thousand years ago, Homer and others praised the heroic adventures of Greek mariners like Odysseus and Jason. Their tales were punctuated by one shipwreck after another in the comparative puddle of the Mediterranean. At the same time in history, these Polynesian master sailors were finding their way with pinpoint accuracy across 2,000 miles of open ocean.

Nainoa Thompson, who keeps the ancient navigating skills alive today as Executive Director of the Polynesian Navigation Society in Hawaii, learned his skills from the adult Mau Piailug. Thompson has guided modern replicas of the Polynesians' crafts over the same courses without resorting even to the sextants of pre-space-age western-style navigation, let alone the short-cut of global positioning satellites. The full significance of that achievement is borne home when you see what kind of vessels these replicas are. Constructed by hand with no modern materials, they reach 60 feet in length, weigh up to 12 tons and are capable of crossing earth's widest ocean with everything needed to settle a new land.

History, of course, is told by the victors. But the Europeans whose gunships eventually conquered the Pacific, laboriously logging each day's advance by the imaginary squared lines of latitude and longitude on a two-dimensional paper chart, were themselves vision-impaired. They were unaware of either the Polynesians' dazzling seafaring accomplishments or the sea's hidden texts read by men and women like Mau.

In the nineteenth-century, a famous navigator saved the Royal Flotilla of Tonga from disaster when a massive storm blew it leagues off course and confounded the dead reckoning of other younger sailors. He then directed the fleet to the nearest atoll in the Fijian archipelago, even correctly estimating its time of landfall. The most startling thing about the feat: this Polynesian navigator was totally blind. His accomplishment is a matter of record.

The Polynesian wayfinders have much to teach us. Although the French colonialists were to ban traditional craft to keep their island subjects under control, these people remained true seafarers. Crucially, Mau learned that a navigator—a leader—must be able to listen across many channels. For the ocean traveler there are the many complex channels between islands but also the diverse channels of awareness of natural signs. Both are significant.

Whether you're a lone sailor or a captain of industry, it's easy to feel lost at sea. Tossed about in this modern tsunami of clashing information, we'd all love to have a little of what Mau had: the capacity to close our eyes, feel the wind, taste the waves, and know exactly which way to steer.

The truth is: we all do! More precisely, we all have what it takes to develop the capacity to read below and above the surface flood of data, and find a reliable direction.

The Polynesian seafarers were imaginative. They were visionaries who were humble in their recognition of a great mystery. They knew they could never know it all. Because of this they were driven to learn and observe with incredible **focus and will**. These are two of the underpinnings of an enhanced imagination, and we're back to Jim Collins's characteristics of great leaders.

In a century with huge technical acceleration, imagination remains invaluable. For anyone responsible for the deployment of significant capital and human assets, it's an essential attribute, demanded at the very highest, Mau-worthy level of performance. As the all-but-lost art of Polynesian navigating illustrates, however, it's a capacity that we seem fated to neglect and forget—only to be driven to rediscover it once more.

Most of us are not sailing across the Pacific. Nevertheless, many of us are piloting uncharted waters, or we feel we are. Much like those navigators from the past, we feel in our bones that time is not on our side, that the wrong choice means disaster. In light of this, it's worth asking oneself how it is the early wayfarers managed to discover new worlds? How did a blind man extract crucial meaning from such diverse sources of information? Can we learn something about his processing skills to help us navigate? How blind are **we** to the real opportunities of our times?

Exploring multiple dimensions

Jill Bolte Taylor recommends that we learn to pay closer attention to a variety of sensory signals. For example, we can train our sense of smell to be much more discriminating. We can pause to feel the breeze on our skin, shift our awareness to more subtle perceptions. Jill suggests these will reawaken us to nature and to another side of our nature. She teaches us that we've been accessing an incredibly limited amount of data out there and so leading narrow, overly focused lives, driven by a demanding and perhaps sometimes tyrannical brain.

It's now almost a cliché to paraphrase Einstein; that a problem can't be solved on the same level of consciousness that it was created. Most of us accept this, without thinking about what a **new level** means. At best we may agree to look at a problem from a different **angle** but by doing things this way, how much can we really hope to achieve? This is where so much of modern writing on business is stuck—looking for new angles to do the same thing. We need much more than that.

While Mau is one of the best examples of how to see the profound possibilities of thinking things through on new levels—in new ways—the following is another way of thinking outside the box.

Nearly a hundred years ago the eccentric Russian writer, Peter Ouspensky, was writing about the following thought experiment. Here's his thinking on dimensionality.

The observer lives in flatland—a world that has no dimension of depth, a flat 2-D world. Let's imagine that somehow, from the 3-D world, a spoked wheel is being turned in a clockwise direction for the observer, as it is in the illustration below. In the diagram, I'm also limiting the observer's eye to an arc of view shown in lighter shading. By stretching ourselves a little, we can imagine that the flatland observer might encounter a permanent, unchanging dot in front of him where the rim continuously intersects with the visible plane. As the wheel rotates, the first spoke to intersect with the plane will be the red one, followed by the blue and green, with the pattern repeating over time. The observer will see a red flash, then blue, and then a green one as the spokes pass through this horizon.[132]

After some time, Ouspensky's observer would be able to predict the sequence of these flashes and announce the discovery of a "Science" based on his mastery of what seemed random to others. He has found a predictable order in nature. He could start a research institution and seek government funding. A smart spiritual entrepreneur might start a temple where predictions about the timing and color of the next flashes from the "invisible" or the "source" or "the heavens" would gain him great power and wealth and possibly some devoted adherents. Like many followers, they would need a limited vertical range themselves. Big things could be arranged around the next flash, with opportunities for ceremonies and community bonding as well as the enforcement of any needed discipline amongst the unorthodox.

As long as the wheel's rotation remains constant, all will be well. The observer will see the time between flashes (that is a function of the speed of rotation and the distance between spokes—of time **and** space) as pure **time and time alone**. The spatial component, which is a key underlying

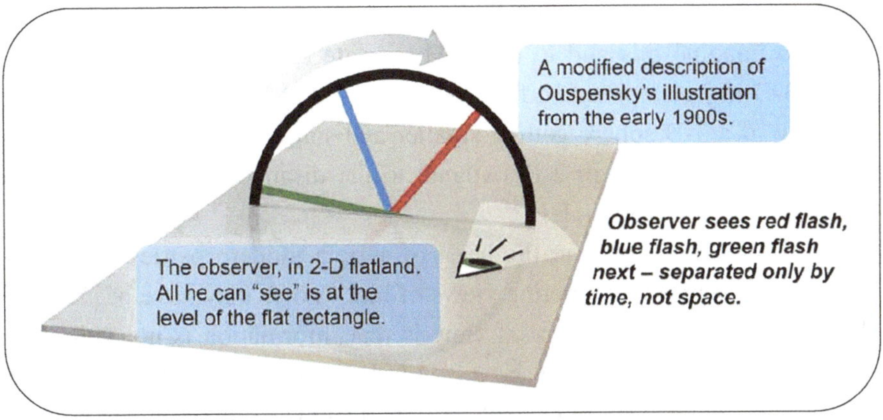

Figure 11 - Dimensions as Thought Boundaries

cause of the intervals, will be unknowable to him. Ouspensky said that time was, in fact, another spatial dimension, "imperfectly perceived." He meant that our horizons were literally limited. This raises the question of how much of what we see as pure time in three dimensions has a spatial component.

We know from another classic Einstein thought experiment that the experience of time differs dramatically, depending on the conditions of the observer. To illustrate this, imagine traveling on a beam of light that has bounced off the hands of a clock on earth as you speed away on the light beam. The hands of the clock back on earth won't change for you because you're riding on the beam that was reflected when the hands were at a specific time. For those back on earth, things will proceed normally, but you won't see any changes when you look back. Things on earth will appear frozen in time for you. Your own local clock will be normal.

So the relativity of time is not hard to grasp at this stage. When you look into 4-D models, they are in fact spatially extended versions of the 3-D world we occupy. One way of viewing them is as dense, extended versions of the 3-D shape, stretched over how they appeared in the time dimension "at right angles" to the world of 3-D.

The apparent density of a 4-D shape gets close conceptually to the density of a hologram, which contains all the elements of the whole in any portion but—a fact often ignored—at lower resolution. Things that are in 4-D "miraculously" appear and disappear in our 3-D world for those with the ability to imagine this and to those who create computer simulations. This echoes 3-D objects appearing from nowhere in 2-D.[133] I've wondered at the similarity of a 3-D sphere getting smaller and smaller and disappearing at a point as it passes through 2-D flatland, to the disappearance of matter and information into a black hole! [134]

Dimensionality is at the heart of certain modern battles in physics. The struggle between competing views of black holes may have been lost by Stephen Hawking as one current view is that information is not "lost" in a black hole but that there may be a 2-D hologram-like rendition of our 3-D world at its "edge." Some current theories in physics require several more dimensions in which to operate.

It's been argued that consciousness is a function of how we perceive higher dimensions. Art historians point out that the portrayal of perspective in drawing (a 2-D representation of 3-D) was a revelation in the Middle Ages and changed the trajectory of art. As time passed, an experience of depth on a flat surface occurred for more and more people until it became an obvious translation of the viewers' reality.

Ouspensky said flatly (so to speak!) that as consciousness changes, the sense of space itself changes. In his introduction to Ouspensky's *Tertium Organum*, Claude Bragnon summarizes Ouspensky's real goal—towards a new consciousness, reflected by consciousness of other dimensions.

> Ouspensky...conceives of space as the multi-dimen-sional mirror of consciousness. Time and motion are illusion—what appears to be time and motion being in reality only the movement of consciousness upon a higher space.[135]

I've worked with people who were comfortable envisioning in four dimensions. The late mathematician and Fields Medalist, William Thurston of Princeton could "see" in five dimensions. Is this an evolving human capability?

What's central here, in terms of this discussion, is the development of the human imagination to perceive higher dimensions and the implications of this. For thousands of years, it's been suggested that our imaginations can evolve, possibly attain much greater freedom. Over time, we've used various attempts at visualizing these other dimensions in science and the arts. We've used metaphor for imagining this process and, as it turns out, achieving results.

However, I don't want to leave the impression that we've exhausted the limits of our 3-D world. There are currently advances in imagining and building very complex self-assembly capabilities even in 3-D. The ability to envision and then create something from complex spatial folding techniques lies at the heart of what may become a revolution in nano-robotics. MIT professor and prodigy Erik Demaine and his colleagues are working on mini robots[136] that are stamped out of a single sheet, and then self-assemble in microseconds into complex 3-D shapes. He proved that a box pleat could form the basis of a universal 3-D pixel (called a voxel). Self-assembled robots could be used for a targeted approach to repairing biological components in the human body.

A parallel but accessible world is a central theme of Plato.[137] He helps us imagine this by also resorting to thought experiments on dimensionality. Plato uses a flat 2-D shadow projection on a cave wall and equates it to our limited normal worldview. In his classic parable, the world is a cave where we resemble prisoners chained to a stark and limited view of that cave. A fire burns in the cave behind them, casting flickering and deceptive shadows. There are people moving behind the chained prisoners, but a barrier obscures the outlines of their bodies from being projected onto the cave wall. Only the moving shadows of the objects balanced on their heads are projected onto the wall in front of the observing prisoners. The arrangement in the cave is a little complex and easily confused, but for our purposes what's important is that the prisoners can't see the outlines of the people, only the flat, grey shadows of the **burdens** being carried on their heads.

If we were to tell the prisoners about the colorful 3-D world outside, they wouldn't believe us. How could they? If they were suddenly released and taken out into the light of day, they'd be blinded. According to Socrates, "To them, … the truth would be literally nothing but the shadows of the images." We're condemned to a form of Flatland.

The parable encompasses the flatness and grayness of jaded perception, but also a possible turn towards the light and the blinding of those unprepared for renewal. I believe this is connected to our failure to see the truth when we only recognize the shadow or darker aspects of another. It serves as a cautionary tale. Because we tend to project our own "stuff," the sunlit, magnificently colored, spacious garden is closed to some.[138] Can we choose to step out into the light at the entrance of the cave, deal with the shock and wonder, and prepare to live in a complex but unimaginably richer world? Are we willing to face this brave new world?[139]

The Vertical Dimension

There are many ways of approaching dimensionality. What's key is that time can play a reduced role as the number of dimensions increase. Extending this line of thought and exploring beyond our 3-D limitations, I'd like to talk briefly about the worlds of the poets and mystics to investigate timelessness.

Joseph Campbell used the shorthand term "vertical dimension" to describe a timeless zone. He spoke in a lecture of a remarkable and unexpected personal experience of it.

One evening, entering a concert of Indian music, he found himself baffled by the way some of the musicians casually walked onto the stage in mid performance as others packed up their instruments and walked off. Realizing, after a time, that the players and audience didn't seem in the least disrupted by these appearing and disappearing bodies, moving with the ebb and flow of the various musical notes created by the changing instruments, he began to relax. He let go of thoughts on how the concert should be conducted and the more he unwound, the more aware he became that what was apparently going on in "real time" wasn't exactly what was going on at all.

The rotation of people on stage wasn't what mattered. He was to allow the music to take over. Navigating this musical scale until those notes combined to resonate with what seemed the very Music of the Spheres, he found himself swept into an ever-present stream. There seemed an eternal flow of energy he could choose to step into and out of, just as the musicians themselves were doing on stage. It was "there" regardless, and he had the freedom to tune into it. Or perhaps it's better said, to tune up to it! Musicians and audience were free to visit and participate with this living force.

Campbell's is a powerful image of a continuous undercurrent of energy that has various names, including: the ground of being, the source of sub-atomic creation and destruction, the vertical dimension. What's important is to remember that this vertical dimension has vastly different qualities to a purely perpendicular extension of our world.

Like Campbell, the English poet and critic T.S. Eliot saw our liberation from the inevitable stresses of linear time emerging in moments of revelation. But he believed most of us could only handle momentary hints of this kind of intensity, that "Mankind cannot bear too much reality."[140] Eliot felt humans needed to be sensitive to the fleeting nature of the intersection.

Dimensions and emotions

There is an emotional connection to limited dimensions that clearly demonstrates the benefit of breaking free of their constraints. When one is involved in repetitive loops there is no **depth or height**—only the same old thoughts and feelings. For example, an inner dialogue of what I should have said, what they conveniently forgot to mention, etc. seems to go nowhere except around some form of emotional Möbius Strip, returning to its starting place on a flat surface with no new perspective as promised by its shape.

Rumi speaks of this, and the need to get out of that place.

Don't be addicted to subtle discussions,
Tying and untying knots, posing difficulties
that then you resolve.

Doing that, you're like a bird
Who learns how to loosen the snare
And then fastens it again,
To show off his strange, new skill.

Don't forget that the point is to escape!
Remember how it feels to sail the mountain air
And smell the sweetness of the high meadows.

Rumi has covered wide ground here—as is often the case. This poem, with the help of all those others created by our Sufi mystic, becomes a hologram, mysteriously forming out of a rich body of interconnecting and self-reinforcing images. Here, he builds a three dimensional space that we're able to enter, visit and experience, and then leave if we choose. He sets up an emotional domain, the experience of neurosis. We know what he's talking about, what it means to be caught in those hopeless feelings; the endless cycling through past events with a compulsion that Jill identified as the left brain running rampant. It's the part of our brain that asserts that same dominance Cesar insists we need to contain. To clear away the debris of repetitive circular patterns, Rumi reminds us "...the point is to escape!" He knows we can break away. We can be free. Suddenly we do remember what it means "...to sail the mountain air / And smell the sweetness of the high meadows." And we know it's what we're to do.

Imagine how things would look if, like Rumi, we could invoke other **dimensions** to deal with the problems that result from lack of vision. These dimensions need not be spatial—enhanced sound such as Campbell's concert experience is another dimension, and so are enhanced feelings, those connected to intuition, for example.

This amplified world is all around us. We're living in it with different species perceiving other realities. A dog lives in an olfactory world with unimaginable shifts going on. With one hundred times more smell sensors (about a quarter of a billion—compared to our three million) the world must be layered in amazingly distinct levels of smell on a vastly expanded dimension. Unlike humans, sharks detect muscles firing, while snakes see heat. There are fragile butterflies in Europe that cover the same distance in equal time as much faster and stronger birds. They do this through an ability to sense and use subtle changes in air currents at varying altitudes. The birds barrel through with a more single-minded strategy but they use far more energy. Sounds a little like the difference between the stereotypes of the average Buddhist and a typical Texan![141]

We've seen that dogs have an uncanny ability to read humans, making them extraordinarily insightful teachers. Cesar Milan has given full credit to the fact that he could not have achieved what he has without the "insights" of his great attendant dogs, such as the universally beloved

"Daddy."[142] Certain dogs accompany him on tough missions to help create more effective climates to rehabilitate other dogs. How this works is not fully understood.

Multiple dimensions of achievement

I've mentioned the shallowness of equating single-measure sports outcomes to organizational success and life success. "Set a single goal, pursue your passion, and all will be well" seems to be a potential recipe for monomania, self-absorption and a lonely old age.

Recently an article on this comparison between sports and life caught my attention. In this case, it involved a decathlete and suggested that the decathlon might provide some useful analogies for the complex task of reading multiple signals in our daily lives. It occurred to me as I sat down to read it that this might be a better argument for the sports analogy than that of a single focused sport. I wasn't sure.

Participants in the decathlon do have a clear measure of success, but can't allow themselves to become overly absorbed in any single challenge, as they need to optimize results in 10 separate fields. Stamina and all-round capabilities are more important than specialized skills in this kind of multidimensional challenge. Consistency is also a critical quality.

A key issue for these well-rounded athletes is that they have to accept the fact that, in some events, they are not at the standard they'd like to be. Still they must compete in these events, and usually in front of large audiences.

As I thought about the challenge of the decathlon, it seemed that in some respects it was a good analogy for the rest of us. It turns out that we all need to grasp the fact that our efforts to change are very likely to make us feel vulnerable, maybe too vulnerable. We're likely to feel uncomfortable as our new, rather undeveloped skills will not be in the same league as our more obvious practiced strengths. A brilliant systems engineer can look clumsy as she learns to handle a meeting. But, like those athletes competing in arenas where they're not as comfortable as they'd like to be, we too need to press on. That's why these athletes use personal trainers, to help them through the tough and challenging aspects of what they're trying to do and, like them, we also need help. The guides are here to help us learn consistency and develop intent. Through them we just might enlarge our potential. We may begin to create a renaissance of our own.

What is a renaissance?

Building on the foundations of tradition

The Renaissance is regarded as that time in European civilization immediately following the Middle Ages. Historians argue this intellectual transformation was the bridge to Modern history. Global exploration flourished and the great revolution in astronomy from Ptolemy to Copernicus shattered our self-centered role in the universe. Although, to some on Facebook, this may not yet be apparent! It was a time of major rejuvenation and widespread education—a knowledge revolution. There was great interest and advancement in music, painting, sculpture, architecture, literature and the sciences. Joseph Campbell argued this period was directly connected to a central change in human consciousness, which is still playing out.

Think of the Gothic cathedrals built around 1,000 years ago. They harnessed the new technology of the day (the pointed arch and the flying buttress) to build thinner, higher frames. But frames for what? Light! These were structures conceived and erected to capture the soaring effect of light refracted through myriads of stained glass prisms to tell the classic stories in shimmering new forms. Some cathedrals took 100 years to build. The faith lived on from one architect and set of artisans and painters to another. These massive churches were built to a scale that could have housed the Statue of Liberty. The extraordinary recovery of the light (literally) in the explosion of Gothic Cathedrals was a spectacular physical rise of a light-based cultural rebirth. The architects were moved by the Greek insights into proportion and number and looked back 1,400 years for inspiration.

When I look at this outpouring of energy, I'm reminded of the Cambrian explosion in biology. The results of both periods changed the fabric of history.

The cultural blossoming in Europe owes a great deal to a renewed interest in classic learning and values. The discovery of some of the lost translations of the Greeks and the opening of northern trade routes were instrumental in advancing Western Civilization. In the following passage, Kathleen Raine reminds us how this flood of creativity resulted from the impetus of ancient traditions. Because they hold the possibility of being more immediate than what we've chosen to call reality, Raine insists

> These...are not reflections of nature but immediate creations of that mental ground of which natural forms are themselves images...[therefore] what we experience can seem more real than reality; it comes from the source.[143]

So, you may ask, what does all this have to do with me? After all, Plato, Socrates, Roman Emperor Marcus Aurelius, and artists and leaders from the Middle Ages lived long before our time. The phenomenal Renaissance that led the world out of comparative darkness happened ages ago. But others every bit as inspirational—Einstein, Mandela, the Dalai Lama and Jill Bolte Taylor are from modern times. And that's the point. The traditions and knowledge of those from any era can be instructive. They are teachers ready to **serve**, to show that we can orient ourselves to have longer, wider and deeper connections to "the source."

They tell us this is the way to the garden-consciousness of any renaissance. This is rebirth.

12
Fate, Fractals and the Feminine

...What is the connection between
what lives in time and what lives in eternity?

If I kept talking about Love,
A hundred new combinings would happen,
and still I would not say the Mystery.
...
... Theologians mumble, rumble dumble,
necessity and free will,
while lover and Beloved
                    pull themselves
Into each other.

Rumi

This chapter takes us to a major question: how do we spend the rest of our lives? As most of us can now look forward to living longer, it's especially relevant.

Fate and destiny help us recognize the areas of our lives where we can have some scope. Then the science of **fractals** cautions us not to become distracted by issues of scale at the outset of any venture. The presence of **feminine** qualities such as empathy helps us redirect our energy. If we can combine specific qualities, with transformed energy, things can self-replicate, and we just might end up on our way to another renaissance. Our actions could even play a part in preventing a global implosion.

Fate, destiny and will

As you'll recall, fate includes what we inherit from the family gene pool and what we're exposed to in our surrounding environment. It's all about who mom and dad were and how they and others influenced our lives. Our fate is with us long before we stumble to take those first few steps, and it remains with us whether we like it or not. Fair, not fair—none of this matters. We don't have a say in it.

The following diagram constitutes an expanded view of our fate. It is "the hand we have been dealt," or what Marcus referred to as the "web of fate." Going back to the Greeks for a moment, they believed a combination of the following three things made up our fate. The first component was our character, which they concluded was formed by influences we've mentioned, including genetics. The second included that always-present, undeniable possibility to "miss the mark," to make errors in judgment. Finally, they argued, there was our propensity for hubris or pride.

The surface of the diagram portrays our destiny, the very small area in which we have some say. In the face of the massive inevitable forces from beneath, what we do here is crucial. We can embrace those aspects of consciousness that are amenable to change, or not. In this way, we can play our part in nudging evolution into some more sustainable and productive patterns, or not. Here lies the home of whatever free will we might have, where we grasp our potential and act in those opportune moments. Or not.

Driven by what's within the power of our wills, the big question is: how creative can I be in the face of predetermination? We know we'll "lose" in the end if we see this simply as a battle with death.

My diagram shows how vast fate's region is—how much is not in our control. Note the small craft (that's us!) doing its best to sail the waves of this mighty ocean. When we look below the surface we see that this question of free will is profound.

On the left of the diagram are some categories of influences on our lives. These go well beyond family and culture. Beneath the top levels are the ranges of deeply ingrained primal patterns. Some are older than the human species.

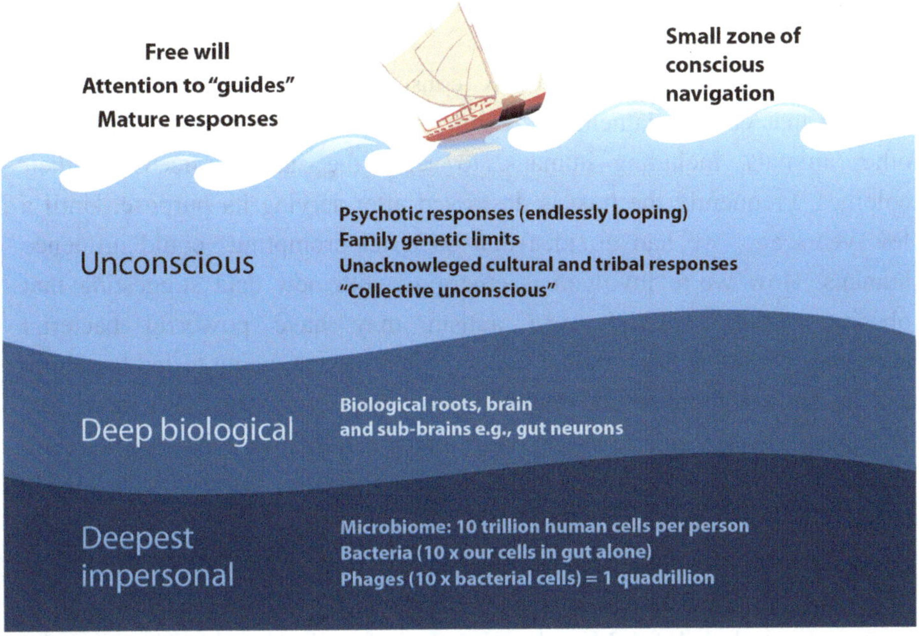

Figure 12 - Levels of Influence

Going down the list, we pass through the first layer of the **unconscious**, where fate gets a foothold—where family and genetics and the highly influential proteomics get to play out. The latter adds vastly greater complexity because our proteome helps determine how inherited genes will express themselves and varies from time to time and cell to cell. In extreme cases, a single gene can code for 1,000 proteins. Next are the tribal and racial aspects, playing out unconsciously and consciously in the world. The "collective unconscious" is the zone of deep structures proposed by Jung, and others, where we share a pool of common imagery and symbols. Here is the home of those composite archetypes, apparently found throughout all cultures, which are projected unconsciously—the magical infant, the anima and animus and so on.[144]

Then we drop down to deeper roots—the deep biological—within our nervous systems. This level includes not only different areas of the brain that are consciously involved, but the autonomic systems, which are out of conscious control. These are essential for every one of our four billion lifetime heartbeats.

Last and furthest from any conscious grasp are the colonies of bacteria that can fundamentally rewire the behavior of insects, birds, and other animals, including humans, to serve the survival needs of their colonies. Frequently the host is destroyed after serving its purpose. Until a few years ago, we had no idea that bacterial promptings could influence humans. How we're involved is emerging with new data suggesting that obesity, depression and even autism may have powerful bacterial correlates.[145] These days, radically new techniques are being tested to simply and instantly repopulate our internal microbiome ecosystems. We have over 10 times as many bacteria in and on us than we do human cells, and there are again ten times as many bacteriophages. These are viruses that invade bacteria. We are super hosts. Every two days, half of the bacteria in the world are said to be killed by phages; the bacteria then regenerate.[146] Are we a major way in which microbes spread? I think so. The invention of the jet has been particularly helpful. Microbes have been found independently riding the jet stream. Vincent Fischetti, a microbiologist at Rockefeller University and leading researcher in phages, comments in a *Scientific American* article that "...what's really in control of the planet are the bacteriophages. They control everything."

This is truly a new set of dimensions, with the potential to identify unimagined drivers of human life on earth. On the conceivably positive side, some genetically engineered nano-scale creatures are being harnessed to power electrical devices in or around our bodies so they can convert pulses of energy to electricity and vice versa. They self-assemble and then function at minute scales with total precision.

In her book *Love 2.0*[147] Barbara Frederickson reminds us of the 50 year-old studies of her fellow Stanford psychologist Walter Mischel on the famous marshmallow test. It's just one example of predetermination and involves giving four-year-olds the option of having one marshmallow now, or two after waiting 20 minutes. A key finding from these studies is that the behavior of the subjects was the best predictor of success in later life—better than IQ, better than income level. There are later windows where change can happen, but generally speaking, if a child could withstand the temptation of the marshmallows, not succumb to instant gratification, he or she was more likely to be successful socially and academically. It's about a key element of emotional intelligence called impulse control and some of us have more of it than others.

So it's up to us to be creative. Our choice! Can we embrace the challenge, while accepting the limitations? Can we bravely fill the sails of that small craft, navigate those reefs and lead the life we were destined to lead?

Because we're all limited in profound ways—while gifted in others—what we bring to our lives needs a true sense of humility and a resolute, but never rigid, will. How could Nelson Mandela flourish and coach his colleagues in a South African prison and emerge as the world's most respected leader? How did Mandela know that he had to maintain a calm assertive stance? He practiced this, even to the extent of dictating the pace at which he walked, while earning the respect of his jailers. And in prison, where these "terrorists" were all forced to choose one book, it's intriguing that they chose the collected works of Shakespeare. Mandela signed his favorite portion of this much-valued collection, later displayed in London, to reflect the lifelong connection he felt to Julius Caesar—another man with a destiny of leadership. If you need an example of someone with a core sense of will and humility, Mandela's your man.

A crucial intersection

The cross is an ancient symbol that lies at the center of many theologies and mythologies. In some religious systems, the point of intersection is viewed as eternal or timeless. For our purposes, I'd like to look at this juncture in terms of fate and destiny. The following diagram shows the two fundamental axes and highlights their meeting point. The intersection of fate and destiny is the dimension of imaginative possibilities.

1. **Fate**—the horizontal axis is our world of space and time.

2. **Destiny**—the vertical axis represents timelessness and contains infinite possibilities, including our **potential**. Here destiny and potential are equated.

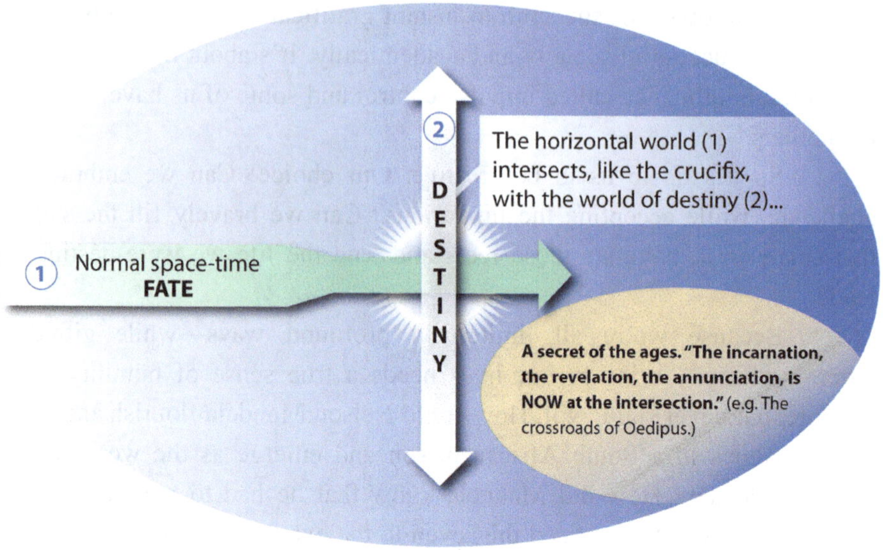

Figure 13 - A Crucial Intersection

Fractals

The following collage by Alexis Cawood features a classic Annunciation painting (by Fra Angelia from the thirteenth-century) woven into a world of fractals.

The theme of Annunciation demonstrates the earlier point that scale is not important, and the intuitive perception that every moment of our lives **is** an annunciation. It may be that our modern sense of chaos comes in part from a loss of the awareness of sacred patterns, such as this. Or, put another way, a loss of faith in that whatever is happening now, actually matters. It's unbelievably important.

The present moment is a fractal, a part of a self-replicating pattern that will make up the larger pattern—the motif of our lives. It embodies our potential and our destiny. Although the collage is not meant as particularly Christian, it is spiritual in its message that here, in this intensely beautiful moment—in every moment—eternity embraces time. There is no real separation.

Figure 14 - The Annunciation

The meeting of the two figures is the eternal nature of love, that dimension of imaginative possibility, where our lives take shape.

In a different age, this insight would have been comfortably conveyed in religious terms using words like annunciation, revelation, or epiphany. Today, we're likely to use more psychological language. But nothing basic has changed. Those Renaissance paintings of the Angel descending with the blessing of God were both religious and, if you think about it, psychological. By this I mean they were not just about announcing the conception, but presented the very real possibility of an ongoing real-time incarnation, as inspiration is delivered into the world.

The collage represents Joseph Campbell's experience of the music that night. That other dimension is "here," in our everyday world, whether we know it or not. The pickup in rhythm in "Samba Pa Ti" from the album *Abraxas* by Santana is another example of musicians celebrating this intersection, of being in the moment, or groove. The final chords of Sibelius's last symphony, the opening chords of *Das Rheingold,* are packed with a complex interplay of harmonics that suggests a moment of perfection, at least while the notes last.

The feminine

We've seen lots of movies and plays, read novels too, suggesting that single-focus thinking can be a problem. If we are to enlarge the space or domain in which we practice strength, we need to be open to more dimensions, some of them emotional. Some form of awakening has to happen, and this can take shape in any number of ways. Think about Jill Bolte Taylor, that jolt or push into another and larger domain came about through a physical crisis. Her stroke gave rise to brain changes that forced her to experience something more than the usual left brain dominance the rest of us have been led to believe is how it has to be. She came back to tell us something different. Sometimes it's the wreckage of a different kind of brain assault,[148] like the sudden hit on the head that changed Jason Padgett, making him a mathematics savant. One of Padgett's brain experts believes we all have his potential—our "inherited software"—but few access it.

Those are two examples involving catastrophe. Other causes may involve tragedies of another sort, social crises, and economic crunches. The irony is that some of us seem to need a crunch, or personal tragedy, before recognizing the healing powers of these desperate states. But can we make the change without a crisis? Initially I wasn't sure this was possible. I've since changed my mind, which is what this book is about. If we follow our guides' suggestions, do the work of the present moment where every decision involves values, while not being sidetracked by distractions, we can do this without a meltdown. We can develop the necessary qualities for creating a climate of imaginative awakening. We can make these shifts, but there's one more thing. We need to invoke and honor the feminine.

Let's take a moment to see again how the feminine plays out in much of the source material. The voices and influences of women frequently propel the narratives for successful outcomes. When death and disgrace are part of the outcome in *Howards End,* it's because of the failure of a rigid man to tolerate or allow the influence of an intuitive, caring woman. He won't have it. In *As Good as it Gets*, a competent, hard-working woman brings out compassionate qualities in two dramatically different men—one macho, the other gay. *American Beauty* tells a story that includes an inappropriate projection of the feminine onto a daughter's young friend. But a compelling late scene between the father and this young woman leads to a mutual recognition of the ways in which each has felt isolated and excluded from relationship. Or you could say, from the living feminine qualities we all need.

Shakespeare's Cordelia is a most amazing character. Although she is referred to frequently, she only appears briefly at the beginning and end of the play. Yet her impact is felt throughout. Her presence reaches across the whole performance, and across the subsequent four centuries. This is an example of the feminine's enduring power to stir our imagination. She demonstrates with striking clarity that something does not need to be visible to be present. She embodies possibility.

Goddard has done us an extraordinary service through recognizing and elevating Cordelia and the role of the feminine in his essay on *King Lear*. But, according to Goddard, the play goes further and captures one of the most important messages for our time. If he stresses something, I pay full attention!

He begins the ascent to this insight by pointing out that, in his early plays, Shakespeare seemed an "Enlightenment figure," believing that reason alone could counter force. In simplified terms, this would be to say that the left brain can deal with the lizard brain. If this were the case, the United Nations would have convinced key Arab leaders to share power in January 2011, and there would have been no need for the Arab Spring of uprisings.

How does one temper force? In his earlier works, even in *Hamlet*, Shakespeare still contrasted reason with force. But, like Lear, Shakespeare himself learned to "See better!" As he gained experience, came to see more, he no longer argued that reason is our primary hope against tyranny. It's not that reason has no place. Only that it needs to be held in its place. Reason is what we have to "fall back on when imagination fails," as is touch, when vision fails. But reason alone is not enough. It's reason, Goddard argues, that saves us from plunging into the chasm, but alone, it's not enough to soar.

King Lear points to nothing less than the end of civilization unless other tempering forces are invoked. In the play Albany says:

> It will come,
> Humanity must perforce prey on itself,
> Like monsters of the deep.

Even the echo of the word *force* in *perforce* (meaning inevitably) is no accident—this is the force of unregulated ambition and greed. Albany's monsters of the deep present an even darker image than those lizards I've referred to earlier. Shakespeare believed that unregulated human passion would destroy the species. But there is one caveat. It is the crucial "unless"—unless something descends from a realm other than the visible to save us. Shakespeare held the radical view that the powers inherent in fragile forces can save us.

> If that the heavens do not their visible spirits
> Send quickly down to tame these vile offences,
> It will come...

So what can supplement reason, which we've seen to be inadequate? Goddard names qualities that have a fragile but infinitely redeeming power:

love, tenderness, patience and forgiveness—qualities found in Cordelia and in many characters throughout Shakespeare's work. Characters like Juliet, Desdemona, Portia, Miranda, the sprite Ariel, also embody many of these qualities or attributes.

There is a potent dynamic between force and imagination. Goddard points out, "In play after play [Shakespeare] pits some seemingly fragile representative of beauty against the forces of inertia and destruction: a dream, the spirit of innocence or play, love, art—whether as poetry, drama or music especially." And there is a chance the higher powers can prevail.

So the power of imagination can invoke and realize feminine qualities. These qualities call to our imaginations as we feel the guides' influence. This is truly a virtuous circle, with the potential to counter force and free us to live our full potential.

It's up to us to be creative. Our choice! Can we embrace the challenge, while accepting the limitations? Can we bravely fill the sails of that small craft, navigate those reefs and lead the life we were destined to lead?

13
See Better to Do Better!

At last, you've shaken your wings
And broken the cage apart and
Flown off into the unseen.

Rumi

To this point I've advocated a change of heart for regaining compassion to learn new ways of seeing and serving. But, if we're to talk of a true renaissance, freedom and openness are also to be prized in this new world of ours. As well as compassion, these values must be present and instilled by those courageous enough to act on their insights.

I'm interested in working in the worlds of organizations and applied science. But I've been unable to let go of my need to see the treasure houses of the humanities protected, saved and applied in everyday life. My concern includes framing the big questions and commitments in our lives—such as our individual quests. Seeing better may involve profound change but I feel the point of any new perspective is to **do better**. I've argued consistently that the journey begins at home, within each of us.

Flying freer

Perhaps you've experienced the stirrings of some newfound freedom as you try letting go of past judgments and old desires and practice a state of inner calm. As Rumi and many others see it, personal change often demands a personal shake-up, a dismantling of current relationships, bondages and sometimes obligations.

Einstein's elegantly simple thought experiment from Chapter 11 describing his passage into relativity theory serves us here as a way of talking about a change of perspective. He imagined himself, you will recall, flying out of the bounds of earth's time limitations on a beam of light to a point in space where he could look back and imagine something he could never have realized while still inside the old box of time and space. Through his imaginative journey, Einstein discovered that time back on earth would be frozen for the light beam traveler as long as he continued traveling at the speed of light.

The idea of thinking in terms of imaginative journeys remains popular on the Course. It's a way of bridging different disciplines. For some participants it proved helpful to see themselves navigating with the aid of an image. For instance, a few resonated with the Polynesians in the Pacific because they were fascinated to learn some of the old navigators used to imagine that their canoes just had to be headed in the right direction. These early adventurers envisioned themselves committed to placing their vessel in the right relationship to the waves and to that vast ocean which rolled continuously towards them. At all times, reaching their destination was about sailing with an absolute sense of **orientation**.

That idea gets us to our question: **how do we choose to orient ourselves?** If these sailors sought and found crucial clues to finding their way in those unknown waters, then what can we do? How do we choose to navigate or orient ourselves in line with the guides we have chosen? And further, do the points of guidance laid out in these pages provide an adequate map?

In a number of ways, Einstein is helpful here, as he imaginatively rode the wave of light beams into space. Like the Polynesians reading their way while riding that wave, he teaches us something about imagination and orientation. But Einstein also shares an astonishing similarity to Rumi's imagery. In the lines quoted in the epigraph to this chapter, Rumi offers a breathtaking image of liberation. We fly on the wings of the poet out of that cage and into the unknown.

It's fascinating that the poet and the physicist have adopted a harmony of imagery from different places in time and space. Both have used an image of flight from the boxes of our known experiences and habits of mind. In each case when we look back we see a smaller, time-defined semblance of ourselves. We've taken flight on imaginative waves to see and experience other dimensions and have gained greater perspective.

We've all been trained. We've become dependent and much of our creative potential has been stifled until, by now, a part of us feels caged. Our flight is in search of freedom from unconscious servitude and so it helps to see and feel what we're leaving behind so as not to stumble back into the familiar. The "unseen" in Rumi's poem is all that we were previously blind to or could not have imagined.

When you've stepped out of old frames, the feeling of the "unseen" can be bleak and lonely. There's a tendency to revert to the safe and reliably supplied cage. The attraction can easily be to a familiar emotional tone, to that of our past. It's even likely that we'll be drawn to those old comfortable days played out in our childhood family living rooms, where at least we knew the rules of the game. Rather than risking a sense of being out there alone in an unfamiliar world, it's more likely to be: Quick, back into the cage—especially at dinnertime! For some people, the restoration of the familiar familial atmosphere of childhood has proved a useful model to see how they recreate boxes and cages from tired old narratives of who did what.

In *The Tempest,* Prospero, from his new vantage point suggested by his liberated imagination, could step back in time and be precise in detailing what each of his enemies had inflicted upon him. But it was time to take a new stand, and let their offenses be confined to that cage of the past. He was able to pursue freedom and to explore a different future without needing his old structured learning or to control and exploit his imagination for purely personal gain. Only when he had reached this stage was his imagination liberated.

But the escape out of the cage and its acquired vistas is only a stage of our journey. These new ways of seeing can go on to contribute to real-world solutions.

One way of staying in touch with the challenges of practicing this unaccustomed freedom is to repeat the identical question we initially asked to help us change our old ways: "Who do I serve?" The question helps us to live with a sense of liberation and clarity. It can also point to which exemplars one chooses in future. Many fellow voyagers have gone beyond their fate and managed to make all kinds of contributions. Some convey that this is an ongoing process—never a done deal. So when you begin locating those happier friends that Rumi speaks of, how will you return to the real world of the castle and function with integrity? You might hope that your own fractals of influence can replicate and evolve.

As Bob Dylan reminded us earlier, we all gotta serve somebody and happily these days, many feel that in the last (and now hugely extended) half or third of life, they have more potential for renewed service than simply deciding which cruise packages offer the most appealing distractions. That change of heart and circumstance has fueled this search for some larger meaning.

The questions of who we serve, and how we serve, are undergoing profound changes in society today. Many of those passing through midlife, and others transitioning into new life phases, are doing so with rich stores of experience, and sometimes, enhanced assets and resources of time. Where they have served in the past they've also mastered as never before what it means to seek accountability. Some know more about effectiveness (doing the right things) and efficiency (doing things right) than any previous generation. When they decide to serve, they want to ensure that their resources and efforts are going to the intended places and causes. This is a continuing and fascinating quest.

The Postscript that follows this chapter has examples of what have proven effective adaptation strategies over time. In the classic Grant Study, which I've admired for decades, the research extends over entire lifetimes. I also discuss some specifics of philanthropy, which link to one of the study's findings of generativity. I present examples of people choosing to operate on vastly different scales. Some are billionaires serving across continents; others are making a difference with loans in increments of $25 to single entrepreneurs in African villages.

The point I try to stress is that it's important for each of us to think about the **direction, scale, intensity and accountability** of our own unique emerging path. You'll recall that the Grail stories stress this aspect of uniqueness. To follow another's path was not only misguided—it was shameful. The journey not only needs your commitment, but a commitment based on **your** values.

Coming home in a different space

We've learned that some people have not only escaped from a constrained life but have in turn discovered an enhanced way of serving in the world. In contrast, others hold on to old relationships with old patterns. Henry Wilcox in *Howards End* was holding on to his privileged role in England's overseas expansion; he couldn't let go to hear his wife's pleas in time to avert a series of catastrophes involving broken lives and shattered hearts.

Both men in *As Good as it Gets* uncover a truer path as they pursue their creative lives. Having experienced authentic love, the Jack Nicholson character is finally able to write about it. Of course, there are no guarantees that his old, financially successful and formulaic style of writing will any longer satisfy him, nor that his new style will please his old readers! In *The Fisher King*, both men and both extremely diverse women find a resurgence of energy in their renewed ability to connect beyond notions of self.

With help, the people in these dramas shake their wings and imaginations ignite. Breaking from their old unconscious ways, they find they can break those cages apart and **take flight on their own imaginative journeys**. They've learned to embrace their fates, leaving them free to follow their destinies. We can join them.

Earlier chapters have made the point that time may not be as linear as we've been taught. It seems it's possible for some to nurture living links with people from the past; with those who are no longer alive. Using their wisdom, perhaps we can build bridges from earlier times in ways yet to be imagined. These links transcend logic and ordinary time through an emotional bond of some kind. We've seen that emotions like empathy can play a key role in helping us replace narrow survival concerns with a much wider sense of relatedness. Recently I read a piece on the 100th anniversary of the onset of World War 1, which led me to think of just these links. Susan Hampson of *The Globe and Mail* had just uncovered the war diaries of her great grandfather. In reading them, she came to appreciate the reality and power of enduring bonds over the span of a century. She reflected:

> Emotions help to collapse time. They are the powerful forces that bring us all to one level playing field, across time and space,

> background and ethnicity. They are what connect us, because we all feel what it means to be alive and to suffer.[149]

When the anthropologist and writer Ernest Becker finished his classic Pulitzer Prize winner *The Denial of Death,* he conceded that no one could predict the forward momentum of life. According to Becker, "The most that any one of us can seem to do is to fashion something—an object or ourselves—and drop it into the confusion, make an offering of it, so to speak, to the life force."[150] Our fractal imagery backs this up and suggests to me that spending too much time on self-promotion, personal branding and other forms of shallow replication can trap us. Avoiding the necessary changes in our lives by pursuing superficial ends can only promise something much less than Becker's possible fashioned offering.

In another poem Rumi reminds us to "Wake into the sobriety / that says, 'I am sustained from within.'" Here he gives us a real clue to Becker's idea of how we might make our offering "to the life force." He expands on Becker's thesis and returns us to that earlier point where I stressed that this work must begin with the self. I think what Rumi suggests here is that before we're likely to be effective in the world, our presence must be dignified by a kind of self-restraint that can only come through self-awareness.

It's interesting, too, that we have another example of how our guides speak to one another and in turn to those of us who will listen as they reach to take our hand and shepherd us on our way. In that handheld guidance, it's as though they weave a kind of safety net. While we teeter on some precipice, struggling not to fall, they weave the elements that guide us in our pursuit—our lives.

Speaking of the guides reaching across time and space in their roles as teachers and defenders, I can't help but think of Rumi and the Owain story. The way our poet expands on the ending of the tale reminds us of our need to finally return to the world. To remain aloof, unattached or unaware of that larger world to which we belong, is to miss the chance to participate and "wake into the sobriety" of our daily lives. To stay asleep through any form of escapism: false pride, beefed up superiority—whatever—is to be lost. Owain, having awakened to the countess, has gained knowledge and vision through this reunion, and the return to the castle at last takes the form of an offering. In the service to something much larger, Owain and the countess together contribute their insights and strength in order to effect an integration of the worlds of the castle and garden. This is an incredibly important caveat. Not to leave the field of the world, but to remain to fulfill one's personal heartfelt contribution, is to choose better by seeing better.

And while we're on the subject of choice and vision, destiny and fulfillment, in another of his poems, Rumi asks: "How long do you plan to stay in your ecstasy, / Where all you can say is, 'I don't know *anything*?'" [Emphasis in original.] And then, before the reader has a chance to catch his breath, to think of some speedy reply, Rumi (in the next line of the poem) quickly directs us to "Let your *I don't see* become *I see*." He can be prescriptive, saying what we are to do or to become. Although ecstasy is a state that comes up frequently in Rumi's work and is an experience he believes in, it's not to be the means to escape our awakening. To become Rumi's "I see" is again a way of talking about choosing better by seeing better.

The future of these ideas

As a young man I was influenced by people who had met and come to know the Jesuit theologian and anthropologist Pierre Teilhard de Chardin, when he visited South Africa. Unfortunately, de Chardin had run into massive roadblocks from his superiors, and his key work, *The Phenomenon of Man,* was only published posthumously, not until the mid 1950s.[151] He had attempted a dramatic and visionary synthesis of science and the humanities in this work.

Long before there was any indication of the worldwide web, de Chardin envisaged a future spiral of increasing interconnectedness reaching across the globe. He believed "No evolutionary future awaits anyone except in association with everyone else." In his conception, the increase in complexity and density would culminate in a transition of human consciousness into a timeless and spaceless phenomenon called "The Omega Point." His thinking calls up our earlier discussion of timeless transition points. In essence, the Jesuit imagined this phenomenon being "pulled" into being.

de Chardin's work influenced a number of novels, from dramas to science fiction, and many thoughtful people all over the world related to his vision. *The New York Times* rated his book a masterpiece, but his work is less influential today, partly because he's difficult to read even with helpful introductions.

In another startling congruence of imagery, Rumi speaks directly to de Chardin's Omega point. Rumi helps us here to grasp that inexplicable sense of being pulled into being, or being led along.

> Humankind is being led along an evolving course,
> through this migration of intelligences,
> and though we seem to be sleeping,
> there is an inner wakefulness
> that directs the dream,
>
> and that will eventually startle us back
> to the truth of who we are.

These words could be a restatement in poetic terms of de Chardin, except that we hear Rumi's voice first, centuries earlier. I'm not in a position to assess how much of this similarity arises from the brilliance of Coleman Barks's modern translation, but the overlap is astounding. As poet and Jesuit were visionaries, perhaps it's that each glimpsed an aspect of the evolution of consciousness. Both views are truly optimistic regarding where interconnected human intelligences and values can lead and are a counterpoint to the dark view of imaginative decline I surveyed earlier.

Now what?

Although it may be a temptation to go back to the starting point of this book and set a new bunch of goals, or dream up bucket lists; you might just consider pausing! Perhaps this time the best move is to watch and wait for some sign of those sometimes denied, or postponed underground springs. I believe the guides will help direct that flow of newfound energy up to the garden that you're creating alongside (not instead of) the old flat world of duty, and getting and spending. But I think what I've learned from mentors in my life about this place of waiting and tending, is that there may be a real need for patience here. This, I might add, for a Type A driven personality, proved one of the hardest lessons. It's still a challenge for me.

The summing up

Having reached the closing moment of this book it seems fitting to turn the final page and approach Rumi for our ultimate beacon of light. He tells us:

> ...The whole world
> is a form for truth.
>
> When someone does not feel grateful
> To that, the forms appear as he feels.
> They mirror his anger, his greed, and his fear.
> Make peace with the universe. Take joy in it.

Here he turns our last key to this quest and we travel on yet another beam of light. Rumi helps us imagine our way out of the remaining darkness of our interior worlds into the light of day or as he puts it, the light of joy.

He reminds us that so much of what we have discerned in finding our bearings and determining the actual direction of our lives turns on a feeling. A particular experience generated from the heart or soul is, according to Rumi, what it means to find what we've been seeking. It seems without it, we're all more or less lost, left still living in a prison of distorting mirrors. Everywhere we look, different versions of ourselves intrude and distort our take on reality. They become the bars of that cage keeping us from any hope of finding "a form for truth," of ever flying into the unseen. We live through our projections and so can never fulfill our destiny.

With **gratitude,** we can help ourselves displace projections and perhaps better see the world, or see it at least to the degree that it no longer merely reflects our issues.

But on top of this, Rumi, in his amazing way, not only shows what the key emotional guide is to seeing better in hopes of doing better but takes us further out of ourselves. He shows us how to generate gratitude. No longer adding our troubled issues to the picture, we are to "Make peace with the universe," to appreciate, venerate, even to celebrate the fact of this whole immense creation in all its complexity. He reminds us we're alive, and although we can never apprehend this vastness we can "Take joy in it." If we do, he promises:

> It will turn to gold. Resurrection
> Will be now. Every moment,
> A new beauty.

And he suggests that if we live in this potential, with this change of heart, and orient ourselves in this field of the world, we are that bird breaking from its cage. We are the phoenix.

Gratitude is the center, the golden mean. Forgiveness and joy coalesce to burn in the furnace of transformation, turning the present moment to gold—an ongoing experience of our lives as they are meant to be, will be. Every moment is rebirth where the phoenix rises. Here a new beauty is born. Now our imaginations fly.

Free.

And we come to know that it's only from a state of experienced freedom that we can responsibly recommit.

POSTSCRIPT
Studies and Service

The Canadian band *Rush* sings the way to a new consciousness:

> To sew a new mentality
> Closer to the Heart.

And goes on to imagine "…sailing into destiny."

The proof is in the studies

We're inundated with studies. However, many are based on hapless undergraduates who've been rounded up for someone's thesis. Because it's important to pay attention to work that has lasting value, I've chosen to list two classic studies that have stood the test of time. There are also brief examples below of what a few people have chosen to do when considering Marcus's question of service.

Huxley

The English writer Aldous Huxley attempted the heroic task of synthesizing all of the world's major religious traditions while extracting the universal aspects of each of them. This classic work *The Perennial Philosophy*[152] was written in the 1940s. Critics of this approach include those who argue that one should remain within one's own religious tradition. Students of comparative religion differ, often quoting Max Muller's point that "He who knows one, knows none." Huxley believed that stepping outside these boundaries was the best way of discovering truth, which is another argument for multidimensional vision. He was not necessarily advocating changing one's cultural inheritance.

Huxley's introduction to *The Perennial Philosophy* is a masterpiece. Here he argues,

> Knowledge is a function of being. When there is a change in the being of the knower, there is a corresponding change in the nature and amount of knowing.

Of course this is not popular with some in academia who see publication and research credits as the goal. Huxley pointed out that he included few quotes from men of letters or professional philosophers, and went on to say

> But the nature of this one Reality is such that it cannot be directly and immediately appre-hended except by those who have chosen to fulfil certain conditions, making themselves **loving, pure in heart, and poor in spirit**. [Author's emphasis.]

These are the necessary conditions to (in my words) "clear the decks" for the possible apprehension of higher truths. Here it's worth noting the role of the fourth energy center.

Nowadays we might expect a modern Huxley to present studies from brain research to support his challenging statement. And in fact, there is mounting evidence that states of being determine states of perception, as each of our diverse guides shows. But Huxley had a much more elegant idea. Just as we have no intuitive idea how oxygen and hydrogen combine to produce the unpredictable state of water, similarly, we have no real knowledge of the chemistry or alchemy of Huxley's three listed conditions.

Huxley drew on 3,000 years of evidence gathered from every corner of the globe. His book covers a huge terrain; enormous topics like truth, self-knowledge, and perseverance. His list of recommended books was a tour de force in his day, and many remain pertinent and relatively untrammeled by modernity.

As far as he was concerned, people can't be expected to transcend their normal and "unmodified condition" without knowledge of certain states of being. They can't be expected to know about other realities, as only someone in a state of **"detachment, charity and humility"** can hope to have such experiences. There's the "h" word again!

The Grant Study

Although it was published a generation ago (and later updated), I've found George Vaillant's *Adaptation to Life*[153] to be immensely helpful. It's a complement to Huxley's review of classic writings. By contrast, Vaillant based his book on detailed studies of many people over their lifetimes.

There are thousands of studies of people who have not "made it" in life. But the philanthropist William T. Grant wisely decided in 1937 to fund a different major longitudinal study (seven decades!) including 237 Harvard sophomores from the WW II classes and 323 inner city youths from Boston.

Because Vaillant needed a model to structure his findings he used the Freudian mechanisms of defense approach, which was highly topical at the time. Daily speech now includes many of these terms, and key examples will be reviewed below.

We do all have crunches!

The essence of his findings was that every life has its trials. We all have our Owain moments of being thrown out into the night. What's key is how we **adapt** to these crunches. The concept of adaptation is crucial to Vaillant, and to *The Secret Sabbatical*. I hope the tools and guides offer helpful ideas in this regard. It's adaptation and resilience (a current favorite word again) that's required to navigate successfully around the inevitable shoals and whirlpools of our lives.

The key findings

Vaillant has a graphically elegant set of charts that summarize his findings. In the diagram below, I've added only color.

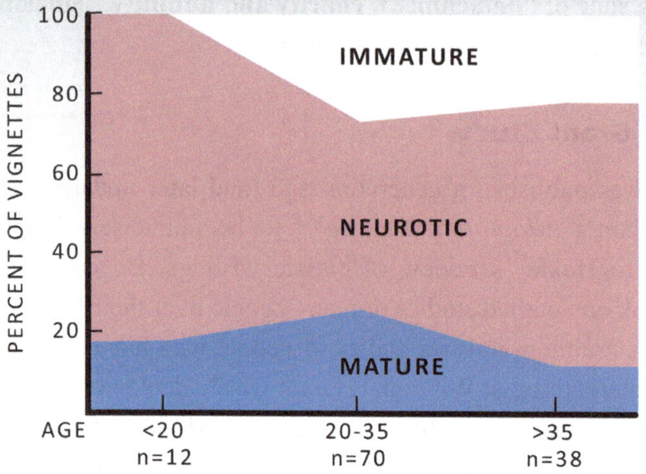

Shifts in Defensive Styles During the Adult Lives of Perpetual Boys.

The figure shows the defensive shifts of the seven Study subjects who never really entered the adult life cycle.

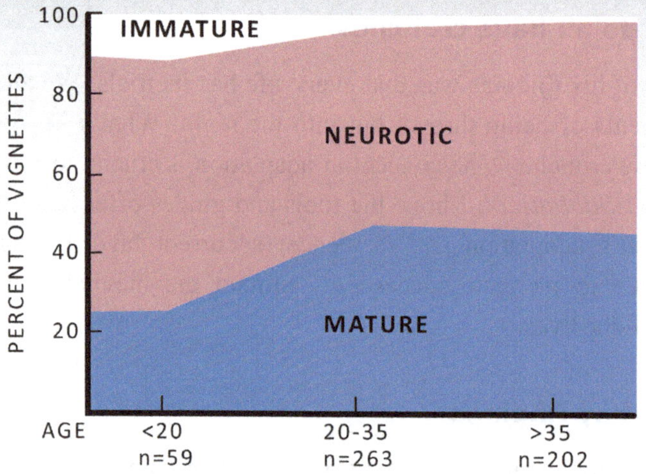

Shifts in Defensive Styles During the Adult Lives of Generative Men.

Defensive shifts of the thirty Best Outcomes.

Figure 15 - Adaptations to Life

Responses to life were measured in vignettes rated on very comprehensive questionnaires and interviews—these are fully reproduced in his book. Topics included childhood issues, social skills, physical and mental health, marital success and the key "maturity of defenses" scale.

Vaillant listed three levels of response in these diagrams. The top chart shows results for the "perpetual boys"—those who never entered fully into the challenges of adult life. As time passed, the percentage of "mature" responses declined—peaking in the subjects' late 20s. The percentage of neurotic responses increased over time.

By contrast, the lower chart shows the top 30 outcomes. Here the respondents used an increasing number of mature defenses as they moved into mid-life. Note that the neurotic responses don't go away! We never get it all right! Keep navigating!

Immature responses

These included the projections I've discussed: passive aggression, hypochondria and acting out in temper tantrums.

Neurotic responses

These are: intellectualization, repression (including inexplicable memory loss) and disassociation (where we drift off to avoid emotional distress for example.) Any of them sound familiar? It's likely, because even the best-adapted subjects still used a number of these to cope.

Mature responses

Although often listed in Freudian terms of the day, some of these are similar to what I've advocated in this book.

- ★ **Altruism** has a direct link to power-for others. When combined with the arts, it also connects to the esthetic concerns I've listed. When combined with charity work, it helps take people out of immediate survival concerns in the hope that higher centers can be activated. It includes the happily growing number of Foundations I'll mention.

- **Humor** is another way of adding dimension to a situation and is an incredibly creative adaptation. Not all humor has to be light—in fact the darkest frequently has the most power to cut through defenses. A New Yorker cartoon showed an embittered woman talking to an acquaintance saying simply, "He died of a bad case of me."

  Rumi was a master of humor and often enjoyed light and enlightening observations. Jon Stewart, Stephen Colbert, *The Big Bang Theory,* some Johnny Carson classics, Monty Python and some newer sources have been staples of my management sessions. I include them mostly because they're fun and, often, they just have a great way of making a point.

- Other mature responses include the ability to defer pleasure or stress and carry on with the task at hand. They include **anticipation, suppression and sublimation**. I've spoken about being able to shift ones' energy from fear, sex or control through the fourth energy center. This is a much richer view than mere sublimation, but it would look like sublimation to an observer using the Freudian model. (This is another example of how our frameworks limit us.)

Marriage and AA!

In a radio interview, Vaillant said the two most effective change programs were a good marriage and Alcoholics Anonymous (AA). I would add that both of these involve a willingness to listen and change. Many long-term marriage partners will attest to rough periods when they needed to work through key issues. Founded on an intervention by Carl Jung, AA linked the crisis of the spirit to a crisis of using spirits. Although I'm told AA's long-term success rate is about 10%, the Program has some amazingly effective and simple slogans designed to help keep one in the moment and on course. In teaching self-awareness, for example, it helps its members to note instances of such things as their own "stinking thinking," which echoes Marcus's awareness of judgments.

Some of the work of personal change is simple in concept but not easy in execution. Huxley and Vaillant knew this.

Examples of Service

One way of staying in touch with the challenges of newfound freedom is to repeat the question we initially asked to help us out of the cage: "Who do I serve?" This question helps us free ourselves to live with this sense of freedom and to realize that we were born free. It can also point to which exemplars one could choose in future. Many fellow voyagers have gone beyond their fate and managed to write, paint, dance, sing—to make some kind of art out of it. Some convey that this is an ongoing process—never a done deal. So when you begin locating those "happier friends" that Rumi speaks of, how will you return to the real world of the castle and try to function with integrity? You might hope that your fractals of influence can replicate and evolve.

Recently I was distressed to see a local charity in my hometown shamed when the directors were found to have enjoyed lavish trips to New York for "research" funded in part by donations—some of which were mine. The intended recipients—the downtown poor—were nothing less than a vehicle for certain members in this group to enjoy a rich lifestyle. Similarly some teachers' unions, as well as other groups, resist being scrutinized to preserve seniority status for the privileged few. They are another holdover from a past that perpetuates privilege over service.[154] Each story of the abuse of privilege can be a danger to our quest. We may react by closing ranks and retreating into our bunkers, which reflects a return to a cage of sorts—but this time with justification, we may feel.

A better solution, I suggest, is to apply our experience and knowledge and advocate—possibly demand—greater accountability in all spheres of society, not just charity or education.

So the final stage of the Course has morphed into a new emphasis—how to research and find causes and organizations that do accomplish meaningful and provable change in line with values we wish to see perpetuated.

I'll start at the top of the asset scale, but stress again that scale seems to be of little significance to what "works" as a satisfying experience for both giver and beneficiary. The power of fractals is another way of imagining that initial scale is not necessarily the key to change. I'll note other examples over time in the blog that accompanies this book.

Compassion with accountability

I had a profound experience watching octogenarian investor Warren Buffett's respond to PBS interviewer Charlie Rose a few years back. Buffet has spent a lifetime generating wealth and creating a legendary community of satisfied investors, but during the interview he made an interesting point, one I hadn't really thought about. Buffet stressed that he, and many of us, have spent a lifetime concerned with the accumulation of assets while spending far less time—if any—researching how our funds are to be allocated in our estates. We have not asked how we would like our efforts and earnings to be distributed back into the world. He made another point too, about himself; he didn't want his family deprived of meaningful work by receiving too much money. They needed the opportunity to make their way in the world. Buffet stressed that he also wanted his hard-earned funds channeled in the way he had become accustomed to in his own successful professional life—this included transparency and accountability. Intense research led him to pass vast sums (85% of his assets) to another wealthy family—the Bill and Melinda Gates Foundation—because they had similar values, including a sterling track record of measurable results.

Whatever reputation Microsoft had, it is unquestionably true that the Gates family has had an extraordinary impact over their lifetimes. Allocating their time and their wealth has resulted in great successes. An article on Bill and Melinda appeared in an online issue of *Fast Company* magazine under the heading: "Bill Gates Says The World Is Getting Vastly Better, While Crushing Myths About Foreign Aid."[155] One of the myths he has begun to demolish is that slashing death rates will lead to greater population growth. The opposite is the case, and he points out that over half of the world's population now lives in middle-class countries that have achieved meaningful improvements in living conditions over the past 50 years.

And it's significant to me (having seen a plethora of new buildings and "brands" emerging on top campuses) that Gates is not interested in building stone and concrete edifices with his name emblazoned on the façade.

In a movement that counters at least some of the justifiable criticism of the 1%, it's also true that over 120 billionaires have pledged to dedicate the majority of their wealth to philanthropy with "The Giving Pledge."[156] One of the first of these was the team of Jim and Marilyn Simons. He has had an extraordinary life, including bridging one of the most prolific careers in advanced mathematics with new hires from physics, cryptography, computational linguistics to form the predecessor to the spectacularly successful Renaissance Technologies investment firm. This was a pioneering interdisciplinary success and one of the origins of so-called big data. His wife, who is an economist, is said to have helped set up a series of philanthropic ventures. Now in his mid-70s, he recently said that this is the side of his life that is accelerating, encompassing massive grants to mathematics education in schools and basic research.[157] Described as "seeker, doer, giver, ponderer," Simons blends academic, practical, philanthropic and reflective qualities.

Another billionaire openly confesses that he seeks the company of fellow big-hitters at an annual gala to fund the biggest anti-poverty set of programs in New York. His fund, "The Robin Hood Foundation," is intriguing in that it does indeed take from the (this time willing) rich and give to the poor, although they don't exactly toss bags of gold onto the streets. Instead, there is an office full of accountants and analysts who measure the effectiveness of every expenditure and program in which the fund invests. Each year, there is turnover of those beneficiaries who have not met the foundation's goals. This benefactor targets his activities in the New York region where he plans to do better by acting locally.

The founder, Paul Tudor Jones, realized at some point in his material success that he had—in his words—"a hole in his soul." This echoes Rumi's sentiments exactly and calls up his wonderful line "You that were soul gazing became soul." Gazing after soul is, I think, another way of describing a longing that will not leave us, or it won't if we're fortunate. It's having that same feeling Tudor Jones had, that something is wrong and must be fixed.

And for Rumi, you may recall, this is the greatest gift of all. To be "called" is to be reminded of what's important.

Tudor Jones freely confesses to having made early mistakes with charitable giving. For instance, a school program in his hometown fell apart through lack of accountability. He tells us this mistake changed him and after much deliberation he decided that he'd have to do things another way. He adopted the way of tough love which, as it turns out, was a good move. What he revealed in a fascinating segment on CBS's *60 Minutes* is that even a seasoned businessperson has much to learn about the world of giving back.[158]

There are hundreds of other models. Using the power of leverage, I've found giving to Kiva.org a remarkable experience. This organization funds microcredit initiatives in many countries. Each credit card donation (starting at $25) gets assigned to the donor's chosen loan seeker and then having contributed, the donor can follow their progress. When the recipient repays their loan, the amount is freed up for further recycling. There is a 98.87% repayment rate, and they lend two million dollars each week. The website "Charity Navigator" gives them its highest rating.

In the late nineteenth-century a Catholic priest, Fr. Michael McGivney, founded a low-key organization named to resonate with the Knights of old. It was a fraternal organization to help provide for the families of poor immigrants who could find support nowhere else. Today the Knights of Columbus has almost two million members, all dedicated to a shared set of principles: charity, unity and fraternity. Though the vast majority of these modern day "knights" are working class men, without the fortunes or connections of a Buffet or Gates, they managed to give $1.5 billion in charitable contributions in the past decade. Grassroots activities are at the heart of this organization, where individual efforts do make a difference.

The City of Vancouver, Canada, is home to The Vancouver Foundation. I've attended an allocation meeting and although my experience is limited, I'd say they do a focused job of stewarding donated funds into specific tightly framed and monitored projects on social and environmental issues.

The bottom line to all this talk about effective giving may be best expressed in another of Rumi's sweeping ideas—that there are "a hundred ways to kneel and kiss the ground."

The narrative continues

Vaillant and others argue that we all need our own narrative—a tale of our lives that frames our efforts to adapt and remain strong. But how do we hold the threads of that tale together and create some semblance of the life we've wished for without losing heart when it doesn't come about exactly as we've hoped? Here the Owain story can serve as an example—a tale of adventure, challenge, suffering, personal change and finally, success. As I see it, besides all of the above, the one other crucial thing we need is for the script to be ours—for the tale to be our own.

About the Author

David Cawood's practice involves three distinct but related fields—organizations, the humanities, and applied science.

Organizations. David worked as a manager, then head office executive, before completing an MBA and Ph.D. and serving on the faculty of a business school. He was a founding member of the first North American Strategic Consulting Group with what is now Deloitte. After a few years, he built an international consulting company, described as the most consistently successful strategic consultancy on the West Coast. This involved several decades of work with very large firms such as HP, De Beers and Deloitte. Clients include a wide range of organizations, from engineering, health care, and infrastructure, to education and research. In addition to the main consulting work, he designed and then handed over executive development workshops for universities and in-house colleges in several countries.

The humanities. The humanities have historically recognized the power of the human imagination and offered successful examples of paths to needed change. David has kept this track of interest alive in his practice by following those who keep evolving the great traditions of the humanities through film, novels and other media. Over the years he's offered ongoing workshops with Continuing Studies adult audiences, Jung Societies and other forums that have relevance to current personal and organizational dilemmas.

Applied science. As an Adjunct Professor of Strategy and Leadership in Applied Science at the University of British Columbia David has taken a keen interest in that key intersecting realm of applied science. But his university and in-house college work can offer only a few ideas from this book, as this material is for readers willing to go on a far-ranging interdisciplinary journey—beyond any single faculty.

He lives on a creek in West Vancouver with his wife, the artist Alexis Cawood.

Notes

1 Harold Goddard. *The Meaning of Shakespeare.* University of Chicago Press, 1951. (Two Volumes.) Goddard has been a major influence on this entire Project. He was a Professor of English, who had a profound impact on his students who became included in a community with him, his wife and daughters. Amongst other books, he wrote an essay on each of the plays of Shakespeare. They are in a different league for me. No other critic has this combination of clarity, deep respect for, and love of, the work, and the ability to range over all of Shakespeare and other greats for perspective.

2 Alan Lakein. *How to Get Control of Your Time and Your Life.* Signet, 1973. I used Lakein as the starting point for self-management courses and he was helpful. His approach was one of the more thorough, but still lacked the needed introspection and deeper enquiry needed for the Course.

3 C.S. Lewis. *An Experiment in Criticism.* Cambridge University Press, 1961. Lewis wrote some interesting pieces, including the famed Narnia children's series, some great criticism and science fiction too. I recommend any collections of his adult writing, in particular *"The Screwtape Letters."*

4 Sam Harris. *Free Will.* Free Press, 2012. http://www.samharris.org/blog/item/life-without-free-will/#sthash.RIg9BAiR.dpuf

5 Henry James. *The American.* Signet Classics, 2005. Originally published: James R. Osgood, 1877. The text is also on Project Gutenberg: http://www.gutenberg.org/ebooks/177

6 Philip Tetlock. *Expert Political Judgment: How Good Is It? How Can We Know?* Princeton University Press, 2005. Tetlock is not as well known as he should be. If he were, many talking heads would disappear. Don't buy blindly into this pundit industry. It turns out that most pundits are worse at prediction than the rest of us. Even more alarmingly, the more certain and focused the expert, the less accurate the predictions.

7 The thirteenth-century poet, Jalaluddin Rumi is quoted throughout this book. His poems were dictated and were not originally titled. We use the translations of Coleman Barks, referred to in the acknowledgements. They are featured in many sources and I found the following helpful: Denise Breton and Christopher Largent.

Love Soul and Freedom: Dancing with Rumi on the Mythic Path. Hazelden, 1998. This is generally a wonderful and respectful initial guide to Rumi.

[8] I recall this concept (this is not his name for it) from the English writer Colin Wilson who told of this insight coming to him on a train journey he took regularly. At the same point in the journey on each trip (about 20 minutes into the ride) he found he was suddenly engaged in the chosen task if he had continued to focus and avoid the distractions associated with putting off that challenging project.

[9] Jim Collins. *Good to Great: Why Some Companies make the Leap and Others Don't.* HarperBusiness, 2001. A beautifully written book that has had very wide circulation. The values are as sustainable as the companies he studied. A gem from the book that is only half humorous; if you see the CEO of a favorite company on the cover of *Fortune*, short the stock!

[10] Huge feasts were not just the stuff of myth. For example, the guests at a feast held in the fifteenth-century at Cawood Castle in York consumed 1,000 capons and 25,000 gallons of wine. The castle is partially restored in the village of Cawood, near York.

[11] Re-told by the author from *The Mabinogion* and from: Heinrich Zimmer. *The King and the Corpse.* Pantheon Books, 1948. This inspired Campbell (who edited the book) and others, and contains our story of Owain, which is called "Owain. The Knight of the Lion."

[12] Aldous Huxley. *The Perennial Philosophy*. Harper and Row, 1944. This a survey by a brilliant and enquiring person of the similarities underlying the world's moral and religious teachers at a deep structural level. *The New York Times* called it "The masterpiece of all anthologies," and I agree. The five page Introduction alone is extraordinary and points out how few academic philosophers made the cut. This book appears again in the Postscript.

[13] The whole question of gender and the Jungian concepts that we will raise can get complex. But for a first run at the topic in this book I'm staying with Jung's gender roles.

[14] Arnold Toynbee. *A Study of History*. The one volume edition revised and abridged by the author and Jane Caplan. Oxford University Press in association with Thames and Hudson, 1972. The original is a massive 12 volume set and was Toynbee's magnum opus. The volume I cite here is wonderfully illustrated and is the recommended entry point to this material if available. Despite his critics, I think this is a great overview. A recent article in *The Times Literary Review* ("Civilized Values: The return of Arnold Toynbee?" October 24, 2104) calls for a

re-appraisal of Toynbee, arguing for example that his views on China were highly prescient. It concludes that it's time to return to his civilizational perspective.

[15] "Workplace Distractions: Here's Why You Won't Finish This Article." *The Wall Street Journal*. December 11, 2012. Of course, if the first observation is accurate, the second implies no further interruptions must occur for at least 23 minutes in order to achieve any progress toward the original task.

[16] http://www.msf-usa.org/motion.html

[17] Proverbs. 29:18 (King James Version).

[18] Plato. *Cratylus.* (MIT Classics). http://classics.mit.edu/Plato/cratylus.html This is a paraphrase by later philosophers. It was actually Plato who wrote (as Socrates): "Heraclitus is supposed to say that all things are in motion and nothing at rest; he compares them to the stream of a river, and says that you cannot go into the same water twice."

[19] William Wordsworth, "Lines composed above Tintern Abbey." *Lyrical Ballads, with a Few Other Poems.* J & A Arch. 1798.

[20] John Dewey, the American philosopher and psychologist, made this clear.

[21] Jacob Hirsh. Quoted on CBC Show in the *Ideas* series, "The Imagination Part 1." October 17, 2012. Also personal communication.

[22] Values, according to the philosopher John Dewey, need to be chosen, prized and *acted upon*, as I've said. Ideals, on the other hand, are *potential* values until brought into action, in this way of framing the distinction.

[23] William Shakespeare. *King Lear.* IV (i).

[24] Ibid. Act IV (i)

[25] Immanuel Kant. *Critique of Pure Reason.* First edition, 1781. I'm not recommending that you rush out to read Kant in the original. However, if you ever have time with a real reading window, you might start with a basic outline guide, and then try the original in sections. It is accessible, while many commentators have been talking about him from secondary sources and making it harder.

[26] There are many references to this "observer effect." One of the most clear, yet fundamental, discussions is by the physicist Neil Turok (now director of the Perimeter Institute in Canada) in *The Universe Within: From Quantum to Cosmos*. The CBC Massey Lectures 2012. House of Anansi Press, 2012. Turok has

collaborated with Hawking and held a chair of mathematical physics at Cambridge.

[27] Gaston Bachelard. *Air & Dreams: An Essay on the Imagination of Movement.* Dallas Institute Publications, 1988. Originally published 1943 in French. Not easy to read for someone trained in a linear way of thinking. His work is highly poetic and filled with extraordinary insight.

[28] C. G. Jung. *Modern Man in Search of a Soul.* Harcourt. First published 1933. A great background on Jung's work was an edition edited by Jung with chapters by various experts. It's called *Man and His Symbols*, and if you can find a hardcover edition, the illustrations are wonderful too. I wish Jung himself had enlisted the aid of an editor as his audience would have been far wider. But it was only late in his life that a much larger general audience discovered him through a BBC interview. His autobiography *Memories, Dreams and Reflections* is very accessible.

[29] James Hillman. *Re-Visioning Psychology.* Harper and Row, 1977. This is regarded by some as his best work and was nominated for the Pulitzer Prize. Hillman was deeply experienced in mythology and Jungian psychology and attending his workshops was always an imaginative journey.

[30] This image is nearly half a century old. I've seen it on many college bulletin boards, thankfully. http://www.nasa.gov/content/forty-fifth-anniversary-of-earthrise-image/#.U_JMjbxdXJI Campbell commented on this at about the time he was involved in interviews with Bill Moyers at Skywalker Ranch after admiring the first *Star Wars* stories. He saw them as examples of the modernization of those ancient themes. It is to me a great pity that the series of films seemed to implode.

[31] O'Toole, J. "Declining Innovation: The Failure of Success, A Summary Report of the Seventh Twenty Year Forecast Project." Los Angeles: Centre for Futures Research, Graduate School of Business, University of Southern California, Los Angeles, 1983. O'Toole used the name "Monolithic Motors" for what was said at the time to be a thin disguise for GM.

[32] Stephen Covey, *The Seven Habits of Highly Effective People.* Free Press, 2004. This is one of the classics in the field and was indeed based on sound values. Recommended by many—practiced by few. This book enlarges on Covey's beautifully phrased idea of "sharpening the saw" as one of his major habits. Some other material in Covey was recycled time management material from Peter Drucker and others. But much management theory is recycled from Peter Drucker!

[33] Rebecca Costa, *The Watchman's Rattle: A Radical New Theory of Collapse.* Vanguard Press, 2012.

[34] Joseph Campbell, *The Hero with a Thousand Faces.* Princeton University Press, 1972. The works of Joseph Campbell are foundational, I believe. He was sometimes criticized by academics because he became increasingly involved in making himself clear to the layperson. His interviews with Bill Moyers were inspirational to thousands. His lectures were truly unforgettable to those of us lucky enough to hear him. Some are preserved on video. His books are highly recommended. *Myths to Live By* is a good start.

[35] Joseph Campbell. *Creative Mythology*. Vol. 4 of *The Masks of God*. Penguin Books, 1991.

[36] The model I'm quoting here is a nine-factor structure going back possibly many centuries. It's called The Enneagram. The book I recommended is by Helen Palmer. *The Enneagram: Understanding Yourself and Others in Your Life.* Thorsons, 1991. Some others turn this model into an entirely positive take on all aspects of behavior and undermine one of the key contributions of the framework which is to see into the excess uses of your style and take steps to change them. People exercising excess control are turned into "leaders" in a particularly egregious example of one of these "keep it positive" variations. This aspect is also highlighted in my workbook based on the Jungian Typology.

[37] Oliver Burkeman, *The Antidote: Happiness for People Who Can't Stand Positive Thinking.* Faber and Faber, 2012.

[38] Miya Tokumitsu. "In the Name of Love." *Jacobin Magazine.* Issue # 13.

[39] Andrew Nikiforuk. "A Big Summer Story You Missed: Soaring Oil Debt." *The Tyee.ca*, 29 Aug 2014. http://thetyee.ca/Opinion/2014/08/29/Soaring-Oil-Debt-Summer/?utm_source=mondayheadlines&utm_medium=email&utm_campaign=010914 Nikiforuk is a powerful and gifted writer on environmental issues and is based in the center of Canada's oil sands industry. In this article he points to the inherent unsustainability of current oil strategies relying on higher cost, higher risk sources.

[40] E.O. Wilson, "Social Studies." *The Globe and Mail*, October 29, 2012.

[41] Thomas Homer-Dixon, "Climate Change's Costs Hit the Plate." *The Globe and Mail*, July 24, 2012.

[42] Robert D. Hare. "*Without Conscience: The Disturbing World of the Psychopaths Among Us.*" Pocket Books, 1995. Dr. Hare is a world leader in this field and an Emeritus Professor at The University of British Columbia. He has been misquoted

on estimates of the prevalence of psychopathy in the Corporate World and his own responses can be found at www.hare.org/comments/comments2.html Bob Hare is now expressing some ambivalence about having released his model to a wider public, including the U.S correctional system where it has a big impact on parole decisions.

[43] Jon Ronson. *"The Psychopath Test: A Journey Through the Madness Industry."* Picador, 2011.

[44] "I Write, Therefore I Am." *The Economist*, September 10, 2011: 56.

[45] Dan Ariely, *Predictably Irrational.* Harper, 2009.

[46] Antonio Domasio. *The Feeling of What Happens: Body and Emotion in the Making of Consciousness*. Harcourt, 2000.

[47] Daniel Kahneman, *Thinking, Fast and Slow.* Doubleday, 2011

[48] Technically, this was defined as the number of transistors that can be placed efficiently on an integrated circuit.

[49] Ray Kurzweil. The *Singularity is Near: When Humans Transcend Biology.* Penguin, 2006. The actual measure used by Kurzweil is the more technical MIPS (millions of instructions per second) per dollar.

[50] Our entire planet and every organism on it is composed of remnants of one or more spectacular supernova explosions.

[51] Numerous books have covered this topic. They include Jonah Lehrer's *How We Decide* and Dan Ariely's *Predictably Irrational.* A much earlier classic was the beautifully written *Dragons of Eden* by Carl Sagan from 1986.

[52] Neil Postman, *Amusing Ourselves to Death*. Penguin, 1986.

[53] Martin Lindstrom, *Brandwashed*. Crown, 2011. This includes reference to a multiyear, multimillion-dollar experiment around Axe male body spray, which proved too successful as schools had to ban the product from eager users.

[54] Robert B. Cialdini, *Influence: The Psychology of Persuasion.* Harper Business, 2006

[55] The Israelis found themselves caught in a double bind during the 2014 summer conflict with Hamas. To justify their thousands of missile attacks they stressed that the missiles were needed because the Israeli population was at grave risk. When Israel's main Ben Gurion airport was shut down after a near miss from a rocket from Gaza the Israelis argued there was no need to re-route flights as the

situation was fully under control. I am not taking sides here—as Hamas itself is no stranger to fear mongering.

[56] "iCrazy: Panic, Depression, Psychosis: How Connection Addiction Is Rewiring Our Brains." *Newsweek*, July 16 2012.

[57] Antonio Gramsci. *Selections from the Prison Notebooks of Antonio Gramsci.* International Publishers. 1971

[58] Stangler D, Arbesman S. "What Does Fortune 500 Turnover Mean?" Ewing Marion Kauffman Foundation. June 2012. This is an interesting analysis of the classic "Fortune turnover" statistics, suggesting that they are easily over-simplified. The number I use is taken from their quote from *Built to Last* by Jim Collins.

[59] Rainer Maria Rilke. "Archaic Torso of Apollo." "Archaiser Torso Apollos." *New Poems (1908) The Other Part*. Translation by the author.

[60] Michael Lewis. *Flash Boys: A Wall Street Revolt.* Norton, 2014.

[61] These include books such as: Ken Wilbur. *The Theory of Everything;* Arthur Young. *The Self Reflexive Universe;* W.B. Yeats. *A Vision*. There are some fascinating comments in a recent biography of Yeats that suggests Yeats's wife shrewdly realized the value of her visions to their relationship.

[62] Sam Harris. *The End of Faith: Religion. Terror and the Future of Reason*. W.W. Norton & Co, 2004.

[63] Peter Senge. *The Fifth Discipline: The Art and Practice of the Learning Organization.* Doubleday,1990. A great and clear book by a gifted thinker and teacher.

[64] Stuart Kauffman. *At Home in the Universe: The Search for the Laws of Self-Organization and Complexity*. Oxford University Press, 1995. This is a wide-ranging and challenging book that shows the interplay between evolution and self-organization.

[65] There are many great books on fractals, and some very good DVDs. Arthur Clarke, for example, made an accessible DVD on this topic. It was called *"The Colours of Infinity"* and is on YouTube: https://www.youtube.com/watch?v=Lk6QU94xAb8. One web site is the fractalfoundation.org.

[66] James Hillman. "The Spindrift Gaze Toward Paradise." Essay in *The Rag and Bone Shop of the Heart*. Harper Collins, 1992. Many of the essays written by the editors of this book: Bly, Hillman and Meade, are wonderfully concise frameworks

for what is a great anthology of poetry aimed at men and admired by several women I know.

[67] Antonio Machado. "The Wind, One Brilliant Day." Translated by Robert Bly. *Times Alone: Selected Poems of Antonio Machado*. Wesleyan University Press, 1987. P. 57

[68] Robert Bly. *Iron John: A Book About Men*. Perseus Books, 1990. This was one of the drivers of a remarkable series of sessions led by Bly, Hillman and others. They themselves decided to end them. A very similar image formed the basis of an unforgettable scene in the wonderful movie *The Mission*. The De Niro character dragged his armor up a massive waterfall as a monumental act of repentance for his mercenary past.

[69] Quoted in *"The Globe and Mail."* August 21. 2012. p A 3.

[70] Jacqueline Murray. Prof of History at the University of Guelph. In op-ed article for *The Globe and Mail.* 22 Aug 2012.p A 11.

[71] Carl Jung (editor). *Man and His Symbols.* Anchor Books, 1964. One of the most accessible accounts of this topic was written by one of Jung's associates, the hugely talented Marie-Louise von Franz. The chapter is called "The Process of Individuation". The hard cover edition of this book is beautifully illustrated.

[72] James Hollis. *What Matters Most: Living a More Considered Life*. Gotham Books, 2009.

[73] D.H. Lawrence. "Healing." *The Complete Poems of D.H. Lawrence*. Wordsworth Editions, 1994.

[74] I was fortunate to hear Campbell speak on this at the University of British Columbia and some other occasions.

[75] Barbara L. Fredrickson. *Love 2.0: How Our Supreme Emotion Affects Everything We Feel, Think, Do, and Become.* Hudson Street Press, 2013. The book provides fascinating support for the timeless intuitions of spiritual leaders. Probably justifiably (after many setbacks from charlatans) our age demands proof of claims affecting mental states and health, and this is now happily becoming increasingly available through real time functional magnetic imaging (fMRI) and other active indicators of physiological processes.

[76] Jonathan Haidt. *The Righteous Mind—Why Good People are Divided by Politics and Religion*. Pantheon, 2012. Interestingly it's the political conservatives who end up with a more "balanced" set of responses on Haidt's fascinating set of six underlying factors.

[77] Iris Murdoch. "The Sublime and the Good." In *The Chicago Review*, Vol 13 Issue 3 (Autumn 1959).

[78] E.M. Forster. *Howards End.* Random House, 1921

[79] Earnings before interest, taxes and depreciation. An accounting measure that tries to isolate factors in management's control to measure their contributions (and sometimes to calculate their bonus). Like most of these measures it is limiting, encourages short term decisions, and can be easily manipulated between time periods.

[80] The number of times EBITDA will be multiplied to set a sales price, given the industry and economic climate.

[81] Often unstated, but clearly visible, motivation. See either "Wall Street" movie.

[82]John Stackhouse Jr. "What's Good about Good Friday?" *The Globe and Mail.* March 29, 2013.

[83] "When Power Goes To Your Head, It may Shut Out Your Heart." Chris Benderev: NPR. Aug 10, 2013 Quoting Dacher Keltner, a social psychologist at UC Berkeley. This article comments on the original journal article "Power Changes How the Brain Responds to Others", by Jeremy Hogeveen, Michael Inzlicht and Sukhvinder Obhi: *Journal of Experimental Psychology*, 2013. 6/6/13

[84] Rollo May. *Love and Will.* W.W. Norton and Co, 1969. A classic. Simply one of the most inspiring books I've read. May made the crucial point that the modern malaise of being disconnected—where one experiences neither love nor will, would lead next to violence as the only way out of this alienated state.

[85] Walter W. Skeat. *The Concise Dictionary of English Etymology*. Wordsworth Reference, 1993.

[86] Robert K. Greenleaf. *Servant Leadership: A journey into the nature of legitimate power and greatness.* Paulist Press. 1977. This has been (to those who follow management writing) one of the great inspirations for a generation. Greenleaf was an executive himself at AT&T who took early retirement to develop his ideas on the change from "top down" power. Of course, the old ways live on too!

[87] Adam Grant. *Give and Take*. Viking, 2013.

[88] Nassim Nichol Taleb. *The Black Swan: The Impact of the Highly Improbable.* Random House, 2007. This book has had extraordinary success, having sold over 3 million copies. Taleb's key point is not to try to anticipate unusual events (by definition they are not predictable). He suggests investigating greater resilience in our lives—not only financially.

---

[89] Sylvia Nasar. *A Beautiful Mind: The Life of Mathematical Genius and Nobel Laureate John Nash.* Simon and Schuster, 1998. A biography of the rise, fall, and the redemption of sorts, of a genius. Russell Crowe played one of his better roles in the movie.

[90] Semir Zeki et al. "The Experience of Mathematical Beauty and its Neural Correlates." *Frontiers in Human Neuroscience,* 13 Feb 2014. jdoi: 10.3389/fnhum.2014.00068, Some author quotes appear in the later article "The Beauty of Math." *Scientific American Mind.* Sep/Oct 2014.

[91] John Keats. "Ode to a Grecian Urn." *Annals of the Fine Arts*, Issue No. 15. Jan 1820,

[92] Nalbantian, Suzanne "Neuroaesthetics: neuroscientific theory and illustration from the arts." *Interdisciplinary Science Reviews* **33**(4): 357–368 December 2008.

[93] Paul Dirac. "The Relation between mathematics and physics." *Proc R Society Edinburgh.* 59, 1212-129,1939. Also quoted in above article.

[94] Claudia Townsend and Sanjay Sood. "Self Affirmation through the Choice of Highly Aesthetic Products." *J. of Consumer Research.* Vol 39, Aug 2012.

[95] Fyodor Dostoevsky. *The Brothers Karamazov* translated by Richard Pevear and Larissa Volokhonsky. Farrar, Straus and Giroux, 1990. It's essential where possible to read the Russians in translations by these two I suggest. Perhaps begin with the chapter called "The Grand Inquisitor," and chapters leading up to this. When Jesus returns, the Church finds his influence will be detrimental to their social order and puts him to death. This is evil incarnate. The subsequent part of the book seems to me sometimes over-written for a modern audience.

[96] *As Good as it Gets.* The movie.

[97] The concept of transforming symbols is central to the work of Carl Jung. He identified "eternal" symbols that populate and influence our deep unconscious minds and that have been revealed across the world in numerous cultures, both ancient and modern. A good introduction is *Man and His Symbols.* Edited by Jung himself. Doubleday, 1964. While the symbols may be universal they have taken on different tones in different cultures over the millennia. The dragon has different connotations in the West than in China, for example, but has been powerful in both.

[98] A great deal was added to the Grail imagery in later times, including an attempt to turn the story into a Christian allegory.

[99] T.S. Eliot. "The Cocktail Party." in *The Complete Poems and Plays of T.S. Eliot*. Faber and Faber, 1930.

[100] Daniel Dennett. "Dangerous Memes." TED talk, Feb 2001.

[101] Seneca. *On the Shortness of Life.* Penguin Great Ideas, 2005.

[102] *The Nature of Things* series on Canada's CBC TV network. This show was called "A Dog's Life" and includes Dr.Carolyn Walsh, Assistant Professor of Psychology at Memorial University of Newfoundland. 21 Nov 2013.

[103] Ferdinand Lot, quoted in Pierre Hadot. *The Inner Citadel*: *The Meditations of Marcus Aurelius.* Translated by Michael Chase. Harvard University Press, 1998.

[104] "Keep calm and think on: How the ancients can save today's world." *The Globe and Mail.* November 25, 2013.

[105] See "other writings" under this entry for James Stockdale. http://en.wikipedia.org/wiki/James_Stockdale

[106] Tom Wolf. *A Man in Full.* Farrar, Straus & Giroux, 1998. A novel that introduces Epictetus in an ingenious way.

[107] Pierre Hadot. *The Inner Citadel: The Meditations of Marcus Aurelius.* Harvard University Press, 1998.

[108] *The Meditations of Marcus Aurelius Antoninus.* Translated by George Long. Circa 1890. I have modernized archaic words, such as "thee." Available on the web at several sites including the Internet Archive from The University of Toronto. https://archive.org/details/meditationsofemp00marcuoft

[109] D.H. Lawrence. *A Selection from Phoenix*. Penguin, 1971.

[110] The wildly popular BBC show *Top Gear* is becoming increasingly desperate for content as it proves less and less interesting to compare one over-priced 550 horsepower car with another over-priced 600 horsepower car. Neither can be driven to a fraction of their potential outside a racetrack.

[111] Friedriche Nietzsche. *Ecce Homo*. Cambridge University Press, 2005. Translation by the author.

[112] James Hollis. *What Matters Most: Living a More Considered Life.* Gotham Books, 2009. Hollis has a justifiably loyal workshop following and is a deep expert on the works of Carl Jung, as well as a practising therapist and author.

[113] William James. *Principles of Psychology*. First published, 1890. This book is a masterpiece of insight and research. It's a true classic still often re-read by

current leaders in the field. The chapter with my reference is called "The Perception of Time." Re-published by Cosimo Classic, 2013.

[114] *The Meditations of Marcus Aurelius Antoninus.* Ibid.

[115] William Shakespeare. *Hamlet.* 2 (ii). In much of what Hamlet says (especially to the characters in this scene) there's a level of irony at play. This doesn't detract from these lines in a broader sense.

[116] *The Meditations of Marcus Aurelius Antoninus.* Ibid.

[117] *The I Ching.* Ancient book of Changes from China. There are many translations and Carl Jung was a great admirer. He wrote an introduction to a classic translation by Richard Wilhelm and linked it to his ideas on synchronicity and interconnectedness. The material can easily be perverted into a simplistic form of prophesy but the underlying wisdom from Confucius is profound. A helpful introduction to its potential levels is Carol K. Anthony. *The Philosophy of the I Ching*. Anthony Publishing Co., 1981.

[118] Edward de Bono. *Lateral Thinking: A Textbook on Creativity.* Penguin Books, 1977. This book by the Maltese physician and consultant was the classic beginning of a stream of books by creativity gurus, most of them based on "out of the box" metaphors. Many are repetitious and I feel there are limits to capturing the imaginative process in conceptual webs.

[119] Idries Shah. *The Exploits of the Incomparable Mulla Nasrudin.* Octagon Press, 1983. I've paraphrased the story. Shah was a complex and controversial character. His work on bringing the wisdom of the Sufis to the West was highly regarded. He influenced many Western thinkers including the novelist Doris Lessing who appreciated his clarity. The Nasrudin character is one of those wise fools who point to the absurdity of some of our beliefs and attitudes in the tradition of the Court fools and of people like Shakespeare's Falstaff. He pricks vanity and helps with perspective.

[120] Bob Dylan. "You Gotta Serve Somebody." Lyric.

[121] Pierre Hadot. *The Inner Citadel: The Meditations of Marcus Aurelius.* Harvard University Press, 1998.

[122] Harold Goddard. *The Meaning of Shakespeare. Vol 2.* "King Lear." University of Chicago Press, 1951

[123] Jill Bolte Taylor. *My Stroke of Insight: A Brain Scientist's Personal Journey.* Viking Adult, 2008.

[124] Newberg and D'Aquili. *Why God Won't Go Away: Brain Science and the Biology of Belief.* Ballantine Books, 2001.

[125] Charles Muses. In an interview on *Thinking Allowed* TV series with Jeffrey Mishlove.

[126] Jill Bolte Taylor. *My Stroke of Insight: A Brain Scientist's Personal Journey*. Viking Adult, 2008.

[127] Immanuel Kant. *Critique of Pure Reason.* First edition, 1781

[128] James Hollis *What Matters Most: Living a More Considered Life*. Gotham Books, 2009.

[129] Shaun Tomson with Patrick Moser. *Surfer's Code*. Gibbs Smith, 2006.

[130] Jill Bolte Taylor. "My Stroke of Insight" presentation. TED network http://www.ted.com/talks/jill_bolte_taylor_s_powerful_stroke_of_insight.html

[131] *How the Earth Changed History*. A BBC miniseries with Iain Stewart. "The Skies Above", season 1, episode 3.

[132] Peter Ouspensky. *Tertium Organum: The Fourth Dimension as the Esoteric Nature of reality.* Alfred A Knopf. Originally published in the early 1920s, it remains in print today in new versions. It has passages of unsupported mysticism that were prevalent at that time. I'm not of course claiming that this is the most current reference on the physics of time, but feel his description of **dimensionality's relation to time** was remarkably lucid and I've not seen it explained more clearly. I've made some slight changes to his diagram for greater clarity. The book was a huge success and was read by T.S. Eliot, Aldous Huxley and other great writers of the time.

[133] There are some fascinating computer simulations of the emergence of 3-D shapes, such as prisms and octahedrons from the "slicing" into 3-D images of the elements of a 4-D hypercube.

[134] This is purely an imaginative connection on my part, and I don't of course claim any credentials in astrophysics.

[135] Peter Ouspensky. *Tertium Organum: The Fourth Dimension as the Esoteric Nature of reality.* Alfred A Knopf. Originally published in the early 1920s.

[136] Erik Demaine. MIT Computer Science and AI Lab. https://www.csail.mit.edu/user/666 A clear description of some of Demaine's work can be found at "Secrets of the Fold" *Bloomberg Business Week.* May 7-13, 2012.

---

137 Plato. *The Republic.* Translated by Benjamin Jowett. Book VII. There are an amazing number of misinterpretations of the situation Plato proposed, let alone the meanings attributed to them. A longer description of the setup is as follows: There's a fire in the cave behind the prisoners and they see shadows from the firelight projected onto the wall. Between them and the fire there's a barrier, also behind them, of the same height as people. Other people, with objects on their heads, pass between the barrier and the fire behind our chained observers. These prisoners can't see the outlines of the people but only the flat, grey shadows of the burdens being carried on their heads as these objects alone project above the barrier. There are over 100 images of the cave layout on the web and not all are accurate. Here's one that is not graphically elegant but has the basic structural layout correct: http://thetopthreepercent.wordpress.com/2012/12/24/philosophy-weekly-platos-allegory-of-the-cave/allegory-of-the-cave-image/

138 It is said the Plato may have attended the Eleusinian Mystery Ceremonies which involved personal preparation and then the experience of ceremonies in dark caves. Kykeon, was a beverage they were handed and it might have been based on hallucinogens from ergot which is a fungus found on rye and related plants. "Mixing the Kykeon." *ELEUSIS: Journal of Psychoactive Plants and Compounds*. New Series 4, 2000.

139 Shakespeare. *The Tempest.* V (i). "O, brave new world..." Both the courage needed and the potential thrill are implied in the famous quote as a young woman's world suddenly opens to a new love, or, in Jungian terms, with a positive projection of her ideal man (or animus). Aldous Huxley borrowed the phrase and added dark irony when he titled his cautionary novel *Brave New World* in 1932.

140 T.S. Eliot. *The Four Quartets. The Complete Poems and Plays of T.S. Eliot.* Faber and Faber, 1969. Some Course participants related very well to selections from this masterpiece, including one particular section on time and motion standing still in some moments of artistic appreciation.

141 With respect to the people of Texas, who also have some of the best beaches for kiteboarding!

142 Daddy achieved great respect for playing a big role in rehabilitating the image of pit bulls. Millan argued their ferocity was the result of wrong-headed training. The beautifully balanced Daddy was in fact a gift from a rapper.

143 Kathleen Raine. *Defending Ancient Springs: Essays.* Oxford University Press, 1967. It is also lamentably out of print. A wonderful book on many fronts.

[144] C. G Jung. *The Archetypes and the Collective Unconscious.* Original edition published by Bollingen Foundation, 1959.

[145] B. Brett Finlay. "Bugs R Us: The role of Microbes in Disease, Health and Society." Talk by this University of British Columbia microbiologist at the Peter Wall Institute for Advanced Studies in Vancouver. This YouTube lecture is particularly accessible and was delivered in Sep 2013. A key book that first brought this undiscovered country to a wider audience was *Parasite Rex: Inside the Bizarre World of Nature's Most Dangerous Creatures* by Carl Zimmer, Astria Paperback, published in 2000 and reissued with some additions in 2011.

[146] Vincent Fischetti. Quoted in "The Phage Factor." *Scientific American.* August 2012.

[147] Barbara Frederickson. *Love 2.0: How Our Supreme Emotion Affects Everything We Feel, Think, Do and Become.* Hudson Street Press, 2013.

[148] Jason Padgett and Maureen Seaberg. *Struck by Genius: How a Brain Injury Made Me a Mathematical Marvel.* Headline Publishing Group (U.K.), 2014. Padgett's book also stresses the centrality of fractals to his understanding and perception of the entire world at all scales. He was also impressed by the Arthur C Clarke video on fractals, which I had also found to be a great source. Padgett's "acquired by crisis" savant skills sees him grasping the nature of how mathematical relationships shape the construction of the world in some ways that echo the amazing skills and gifts of Pythagoras. But it's only in the age of computers that the full power of fractals can be demonstrated—as the modern "discoverer" Mandelbrot said from his IBM base. This is an endlessly fascinating topic and may change the way you see everything.

[149] Sarah Hampson. "Back to the Future" in *The Globe and Mail.* August 2, 2104. This entire piece has some reflections on the power of memory that would be a good introduction to how Proust framed his recollections in the classic *In Search of Lost Time.*

[150] Ernest Becker. *The Denial of Death.* The Free Press, 1973.

[151] Pierre Teilhard de Chardin. *The Phenomenon of Man.* First published in English by Wm. Collins Sons & Co., Ltd. London, 1959.

[152] Aldous Huxley. *The Perennial Philosophy.* Perennial Books, 1970. First published 1944.

[153] George E Vaillant. *Adaptation to Life.* Little Brown, 1977. Updated by the author in *Aging Well* in 2002.

[154] Gary Mason. "Imagine the uproar if we weeded out bad teachers." *The Globe and Mail*, May 9, 2014. A Task Force report on the Alberta Education system pointed out that not a single teacher had lost their job for incompetence in the previous 10 years. It suggested re-certification every five years. The Teachers' Association said the plan was an all-out "assault" on its members.

[155] *Fast Company* Magazine. Jan 21, 2014. http://www.fastcoexist.com/3025108/bill-gates-says-the-world-is-getting-vastly-better-while-crushing-myths-of-foreign-aid. Gates has a more nuanced approach than I have space for here. For example he points out that even if there is waste in the disposal of funds it's still worth doing it. But Buffet argued that the Gates organization passed his own strict scrutiny, and that is what influenced his choice.

[156] www.givingpledge.org

[157] "Seeker, Doer, Giver, Ponderer." *The New York Times*. July 7, 2014.

[158] "Modern Day Robin Hood." CBS News. *60 Minutes* April 20, 2014. The show was not available on the web.

CPSIA information can be obtained at www.ICGtesting.com
Printed in the USA
LVOW01s1059100615

441879LV00002B/3/P

9 781634 980517